on track ...

Lynyrd Skynyrd

every album, every song

Chris Salisbury

sonicbondpublishing.com

Sonicbond Publishing Limited
www.sonicbondpublishing.co.uk
Email: info@sonicbondpublishing.co.uk

First Published in the United Kingdom 2026
First Published in the United States 2026

British Library Cataloguing in Publication Data:
A Catalogue record for this book is available from the British Library

Copyright Chris Salisbury 2026

ISBN 978-1-78952-472-7

Typeset in ITC Garamond Std & ITC Avant Garde Gothic
Printed and bound in England

Graphic design and typesetting: Full Moon Media

Follow us on social media:
Twitter: https://twitter.com/SonicbondP
Instagram: www.instagram.com/sonicbondpublishing_/
Facebook: www.facebook.com/SonicbondPublishing/

Linktree QR code:

on track ...

Lynyrd Skynyrd

every album, every song

Chris Salisbury

sonicbondpublishing.com

Acknowledgements

Thanks to Sarah for all that you do and for putting up with me. Thanks to Nigel White for your generosity and Mike Estes for your help and recollections.

Dedication

In memory of Mum and Dad, Audrey and Ken. I think you would be proud. Sam, Talia and Leah, you are the best kids I could have asked for. Also dedicated to the memory of Andrew Meulenbergs – fly high, Freebird.

on track ...
Lynyrd Skynyrd

Contents

Introduction

The 50th anniversary of Lynyrd Skynyrd's debut album *Pronounced 'Lĕh-'nérd 'Skin-'nérd* was marked in 2023, although the genesis of the band dates back further to 1964. The band may have had a humble beginning, but despite tragedy and reunion, they earned their place on *Rolling Stone*'s list of 100 Greatest Artists of All Time.

Understanding how the band began illuminates their recorded works in context and gives a perspective on the controversy surrounding the band's reformation and continuation, following the tragic events of 20 October 1977, when the band were decimated in a plane crash.

In the summer of 1964, a young Bob Burns was watching a local baseball match in Jacksonville, Florida, when a young batter called Ronnie Van Zant, playing on the Green Pigs team, hit a line drive that knocked Bob unconscious. Bob played for a team called the Bugs, and he had been watching the game with his 12-year-old friend Garry Rossington, also a player but for the Lakeshore Rebels.

Ronnie felt bad about the incident, but it led to a friendship between the three, who, it transpired, also shared a love of music. Despite their young age, Gary had already started to play the guitar, and Bob the drums.

Although both Bob and Gary had initially wanted to play drums, Gary decided to play guitar. Born in Jacksonville on 4 December 1951, the young Rossington was raised by his mother, Berneice, following the passing of Gary's father when he was ten. Gary would later name his Les Paul Sunburst guitar after his mother in tribute to her. Gary saved his money and bought a Sears Silvertone guitar. A local musician, Lloyd Phillips, was dating Gary's older sister Carol, and he gave Gary lessons while he was waiting for her to get ready. Gary and Bob recruited their friend, Larry Junstrom, to play bass, and the three began to practice, calling themselves You, Me and Him.

Following their chance meeting, subsequent friendship and the realisation of their shared interest in music, Ronnie teamed up with the nascent band. They made the decision that they would be a stronger band with the addition of another guitar player. Despite not having heard him play, they set their sights on Allen Collins, who, despite his young age, had already made a name for himself with the kids in the neighbourhood.

Born Larkin Allen Collins, Jr. on 19 July 1952, at St. Luke's Hospital in Jacksonville, Florida, into a turbulent and subsequently divided household, the young, restless Allen initially gravitated to Jacksonville Raceway, which perhaps forged his lifelong love of automobiles and speed. Allen became intrigued with a friend's guitar and was delighted when his mum Eva Strunk managed to save enough money to buy him a Sears Silvertone of his own.

With help from his stepmother, Leila, who taught Allen the rudiments of country and western guitar, the young guitarist made rapid progress and soon formed a band of his own called The Mods. Allen's natural talent was clear from the start, and he was committed to practice, which he was able to do while his mother worked evening shifts.

There are differing accounts of the first meeting with Allen. What is clear is that Ronnie's reputation preceded him, and when they did find Collins, he had either cycled or run away, according to one account, trying to hide up a tree, fearful of receiving a beating at the hands of Van Zant.

Ronald Wayne Van-Zant (which he later spelt Van Zant) was born on 15 January 1948, at St. Vincent's Hospital in Jacksonville, the second child of his father, Lacy, but the first with his second wife, Marion. Ronnie was a driven child who wanted to be the best at what he did. His family attested to the fact that he felt destined to escape the shackles of his neighbourhood on the west side of Jacksonville. This was an area that Ronnie described as rough, particularly at the time he grew up there. He called it Shanty Town and recalled a lot of street fighting and adventure at that time.

From an early age, Ronnie loved to sing and had a knack for imitating singers he heard on the household radio. He had a penchant for country music and, according to brother Donnie, his favourite artist was Merle Haggard. Such was his love for singing that Ronnie's mother once had to go to his elementary school to deal with him for singing 'Beer Drinkin' Daddy' in the classroom. His exposure to country music was supplemented on his trips in his father Lacy's 18-wheeler.

At 14 and while attending Lakeshore Junior High School, Ronnie heard that a group of students were putting together a band, and they needed a singer. In his own indomitable style, he announced himself as their new singer, forgoing the opportunity to join the audition. Even at that age, his reputation as a fighter was established, so the group accepted him as the singer for what became Us. With this band, he was able to win a Battle of the Bands contest, defeating a group featuring the younger Allen Collins. Ronnie had confidence in his own ability and harboured thoughts of becoming a professional singer, clearly an occupation preferable to his employment at that time, bagging groceries. Ronnie decided the best strategy to progress his career would be to front his own band and surround himself with the best musicians that he could find. This was the strategy that led him to play with Gary, Bob, Allen and Larry.

Ronnie's short temper and aggressive nature are well documented and recounted by those who knew him at Robert E. Lee High School, where he frequently sought out confrontations. Although self-aware of his antisocial behaviour, he did little to change his ways. He was often quoted as calling himself 'a boy only a mom could love.'

Ronnie, Gary, Allen, Bob and Larry were rehearsing and had drawn up a set covering songs by The Rolling Stones, amongst others, by the summer of 1964, and they were ready to perform at local parties. The fledgling band performed under a variety of names, including My Backyard, The Noble Five and Conqueror Worm, before settling on The One Percent after seeing a Hell's Angel movie in Gainesville, Florida, in 1968.

Their first paid gig came in 1964, performing as The Noble Five, for the Christmas party of the automotive parts store where Ronnie worked part-time. They commanded a $10 fee, and the gig was successful despite the repetition of a very limited set.

By the time they were known as The One Percent, they were able to secure rehearsal space and gigs at The Comic Book Club in Jacksonville. Many talented bands passed through and played at the club, and the young band took the opportunity to learn from them. The choice of the band's covers limited their wider appeal, so they were grateful for the opportunity the club gave them.

In 1968, the band recorded for the first time, making what became known as the Shade Tree recordings. The initial session led to the recording of two songs, released as the band's first single, a limited promotional pressing of 300 copies of 'Need All My Friends' and 'Michelle'. The band subsequently returned to the studio to cut further songs. During this period, the band changed their name to Lynyrd Skynyrd, although initially the spelling was Lynard Skynard, as they are credited on the initial single.

Ronnie, Gary and Bob all attended the Robert E. Leigh High School and their run-ins with coach Leonard Skinner are well documented. Primarily, Skinner objected to the boy's long hair. The intimidating coach had a reputation amongst the local youth, who had their own Skinner stories. Ronnie jokingly introduced the band as Leonard Skinner, which went down so well that it was adopted, with a spelling change, and the legend was born.

Subsequent recording sessions at Quinvy and Muscle Shoals Studios were important stepping stones for the band. Significant managerial and personnel changes took place before and during these recordings, which were subsequently released on *Collectybles* (with the Shade Tree recordings), *First And ... Last* and *Skynyrd's First: The Complete Muscle Shoals Album*.

Jim Sutton and Tom Markham formed Shade Tree Records in the late 1960s with the hopes that Markham proposed: 'Let's make lots of Money. Maybe we could make millions.' Sutton came up with the Shade Tree name, which the pair agreed on. Markham recalled that it was Sutton, who, in 1968, saw the potential in the then One Percent. They signed the band to a five-year contract, promoting them at grocery stores and shopping centre openings. They offered the band their time and expertise in the recording studio in exchange for publishing rights and royalties. Sutton and Markham were not particularly keen on the band name but thought their subsequent choice of Lynyrd Skynyrd was worse.

Alan Walden had left his brother's Capricorn Records in 1970 and was looking to sign bands, having started his own publishing and management company, Hustlers Inc. An employee of Walden's, Pat Armstrong, arranged an audition where he heard Lynyrd Skynyrd, and he alerted Walden to their potential. Walden invited the band to play for him, about which he said, 'I heard them play 'Free Bird' and I knew from that one song that they were onto something.'

Walden's subsequent deal gave him 30% of the earnings that they would make if signed by a record company, but also gave him the publishing royalties. Walden had to convince Jim Sutton and Tom Markham to release the group from their contract, but they had not had any success themselves, so this was a formality. Sutton was taking a job in Texas and getting married, while Markham was getting a divorce. 'We hadn't gotten them off the ground. We'd pressed records, promoted them, all that, but a spark didn't happen, so we released them', Markham recalled for the *Florida Times-Union*. Years later, they were able to benefit from the publishing rights that they retained for the band's earlier recordings. In *Whiskey Bottles And Brand-New Cars*, author Mark Ribowsky claims that Sutton and Markham put out a single featuring 'I've been Your Fool' and 'Gotta Go'. There is no record of this release. The tracks subsequently appeared on the album *Best Of The Rest*, with production credits for Jimmy Johnson and Tim Smith at Muscle Shoals. They were released in 1982 by MCA as a single.

The next step was for Walden to get the band recorded properly, and he was able to arrange sessions for the band at Muscle Shoals, with the intent of producing recordings of sufficient quality to land a deal with a major record company. These recordings would later surface on the post plane crash albums *Skynyrd's First And ... Last* and *Skynyrd's First: The Complete Muscle Shoals Album*.

Prior to the recordings, there were personnel issues to resolve within the band. Larry Junstrom later recalled that he left the band, but Ronnie fired him. Ronnie had concerns with his image, but also with his commitment to practicing and gigging. Bob Burns, at this point, was homeless and broke. His parents had left him, at 15, to fend for himself and moved to Orlando. It reached a point where Burns had had enough, so he followed his parents. Both were temporarily replaced with Rickey Medlocke on drums and Greg Walker on bass, both from the band Blackfoot.

Although it has been claimed that there was a technical glitch with the tapes, when Allan Walden presented the finished recordings to several major record labels, they were rejected outright. Walden recalled that Atlantic, Warner, Columbia, A&M, RCA, Epic, Elecktra and Polydor all passed on hearing 'Free Bird' and other songs from Muscle Shoals. Ronnie was angry with producer and engineer Jimmie Johnson and felt betrayed on hearing the tapes, feeling that Johnson had deliberately sabotaged them. Muscle Shoals house bass player David Hood recalled the tape had become twisted on the reel, so on playback was muffled. During the recording of the *Pronounced* album, Ronnie became aware that there had been a genuine mistake with the winding of the tape and called Johnson to apologise for his reaction. He swore to put this right by mentioning the Muscle Shoals Rhythm Section, The Swampers, in a song. True to his word, they were immortalised in the lyrics of 'Sweet Home Alabama'.

Although, with hindsight, it seems beyond comprehension that the band were not signed despite the connections that Walden had, their salvation came by chance courtesy of Alan Peter Kuperschmidt, a New York music industry big shot, better known as Al Kooper.

While in Atlanta, Al Kooper had called up his friends who were making a new album. They were now known as The Atlanta Rhythm Section, having formerly been known as the Candymen and working as Roy Orbison's backing band. They were recording in their own recording facility called Studio One and were producing impressive results. Shortly after, having made a deal with Warner Brothers Records, Al booked studio time to produce his own backup band, Frankie and Johnny. The Atlanta Rhythm Section were used as the backing band, and the engineers were Rodney Mills and Bob 'Tub' Langford.

The recordings took place between midday and around eight in the evening, after which Al, Frankie and Johnny would retreat to a downtown rock club called Funnochios on Peachtree Street. They received VIP treatment courtesy of the manager, a former acquaintance of Al's. Al jammed every evening with a band called Boot for a week until their tenure ended and a new band replaced them. Al was struck by the lead singer of the new band, a barefooted, blond-haired singer swinging the mic stand. The faces of the guitarists were hidden by their long hair as they played a set of original songs. Al approached the band after the third night and persuaded the band to let him sit in on a number playing guitar. The band's strategy of calling out the first song as a blues in C# didn't catch Al out, as it was clearly intended to do. Kooper remembered that the band called out the awkward key as an intimidation process to keep jammers offstage, but as a competent musician, Al took it in his stride.

Al struck up a relationship with the band, impressed as he was by their music. They were playing a weird amalgam of blues with second-generation British band influences (Cream, Free, etc.). He recalled, 'The resultant sound was unique and appealed to me. The one song that got me every night was 'I Ain't The One'.'

The last night that they played at the club, Al offered them a record deal with him as producer. The band said they would discuss this and talk to their manager, and left Al in the hope that he would soon hear back. The band were, of course, Lynyrd Skynyrd.

Phil Walden's Capricorn Records, based in Macon, Georgia, realised that there was a new movement in the South. If Capricorn rejected a Southern artist, they had few options. Al recognised an opportunity that other labels had missed and so decided to start his own label based in Atlanta. Al's agent arranged a meeting with MCA, who ultimately signed a deal to distribute the records made by Al's fledgling record company that he named Sounds of the South. At this point, Al heard back from Skynyrd's manager, Alan Walden, who turned out to be the younger brother of Phil Walden. Alan and Al were able to hammer out a deal after two or three months of negotiation. It is interesting to note that Ronnie claimed to have turned down a deal from

Capricorn, as they would have always played second fiddle to the Allman Brothers, but there are other claims that no offer was made.

Charlie Brusco (manager of the Outlaws, and later influential in the reformation of Lynyrd Skynyrd), in Ribowsky's *Whiskey Bottles And Brand-New Cars*, remembered it thus:

Alan tried but could not convince his brother to sign them. Alan Walden was not Phil Walden. He was the kid brother. And Phil wasn't about to bail him out. It was a very difficult thing to get them signed. They weren't really a country-rock act. They were a three-guitar rock band in the country fold, and there just wasn't anything like that around. Phil never considered signing them, a decision I'm sure Phil came to regret.

Alan Walden, according to Ribowsky, recalled that he never asked his brother to sign them and recounted that after seeing Lynyrd Skynyrd in the Grand Slam Club in Macon, Phil claimed the singer was too cocky, couldn't sing, the songs were weak, and they sounded too much like the Allman Brothers. He kept these remarks from Ronnie. It is possible that Ronnie claimed to have turned down a deal with Capricorn to prevent discouragement within the band.

Late one evening, during the negotiations with Walden, Kooper received a phone call from Ronnie Van Zant. The band's equipment had been stolen, and he needed $5,000 to keep the band on the road and to honour commitments. Without hesitation, Kooper agreed to send the money. Ronnie's reply cemented their bond, 'Al, you just bought yourself a band for $5,000.'

Pronounced 'Lĕh-'nérd 'Skin-'nérd (1973)

Personnel:
Ronnie Van Zant: lead vocals
Gary Rossington: guitar
Allen Collins: guitar
Ed King: bass, guitar
Billy Powell: keyboards
Bob Burns: drums
Additional musicians:
Al Kooper ('Roosevelt Gook'): bass, backing vocals, mandolin, bass drum, organ, Mellotron
Robert Nix: drums
Bobbye Hall: percussion
Steve Katz: harmonica
Recorded at Studio One, Doraville, Georgia, US
Producer: Al Kooper
Engineer: Al Kooper, Rodney Mills, Bob 'Tub' Langford
Release date: 13 August 1973
Label: MCA
Chart places: US: 4, UK: did not chart
Running time: 43:05

Pronounced 'Lĕh-'nérd 'Skin-'nérd, the debut album by Lynyrd Skynyrd, was released on 13 August 1973 on the MCA label. Earlier recordings were subsequently issued as albums, but this release was the landmark celebrated as 50 years in 2023.

Kooper's assessment of Ronnie Van Zant was that he was a formidable leader, but a gentleman and a man of his word. Kooper felt that he had a rather pedestrian voice but had a penchant for songwriting. Ronnie acted as mediator between the band and Kooper in his role as producer.

Kooper found the band to be incredibly well-rehearsed, to the point where all the guitar solos were written and rehearsed in advance. He thought they were the best song arrangers he had ever worked with and needed to offer little input with this. Kooper helped them with their studio craft and in understanding the relationship between the bass and drums, to make the songs really rock. He was certainly impressed that, when instruction was required, he only needed to tell the band once. Although he would offer advice, including on the removal of what he felt were weaker songs, the band did not always agree. On one occasion, as Kooper recalled, when the band were reluctant to listen to Kooper's advice, Ronnie said:

Alright. Wait just a second. I think that idea sucks, too, but I will listen to everything Al says. Maybe once in 20 times, he'll have a great idea, but I will suffer the other 19 times because the 20th one will make us sound better, so go easy on the old guy!

Al Kooper was still only 29 at that point in time.

The band Kooper signed had featured Leon Wilkeson on bass, but at the time of recording the album, he had left. The band, remembering Ed King from gigging with Strawberry Alarm Clock, called him and asked him to join on bass. King and Van Zant had gotten along well when Skynyrd had opened for Strawberry Alarm Clock, and Ed had told Ronnie to call him anytime if he needed a guitar or bass player. King said: 'Ronnie Van Zant was the only reason I would ever consider joining the band. He had a quality about him that reeked of greatness.' Ed mostly played the parts that had been written by Wilkeson, but he was a technically accomplished player and added his own flourishes to the parts.

Another addition, and one that delighted Kooper, was Billy Powell on piano. Billy had previously played with Donnie Van Zant in Alice Marr and had been a roadie for the band, but had been promoted upon Ronnie hearing his arrangement for the introduction to 'Free Bird'. He was offered a place once the band could afford to pay another member.

Billy was born in Corpus Christi, Texas. He was from a military family, and he spent several early years in Italy, where his father was stationed with the US Navy. The family returned to the United States to settle in Jacksonville, Florida, after the death of his father from cancer. In elementary school, Powell met Leon Wilkeson, who became a lifelong friend. Billy was the only member of the early band to have formal music training, and he was a gifted pianist. Billy's classical training meant he did tend, initially, to overplay with his left hand. Kooper recalls tying his left hand to the piano bench leg to make his point. However, Billy's piano work, particularly his soloing, was a great asset to the band and became part of their signature sound.

On 26 March 1973, prior to recording the album, Kooper took the band into the studio to record the songs they knew live to two-track tape so that selections could be made to take forward and record for the album. Kooper recalls that the tracks were live with no overdubs and that they were all good songs. Several of these recordings ended up being used on post-crash compilations.

The album was recorded between 27 March and 1 May 1973, in Studio One, Doraville, Georgia. Kooper recalled that the sessions went well and there were only a couple of points on which they clashed. Perhaps unsurprisingly, Kooper lost both arguments. Al mixed the album in New York City, taking three attempts before he was satisfied.

With the help of Sharon Lawrence from Norman Winter Associates, who had been hired to help Kooper's label with press, they were able to organise a huge launch party for the band in Atlanta. They flew in important radio and press personnel along with representatives from MCA. Even Marc Bolan from

T. Rex was a guest. Al presented his band, Mose Jones, along with Lynyrd Skynyrd, who quite simply put on a stunning show. With only weeks before the album's release, Skynyrd had ensured themselves significant radio and press support. Their coup de grace was premiering a new song they had written for the event, 'Workin' For MCA'.

Ed King had the following recollections of the album cover photography when prompted on his *ProBoards* forum:

> The cover shot was the very last picture we took that day. We were standing on Main St. in Jonesboro, Georgia – a storm was coming down from Atlanta. After the guy took the picture, he said 'Cool. I think I got a lightning bolt in that one.' So, yes, the lightning is real. From what I understand, it still looks the same! I haven't been back since. After that was taken, Gary ran over to the curb and threw up. Hangover. And Bob Burns still had residue of blood in his eyes from where he'd gotten brass-knuckled at a bar three weeks prior. I was there and saw that, weird, wild stuff. Wrong place, wrong time.

Skynyrd's penchant for fighting led Kooper to focus on a tough image for the band, and he designed a skull head logo with the band name spelt out in bones. Following the success of the launch party, MCA agreed to a $100,000 ad campaign, which began six weeks prior to the album release. Radio play began three weeks before the album release, which helped the initial album sales.

'I Ain't The One' (Rossington, Van Zant) 3:51
This is the song that first caught Al Kooper's attention when he saw the band play live. Their skill as arrangers is evident from this, the opening track of the album, which kicks off with Ronnie counting the song in and a panning cymbal splash over the instantly recognisable drum pattern. According to King, the unusual effect you can hear was created thus:

> You get that sound by flipping the master tape over, playing the hi-hat track backwards and recording it on an open track with reverb. When you re-flip the master tape back to normal, the reverb happens before the hi-hat. Thanks to Al Kooper, and I'm quite sure he lifted the idea from someone else.

The first guitar enters, playing the intro riff, and is joined after a couple of bars by the second guitar playing a variation. Ronnie's characteristic whistle at 24 seconds signals a change in the rhythm guitars and brings in the first short solo from Allen. Ronnie's vocals differ in sound and style from the original Muscle Shoals version, which saw later release on *Skynyrd's First – The Complete Muscle Shoals Album*, the reverb-drenched snarl having been replaced by a more natural delivery. His skill as a storyteller is evident from the first verse as a tale of a man being pressured into marriage by a pregnant girl unfolds. Ronnie denies his involvement.

Ed came up with the bassline one night at the Hell House while jamming with Ronnie and drinking psilocybin mushroom tea that the singer had prepared. He later wished he could have heard Leon's bassline before he learnt and recorded his. In the band's early days, their noisy rehearsals were often shut down by the police. They were able to find and rent a little shack on a 99-acre farm just outside Jacksonville in a town called Russell, near Black Creek. Here, Ronnie established a brutal practice regime for the band where they wrote and rehearsed in extreme temperatures. This became known as Hell House and is very much part of the Skynyrd legend.

Ed recalled that in addition to his album credits, he made the following contributions:

> I doubled the bass part (using my Strat) on 'Things Goin' On', and there's some of my picking going on behind Billy's solo in 'Tuesdays Gone'. I also doubled my bass part (using the Strat) during the dual guitar solo on 'Simple Man'. Mostly stuff you wouldn't notice. I did it whenever I felt it needed it. You might not hear it, but I sure do. It just fattens up the bass by throwing another octave in the mix.

At 55 seconds, we hear Billy Powell for the first time, his keys subtle and appropriate to the song, but adding an extra layer. At 1:47, we drop to a single guitar as accompaniment as Ronnie tells us it's time for him to put his boots out in the street. This sets us up for the stinging solo from Allen, his clear articulation and quick vibrato evident. At 2:28, the band drop out, leaving a brief doubled guitar solo followed by a build-up, and then the band are back in, Ronnie singing but still with some deft fills from Allen. At 3:16, the band drop out, leaving a single rhythm guitar, then a second guitar and this sets up a typically rowdy song ending lasting for the remaining 30 seconds, with stabs and a fast bass run from Ed and the band building to a crescendo.

'Tuesday's Gone' (Collins, Van Zant) 7:32

'Tuesday's Gone' is a simple but poignant slow-tempo ballad about a relationship that is ending, crafted in the country blues tradition. It seems likely that Tuesday is a woman, given the line 'Tuesday, you see. Oh, she had to be free', although 'Tuesday' could also represent his past life, and a lament that his normal life was ending as the band achieved success. Although this is a song penned by Collins and Van Zant, it features some great lead work from Gary, his slow, laid-back string-bending approach and tasteful vibrato adding much to the feel of the track. Al Kooper, credited as Roosevelt Gook, plays bass, adds texture with the addition of Mellotron, providing orchestral string sounds to the ballad, and also sings backing vocals.

The themes of the wind blowing and leaving on trains might be cliched in other hands, but the writing and performance of Ronnie are outstanding. We are never clear if the singer is leaving Tuesday by choice, to let her be free, or whether he had no choice, but we feel his pain. Clearly, he is putting distance between them: 'The train roll on/A many miles from my home, see I'm/I'm riding my blues away, yeah'. However, they remain stoic, 'Well, when this train ends, I'll try again', but the feeling of melancholy the song conjures up hangs heavy. There was a train track near the place where the band rehearsed, and allegedly, the sound of the trains inspired lead singer Ronnie Van Zant to write the first line.

The song begins gently with hi-hat and keyboards, Gary coming in at 19 seconds and taking us to the beginning of the vocals some 40 seconds in. Gary takes another solo at 1:40, plaintive and slow. Sympathetic drumming from Robert Nix of the Atlanta Rhythm Section is evident throughout. Bob Burns had played on the demo version, included on the extended edition CD release of the album, but did not play on the main album release. According to Ed, the drumming of Burns was not heavy enough, recalling:

Robert Nix leans on his drums when he plays; you can just about hear them creak. Robert's a big boy; he towers over his drum kit. Listen to those drum fills in the verses, especially midway through the last one. For that matter, take a listen to all that old Atlanta Rhythm Section stuff.

At 3:17, we hear a beautiful extended piano section from Billy Powell that adds much to the track. There are quiet guitar parts in the background, supplementing the rhythm, that may be Ed King. At 4:33, Gary follows the piano with a guitar solo, and then once again for the last minute as the song fades, in stark contrast to the ending of the previous song, evoking the image of the train receding into the distance.

Metallica, Phish and Hank Williams Jr. have all covered the song, with Gary Rossington guesting on the Metallica version on their covers album *Garage Inc.*

'Gimme Three Steps' (Collins, Van Zant) 4:30
Gene Odum, in his book *Lynyrd Skynyrd Remembering The Free Birds Of Southern Rock*, hit the nail on the head when he described this track as a bouncing barroom romp. Telling the true story of an occasion in a Jacksonville bar, this lively tongue-in-cheek song was Skynyrd's first commercial single. Although some critics felt the song was comedic, it has endured as a crowd favourite. This song is a Collins/Van Zant creation but features solos from Gary and is further embellished by bongos played by Bobbye Hall, who worked with The Temptations, Marvin Gaye and Stevie Wonder, amongst many others.

The song opens with the signature riff on a solitary guitar before the band all kick in, and a doubled Rossington solo sets the tone and leads us into the first verse. The hero of our song dances with a girl whose partner takes offence and levels a .44 handgun at his head. The plea is made to 'gimme three steps towards the door'. Rossington is on top form, and the tone and phrasing of his solos fit perfectly with the barroom boogie. The song closes by fading out rather than reaching a crescendo. An edited version of the song was released in November 1973, but did not receive any notable chart success. The B-side was one of the pre-production demo tracks, 'Mr. Banker'.

'Simple Man' (Rossington, Van Zant) 5:57
Initially, this was a song that Al Kooper felt should not be recorded for the album. It is claimed that, following a disagreement over the song, Ronnie walked Kooper out to his Bentley, closing the door behind him. He leaned in and said, 'When we are done recording it, we will call you.'

The song is about a mother's advice to her son and feels very personal and heartfelt. Ronnie wrote the words in the shower after the passing of his grandmother, remembering them and never writing them down, as was his style. The song became another band and crowd favourite and has been played in homage to Ronnie and other members of the band as they have passed. The song begins with arpeggios on a fairly clean electric guitar, embellished faintly with the organ playing of Kooper, who came to like the song and had realised his error.

At 1:04, there is a more muscular bridge before settling back to another verse and a heavier chorus. At 3.36, the guitar solos kick in. Gary and Allen are both playing the same parts, rather than a harmony, which became a trademark. The solo, in terms of style and phrasing, sounds like an Allen Collins composition, a notion that Ed agreed with but could not confirm, since it had been written before he joined the band. Other Southern bands, notably the Outlaws and the Allman Brothers band, played harmony rather than doubled lines. The song ends with a fading chorus and a message to 'be a simple kind of man'.

Ed composed the bassline for the song, except for the part under the solo, which was composed by Leon but taught to Ed by Allen. When questioned on the Ed King *ProBoards* forum, Ed recalled:

'Simple Man' was the first song that I learned with the band. It was the last song that the band recorded because we were short one song. It was one of the best songs on the album. It was good enough for a beer commercial.

A version of the song, recorded by Shinedown, was used on a Busch beer commercial decades later. Jasin Todd, original Shinedown guitarist, was married to Melody Van Zant, Ronnie Van Zant's daughter.

'Things Goin' On' (Rossington, Van Zant) 4:57
Although Billy had already made his presence felt on the album, on 'Things Goin' On', his playing brings much to the song and sets the blueprint for the

honky tonk nature of much of the band's subsequent material. Ed King loved the song, but he felt that Billy's approach was novel: 'I don't think Billy even realised what he was doing. He's not too good at listening to the lyrics until the song is long completed. So, his devil-may-care piano work sounds so opposed to Ronnie's complaining about the government. It's hilarious.' The song is a cry out for change from the government to address poverty and environmental damage, themes dear to Ronnie.

For much of the song, the drums are sparse, and there is some additional percussion credited to Bobbye Hall, which is probably the tambourine embellishment that can be heard if you listen closely. The solos are from Rossington again, this time taking them on one of his own compositions. The song fades again, this time over a guitar and piano riff, with Ronnie intoning 'Things goin' on' and then almost inaudibly 'bad things'.

'Mississippi Kid' (Kooper, Van Zant, Burns) 3:57
There is some irony that the only Lynyrd Skynyrd song to give Bob Burns a writing credit is one on which he does not play. This song begins with Al Kooper playing the mandolin, and he also plays the bass drum. Kooper spent several days looking for a mandolin player before going out and buying one and teaching himself the chords he needed. Ed King takes the slide solo, and harmonica is played by Steve Katz, a friend of Al Kooper's from the Blues Project and Blood, Sweat and Tears. There is no credit given for anyone playing the bass on this track, but there is a bassline on the recording, possibly by Kooper. The bass has a softer, less prominent, finger-picked tone with less attack to the notes' timbre than can be heard elsewhere from King.

The lyrics are unusual for Ronnie in that the narrative is not clear. It has been suggested that the reference is to bringing back a black lady to Alabama. Although he wasn't looking for trouble, he would deal with it if it came his way. At the very least, it is a stripped-down, rootsy song, and Bob gets the credit for the title, apparently his first suggestion when they were stuck for ideas.

'Poison Whiskey' (King, Van Zant) 3:11
At 3:11, this is the shortest song on the album, but it is also notable for being the first credited composition by Ed King on the original studio releases. The lyrics are about the perils of alcoholism and particularly the prolonged intake of Johnny Walker's Red. There is some irony here due to the band's penchant for alcohol and substance abuse. Gary takes the lead break, and Billy adds a typically dextrous and instantly recognisable solo at 2:00.

'Poison Whiskey' is another great song on an album with no real filler. The strategy of recording the demo songs in March, choosing the best, working on them and adding new material, before returning to the studio in April, clearly proved effective.

'Free Bird' (Collins, Van Zant) 9:08

'Free Bird' began as a chord progression Allen had written in his teens. According to Gary Rossington, Ronnie initially felt that the song had too many chords to write words to, adding:

> After a few months, we were sitting around, and he asked Allen to play those chords again. After about 20 minutes, Ronnie started singing, 'If I leave here tomorrow', and it fit great. It wasn't anything heavy, just a love song about leaving town, time to move on. Al put the organ on the front, which was a very good idea. He also helped me get the sound of the delayed slide guitar that I play; it's actually me playing the same thing twice, recording one on top of the other, so it sounds kind of slurry, echoey.

The lyrics are about a man explaining to a girl why he can't settle down and make a commitment. The opening lines, 'If I leave here tomorrow, would you still remember me?', were inspired by Allen Collins' girlfriend Kathy, who had asked him this very question during a fight. The song had been recorded previously in several incarnations, including versions with no piano or the tempo shift into what became one of the most quintessential solos of 1970s rock.

On the debut album version, Al Kooper, credited as Roosevelt Gook, starts the song on organ, creating an almost church-like atmosphere. Kooper had the pedigree to pull this off. He was the man, despite having never played electric organ, whose improvised organ riff on Dylan's 'Like A Rolling Stone' has been described by Mark Polizzotti in *Highway 61 Revisited (33/1/3)* as 'One of the great moments of pop music serendipity.' The song gently builds with an acoustic guitar and piano faint in the mix, with Burns punctuating with drum accents. At 35 seconds, Gary joins with his plaintive slide guitar. Never a technical master of the slide, Gary channels his ear for melody and lays down beautiful slide lines. We are over a minute in before Ronnie begins to sing.

There have been criticisms of Ed King's bass playing, largely misplaced and falsely interpreting Ronnie's quote that Ed was the worst bass player he ever heard, where he was showing his humour and wanting Ed to move to guitar upon the return of Leon Wilkeson. Al Kooper was complimentary of Ed's bass, and Ronnie wouldn't have accepted it if he really felt it was substandard. The basslines here are sympathetic and complementary to the music. Several of the basslines Ed played on the album were learned from Leon himself before his return following the album and prior to the recording.

At 4:42, the tempo lifts, and at 4:55, Ronnie utters the word 'Free Bird' for the only time in the song, lighting the touchpaper for Allen's era-defining magnum opus solo. Where the solo has doubled lead parts, they are both played by Allen. At 6.33, stabs punctuate the song, accompanied by Allen's rapid picking. At 7:25, the rhythm changes to more of a gallop with Allen still going strong and the bass building to a climax at 8:13. More melodic soloing follows, and eventually the song fades out in stark contrast to the live versions of the song, which end in dramatic fashion. At 9:18, this is the longest song on the album.

The original version of 'Free Bird' did not have the extended solo section at the end. Gary felt he had been cheated out of royalties, claiming this section was his idea and that it had been borne out of the need for more material to fill time at a gig. In a *Classic Rock* interview, Gary claimed:

> One night, we were playing at a club, and Ronnie said, 'Play that a little longer, my voice is hurting, I need a break.' So, we played for two minutes or three minutes. Then, two days later, his throat was all sore, and he could hardly talk, and we ended up playing it ten minutes at the end, just jamming.

However, Ronnie once said in an interview that it was Allen who came up with the idea, and to further muddy the waters, Bob Burns (through his wife Marsha) said it was Larry:

> During a band practice at Larry Junstrum's parents' house, after the slow part was rehearsed, LJ just kept playing and everyone joined in. It was totally creative and spontaneous. Everyone liked it, so they decided to keep it in and develop it as a permanent part of the song. The rest is history!

'Free Bird' was first released as a single in November 1974 with 'Down South Jukin'' as the B-side. It followed the release of 'Sweet Home Alabama' as a single and reached number 19 in January in the US and number 21 in the UK. It was acclaimed number three on *Guitar World*'s list of greatest guitar solos of all time in 2010 and 2016, and placed number eight in their rankings by 2022.

Second Helping (1974)

Personnel:
Ronnie Van Zant: lead vocals
Gary Rossington: guitar
Allen Collins: guitar
Ed King: guitar, backing vocals, bass on 'I Need You' and 'Don't Ask Me No Questions'
Leon Wilkeson: bass (all tracks except 'I Need You' and 'Don't Ask Me No Questions'), backing vocals
Bob Burns: drums, except 'I Need You'
Billy Powell: keyboards
Additional musicians:
Mike Porter: drums on 'I Need You'
Merry Clayton, Clydie King, Sherlie Matthews: background vocals on 'Sweet Home Alabama'
Bobby Keys, Trevor Lawrence and Steve Madaio: horns on 'Don't Ask Me No Questions' and 'Call Me The Breeze'
Al Kooper: backing vocals, piano on 'Don't Ask Me No Questions' and 'The Ballad Of Curtis Loew'
Recorded at Studio One, Doraville, Georgia (track 1); Record Plant Studios, Los Angeles, California
Producer: Al Kooper
Engineer: Al Kooper, Austin Goodsey, Bob Merritt, Gary Kellgren, Rodney Mills
Release date: 15 April 1974
Label: MCA
Chart places: US: 12, UK: did not chart
Running time: 37:15

The Who were preparing a huge tour for their *Quadrophenia* album. They were also on MCA, and through good fortune, Kooper bumped into Pete Townsend and Who manager Peter Rudge at the MCA offices. Kooper gave them a pressing of the new Skynyrd album and told them the band would be a great support. A young up-and-coming band would provide the opportunity to sell any remaining seats on their tour, so the timing was perfect.

Skynyrd had maybe played to a crowd of a thousand people, and usually much less. Now they were opening a show in front of a crowd 20 times that number. With Kooper mixing live sound for the band, probably to keep an eye on them and their crew as much as to make sure it was done properly, they went down exceptionally well, even getting encores. Al remembered an incredulous Rudge saying he had never seen that happen with any Who opening act. His biggest problem was that he had to mix from the side of the stage, which apparently Townsend insisted on for The Who, so he could whack Bob Pridden, their sound man, if he didn't like something. The Who took Lynyrd Skynyrd in and treated them as equals.

'Gimme Three Steps' made little headway as a single, with 'Free Bird' getting more airplay. However, album sales were building, as was the fanbase. Skynyrd became a popular choice of opening act for arena headliners, helping sell any remaining tickets. ZZ Top, Savoy Brown and Eric Clapton all had Skynyrd open for them. One less successful pairing was when the band opened for Black Sabbath at Nassau Coliseum, Long Island. When a section of the crowd shouted that Ozzy ruled and that they needed to get off the stage and then made a move toward the stage, Leon resolved the situation by drawing his revolver and firing it at them. Although thankfully loaded with blanks, it did the trick.

Leon Wilkeson had been brought in on bass after the departure of Greg Walker, who himself had been brought in to replace the bass parts laid down by Larry Junstrom, who had been fired during the sessions at Muscle Shoals. Although he was devastated at the time, Junstrom was a good bass player and went on to have considerable success with .38 Special and with hindsight, he would be happy with his success, and that he wasn't on the plane that went down in 1977.

Leon had been playing in Dru Lombar's band, the King James Version. The music he played with Lombar, who went on to front Grinderswitch and Dr. Hector and the Groove Injectors, wasn't particularly to Leon's taste, but it helped refine his skills. Leon recalled that one night he was watching Donnie Van Zant and then Skynyrd roadie Billy Powell rehearse their band Alice Marr at the Comic Book Club when Ronnie, Gary and Allen walked in. Allen Collins' words may have caused Leon a little concern: 'Leon, we're fixing to take a ride around the block. Why don't you come ride with us?' However, Ronnie offered Leon, known to most as Thumper, the opportunity to play with the band but made his expectations clear: 'Every time you step up to the plate, you gotta put it out the park. Gotta be a home run.'

Prior to the recording of the first album, Leon got cold feet. He felt too young for fame and was being supported by his parents. At this point, he wasn't making money with Skynyrd and was worried that he was not good enough, especially with the interest being shown by Al Kooper. Although he later realised it wasn't a great choice, he decided to go back to the King James Version, which made money, and got a job at Farm Best Dairy Products. Luckily for Leon, who had kept in touch with the band, Ronnie wanted him back after the first album and so sent Billy and Bob to fetch him and to chat while he fished. Although Ed loved playing bass, and Kooper liked his bass work, Ronnie wanted Leon and King to move to guitar soon after the first album was recorded.

The second album was recorded at the Record Plant in L.A. This was very different to most studios, not least because it had a jacuzzi and three bedrooms. 'Sweet Home Alabama' had already been recorded in Atlanta, but the band had some really strong material, with Kooper recalling that the band had a 'Musical knowledge and maturity far beyond their mid-20s age range.'

While Skynyrd worked in Studio B on *Second Helping*, Bill Szymczyk was producing *On The Border* in Studio C. Twenty years later, the two producers met for lunch, and Kooper made the observation that practically all the then-contemporary country music was founded on one or both of those albums. In his memoir, *Backstage Passes & Backstabbing Bastards*, Kooper mistakenly confuses *Hotel California* for *On The Border*.

Perhaps surprisingly, 'Don't Ask Me No Questions' was released as the first single. The theory was that if it was a hit, 'Sweet Home Alabama' would be an even bigger hit. It bombed. However, the second single, 'Sweet Home Alabama', fared much better.

'Sweet Home Alabama' (King, Rossington, Van Zant) 4:43
This song predated the rest of the album, having been recorded in June 1973 in Studio One, Doraville, Georgia. Ronnie liked the song so much that he was very keen to record it as soon as possible; it was, in fact, recorded before the release of the first album in August 1973, possibly with a view to including it on the first album. The backing vocals were added later in Los Angeles by Kooper without the band's knowledge, featuring Merry Clayton and Clydie King, two of the most prolific and noted studio singers of the time, and Sherlie Matthews. The backing vocals were a great addition, despite early reservations from Clayton. As she recalled to Sam Adams for *AV Club* in 2013:

Clydie King called me – we'd known each other since we were seven or eight years old – and said: 'Baby sister, there's a session going on by these guys called Lynyrd Skynyrd. They want us for this song called 'Sweet Home Alabama'.' I said, 'Oh no, honey, I'm not singing no Alabama for anybody, anytime, anywhere.' And I gave her the whole thing about the civil rights movement and bombing churches and the rest of it. But Curtis (Merry's husband) convinced me that this would be a wonderful platform: 'This could be your protest song. I'm much older than you (Curtis Amy was 19 years Clayton's senior), and I was born in Houston. I've seen people swinging from trees. You need to do this song, Merry. And when you sing it, I want you to do it with everything that's in you.' So, when I go to the session, I said to the girls: 'We're going to sing this song until the walls cry out.' If you listen to it, we're all singing through our teeth, like we're really angry. That's how we got through the recording.

The song begins with a count-in from Ed King, followed by his picked introductory riff, which is one of the most instantly recognisable of all time. You can also hear a studio artefact, deliberately left in place: Ronnie requesting 'Turn it up' to the studio engineer, Rodney Mills, and Al Kooper. His reference was to turn up his monitoring level, but the immortal words have been heeded by fans, turning up the volume as they listen, on innumerable plays of the song all over the world. Subsequently, the intro riff is joined by a simple picked guitar motif, from Rossington, that adds much yet often escapes the attention of artists covering the song. This is probably the riff from Gary that inspired King. Skynyrd were the masters of guitar arrangement, each finding their space and complementing rather than competing. The same is true of the delicate piano flourishes from Billy.

At 43 seconds, the bridge riff begins and leads into the second verse. Straight after Ronnie sings 'Well I heard Mr. Young sing about her', if you listen very closely, Al Kooper can be heard faintly singing 'Southern Man' at 56 seconds. At 1:14, the chords remain the same as the verse, but the style subtly changes and becomes choppier for the chorus.

At 1:30, we have the first of Ed's brilliant solos, both of which he claimed came to him, complete, in a dream. At the time of recording, there was a disagreement about the key of the song. Ed felt that the song was in G, but Al insisted it was in the key of D. In later years, Ed was critical of the approach other players, such as Steve Gaines and Hughie Thomasson, took to the solo in terms of them playing it in the wrong key.

At 2:20, there is another stinging and more extended solo from Ed, which is supplemented by the female backing vocals and takes us to 3:00, the bridge riff and then into another verse. This is where Ronnie was able to mention the Swampers, the team at Muscle Shoals, and pay them a tribute as Ronnie had promised he would, following the misunderstanding over the Muscle Shoals demos.

Right before Billy's piano solo, you can hear 'whoo, whoo': one is Leon, and one is Ed King. At 4:08, Billy's stylistically characteristic piano kicks in and takes us through to the end of the song, which finishes with a fadeout 20 seconds from the end. During the final section of the song, Ronnie can be heard in the background, but the words aren't clear. According to King:

> At the end, Ronnie is saying, 'Montgomery's got the answer.' Kooper always recorded at least two vocal tracks. The first 'Mont' you hear Ronnie say is from the first vocal track. Then, during the mixdown, Kooper shut that track off, and you hear Ronnie say the second 'Mont'. Get it? 'Mont, Montgomery's got the answer'.

Some interpretations suggest it might be a subtle jab at Alabama Governor George Wallace, who was a controversial figure known for his segregationist views. The song also mentions Birmingham, another Alabama city, and its connection to the governor, further fuelling the debate about the song's stance on the South. Birmingham is significant because it was the site of civil rights activism and violence in the 1960s, most notably Martin Luther King's Birmingham campaign. Montgomery is the capital city of Alabama.

Ed King was primarily responsible for the music for 'Sweet Home Alabama' and for its defining riff. Quite remarkably, he wrote it on his first day as the band's third guitarist, following the return of Leon on bass guitar. Gary

Rossington had come up with the D, C, G progression and had been playing it repeatedly for 15 minutes when Ed walked in and added the iconic riff. According to Rossington, Ronnie had the words within the hour. Contrary to what some believe, there was never any animosity between Neil Young and the band; he was, in fact, one of their favourite artists. The song is a riposte to Young's criticism of the South in 'Southern Man' and 'Alabama'. Although Neil Young is name-checked in the song, he liked it and actually played it live himself on a couple of occasions. He did, however, express some regret over the condescending tone of his own lyrics. King claims authorship of the signature riff and choruses but acknowledged that he wouldn't have written his parts without Rossington's inspiration.

According to King on his *ProBoards* forum:

Rossington wrote the guitar part that you can hear him play behind the verses (behind my Strat part). It's sort of a counterpoint to my part, though his part came first. He was playing the guitar figure that you hear in the second verse. When I first heard that, I put my intro lick on top of that and then finished the tune. Without me hearing that riff of his, I wouldn't have written mine. Hearing 'Sweet Home Alabama' on the radio for the first time, that was a great feeling. Ronnie would say, 'That's our 'Ramblin' Man'.'

'Sweet Home Alabama' was released as a single, the second from the album, on 24 June 1974 with 'Don't Ask Me No Questions' as the B-side. This reached number eight in the US charts and number 31 in the UK.

'I Need You' (King, Rossington, Van Zant) 6:55
This is a slow, bluesy ballad and a relatively long song at 6:55. It is frequently overlooked in the band's artistic canon. The band's influence by Free can be heard in the song, but it is in no way derivative. According to King, it was the second song written on the same day as 'Sweet Home Alabama', and it was Leon's first day back in the band after quitting the ice cream factory.

The recording of the song took place some months later. On a day off in L.A., King took the time to show Mike Porter his arrangement of the song, which differed from the earlier version. Porter and King recorded the basic track in sections late one night at the Record Plant, Porter playing drums and King playing bass guitar. Kooper came in the following day and, after hearing it, cut and assembled the song. Although King felt Burns could have probably played the part, he was already familiar with the old arrangement, and Porter's drum track is used on the album. King also wanted a bassline that reflected how he heard it and tied closely to the guitar part. King recorded the rhythm guitar next, using his Fender Stratocaster through Porter's early 1960s Fender Princeton amplifier that provided the tremolo effect heard on the song. There is only one electric rhythm guitar track on the album, but on very close listening, there is possibly a faintly audible acoustic guitar providing some reinforcement. There are no credits for this, although in 2009, King speculated that if there is a part there, it wasn't him and could have been Allen Collins.

The solo sections throughout the song are Allen and Gary, doubled and panned in the audio mix. The feedback sustain that can be heard at points in the song, and predominantly towards the end of the song, is Gary Rossington and his 1959 Les Paul that he had just bought from Gruhn in Nashville. According to Ed, Gary could pick the note once, and the guitar would resonate on A all day long. The sustained feedback notes became a signature of Gary's playing.

When Allen and Gary were recording their solos, Ronnie came into the studio and announced that it was time to do the vocals. According to King's recollection, there was a single microphone placed in the room, and Ronnie did the vocals in one take, with one punch-in to correct a mistake. This was a remarkable achievement given the quality of the vocal track. The lyrical guitar lines are exemplary throughout, as is King's rhythm guitar.

'Don't Ask Me No Questions' (Rossington, Van Zant) 3:29
In the early years of the band, there were many people who were not interested in them when they were struggling. This song was a message to those people who became demanding once the band were successful. The song was written by Rossington and Van Zant while they were out on a fishing trip. Released in April 1974 as the first single from the album to little acclaim and success, it did not chart and was soon overshadowed by the release of the second single, 'Sweet Home Alabama'. The original single version differs from the album version and became available with the reissued CD version of the album. The B side, 'Take Your Time', was also included on the reissue of the album.

The song begins with a single rhythm guitar, which is joined by a slide and understated piano, before the band are all in for a short slide guitar solo from Ed. The vocals come in at 23 seconds, and Ronnie sets the tone for the song, expressing his desire for privacy when he gets to spend some time at home.

At 53 seconds, the bridge is augmented by the horns of Bobby Keys, Trevor Lawrence and Steve Madaio. Subtle subsequent horns embellish the song. Gary kicks in with his solo at 1:43, a solo that was one of Ed King's favourite solos by Gary. Al Kooper's backing vocals are clearly audible as the song begins to end, and Ed delivers a short, simple slide solo. A final piano flourish sounds like Billy, although Al Kooper has a piano credit for the track, perhaps for an earlier backing part in the song. Once again, this song features Ed on bass rather than Leon. Although it's a relatively short song, it is catchy and, as usual, well-crafted and arranged.

'Workin' For MCA' (King, Van Zant) 4:49
In 2009, on his web forum, Ed claimed he originally conceived 'Workin' For MCA' as a mid-tempo R&B tune. He originally wanted a major-key, slower

R&B feel and wasn't particularly pleased with the way the song developed. He gave an insight into the writing process:

> It's a good example of how six people working together can interpret someone's idea. It was just one of those things I came up with. It actually turned out a lot 'harder' than I'd envisioned. But it took on a life of its own. Skynyrd fans love it. I'm ambivalent! Everybody plays it wrong because they don't know that particular chord position (inversion) where I start. Hard to explain, but if you saw it, you'd understand. No one else gets it. I even showed it to Hughie. I guess he doesn't get it either because they're still not doing it right. At least, it doesn't sound right to my ears.

The song was written by Ronnie and Ed to be aired to the record label during a showcase at a Sounds of the South press party held at Richard's in Atlanta on 29 July 1973. The band opened with the song and had the record execs' attention for the remainder of the set. The lyrics were both biographical and judged to perfection, describing the band's signing for MCA and the potential repercussions of non-payment.

> Seven years of hard luck, comin' down on me
> From the Florida border, yes, up to Nashville, Tennessee
> I worked in every joint you can name, mister, every honky tonk
> Along come Mr. Yankee slicker, sayin' 'Maybe you're what I want'

The seven years of hard luck are the band paying their dues between 1966 and 1973. The Yankee slicker is Al Kooper, although that's not how he saw himself. The line 'Oh, nine thousand dollars, that's all we could win/But we smiled at the Yankee slicker with a big ol' Southern grin' reflects the fact that the band actually signed for $9000, and the reference to the repercussions of the record company not meeting their contractual obligations were clear, if possibly tongue in cheek, when he sang 'Just pay me all my money, mister, maybe you won't get a scar'.

The song begins powerfully with rhythm guitar augmented by drum and guitar stabs, followed by Leon unleashing a vocal growl that brings the song in. Rossington and Collins deliver a doubled solo before the vocals begin proper at 22 seconds. Again, the band's innate arrangement skills are evidenced by this dynamic opening that packs a big punch in a short space of time. At 56 seconds, another lead break brings us from the chorus back into the next verse. This one sounds like it is played by Gary. At 1:41, Billy takes a solo on what sounds more like an electric piano, which is followed by a stinging and aggressive lead from Ed. At 2:26, it sounds like Allen takes over lead duties as the guitar tone changes; however, contemporaneous video footage shows it is probably still Ed. This is then followed by dual leads from Rossington and Collins, which transition back into the verse. More dual leads from Rossington and Collins take us to the end, which is once again a fadeout.

'The Ballad Of Curtis Loew' (Collins, Van Zant) 4:51
This song opens side two of the album. As the name suggests, it's a slow ballad and features some of Ed King's best slide work. He always favoured a heavy glass slide, which can be heard on the song, although he used a metal slide for the solo, using a 1965 Strat through a Fender twin.

The song begins with a plaintive slide guitar and a single clean rhythm guitar playing the chords. Once again, the guitars are arranged superbly, creating space. A gentle slide accompanies an electric guitar with tremolo, and an acoustic guitar is low in the mix. Interestingly, Al Kooper is credited with acoustic guitar, but in 2009, Ed said, 'There is a place that I can hear myself playing an acoustic on that song, right before it goes into the Rossington outro. If you can hear an acoustic guitar anywhere else on that song, that'd be me.'

At 37 seconds, the drums come in, but the delivery remains relaxed. At 2:40, there is a slide solo, followed at 3:06 by Gary playing a sweet but typically understated solo that resolves with more slide from Ed. Al Kooper is credited with keyboards, but they are only really evident in the closing bars, and it sounds like Billy.

Lyrically, the song tells the story of a black guitar player, called Curtis Loew, who plays guitar for a boy who has made a little money collecting and returning soda bottles. The boy idolises Curtis, the finest picker to ever play the blues, and goes to see him regularly despite beatings from his mum. Curtis dies, and no one attends the funeral, the local folk considering him to be useless.

As is the case with almost every aspect of Lynyrd Skynyrd, there are multiple and often contradictory accounts of the details, in this case, about who the song is based on. According to Gene Odum, childhood friend of Ronnie, plane crash survivor and part of the band's road crew in the 1970s, he is the young boy 'searching for soda bottles to make myself some dough', and Curtis is the grocery store owner Claude Hammer, a competent guitar player who may have taught Ronnie at one time. According to John Haury, Ronnie said that Curtis was a fictional character, inspired by his memories of Shorty Medlocke, grandfather of Rickey Medlocke, and his front porch jams, but also from a story he heard about Hank Williams, who had been inspired by an old black blues musician. Ronnie explained that Curtis was every old black blues player who had ever taught a trick or two to a young white boy trying to learn the blues. Perhaps significantly, 'Curtis' was also the name of the black blues player who had influenced Merle Haggard in Folsom Prison. Ronnie was a big fan of both Williams and Haggard. Interestingly, though, both Claude and Shorty were white. Ed claimed that the final twist, the spelling of Curtis Loew, was a joke he was able to play by overseeing the album credits and implying that Curtis was a Jewish black man. The pre-crash band only played the song once live, but it was revived for the *Tribute Tour*.

'Swamp Music' (King, Van Zant) 3:31
This is the second shortest song on the album, being just two seconds longer than 'Don't Ask Me No Questions', but it is one that Ed King loved:

> You've got to understand that I'll always love that tune. It was my ode to James Burton. I'd been watching a live Elvis film with the song 'Steamroller Blues'. I was playing around with some of James Burton's licks, and 'Swamp Music' came out of it.

The song begins with Ed's super catchy riff, which is soon joined by a second guitar and the drums. The bassline from Leon, who also adds backing vocals, is perfect, and Bob Burns really hits a great groove on this song. The keys also supplement the rhythm section, and it sounds like Billy is playing an electric piano.

Lyrically, the song is about enjoying the simple pleasures and spending time in nature, fishing and going out with the dogs, capturing the feel of Southern life.

At 1:17, a short keyboard fill takes us into a vocal and guitar call and answer refrain, 'Swamp, Swamp, Swamp music'. Then, at 1:53, Gary takes the solo, despite this being Ed's song, but as he said, 'It always wound up that the best solo was the one that got played. We never fought about it. It was great teamwork. I was very busy with my rhythm part on this one anyway.'
The fills and rhythm work on this song stand as some of Ed's finest work.

'The Needle And The Spoon' (Collins, Van Zant) 3:53
The song title is obviously a reference to injecting heroin, and the lyrics clearly warn of the dangers, talking about 'feelin' so sick inside' and reflecting, 'Got to get better, Lord before I die'. Allen opens the song with a neat, picked riff, which is augmented by picked natural harmonics, before the chordal motif is established at 17 seconds, and once again, Ed's stinging fills are evidenced just 23 seconds in.

One of the most notable aspects of the song is Allen's first solo that begins at 1:40. His wah-wah solo was ranked number 19 in 2015 by *Guitar World* magazine in their list of best wah solos of all time. They said: 'A clear tip of the hat to Eric Clapton's solo from 'White Room', Allen Collins pulls out the wah to blend 1960s psychedelia seamlessly into a bona-fide Southern-rock classic.' Indeed, Collins was heavily influenced by Clapton, a theme echoed in their live renditions of 'Crossroads'. Allen shows clear mastery of the wah pedal, but didn't use it again, or indeed any effects on any original album releases (pre-crash). However, he takes a wah solo on 'Wino', released on *Skynyrd First And ... Last*, and on the album *Thyrty: The 30th Anniversary*

Collection, there is a very early recording by the band of a blues medley. Allen takes a long unaccompanied solo at the end of a song, the final section of which includes wah-wah. Also, demo versions of 'Junkie' and 'He's Alive' from the *Lynyrd Skynyrd – The Definitive Lynyrd Skynyrd Collection* box set also feature the wah.

At 2:13, we have two lead guitars from Ed and Allen. As Ed recalled on his forum: 'I always felt that harmony lines worked best for just parts of the tune. For instance, in the midst of several unison lines, we'd throw in a harmony part. Most of our guitar parts were constructed that way. The end of Allen's solo on 'Needle & Spoon' comes to mind. My idea, so that's why I remembered it.' At 3:05, we have a reverb-laden echo from Ronnie of 'I know, I know', which leads us straight into another Collins lead that continues as the song fades out and ends at 3:56.

'Call Me The Breeze' (J.J. Cale) 5:23
According to Ed, Ronnie loved J.J. Cale, and the band had this tune worked up before he joined. Rossington recalled that they originally tried the song like the original version, but it wasn't working out. Ronnie told him to rearrange the song, come back with the music and he would sing over it. Ed described the intro, created by Rossington, as genius: 'What a cool guitar riff that is, one of the best ever because it suits the song.' Ed claimed the effect on Rossington's guitar is a Uni-Vibe, which is an effect where the sound is phased in multiple stages with each stage at slightly different pitches, which creates a thick, sometimes hypnotic, pulsing sound intended to replicate a rotating Leslie speaker. He also pointed out that they didn't really write traditional 12-bar, three-chord progressions, so 'Call Me The Breeze' was a perfect foil to the rest of their material.

As Ed described, this really is a simple song revolving around only the A, D and E chords. Lyrically, it is easy to see the appeal to Ronnie, and stylistically, the lyrics are like his own. The subject of the song is carefree and passes through like the breeze, no trouble, with no commitments: 'Call me the breeze, I keep blowin' down the road'.

The song has an outstanding arrangement. Gary kicks the song off, Ed adds fills and horns provide colour at 15 seconds, and a snare roll brings the band in at 20 seconds. The band establish a rolling groove, and Ed lays down cool fills before Gary takes a trademark solo from 1:21, joined by hand claps at 1:51; the solo ends at 2:22, with the claps still evident. Billy solos at 2:24, building up speed and being joined by the horns for the remainder of the solo, finishing at 3:55. Ed's fills continue in abundance, all tasteful and seemingly effortless but creative. The horns build up to a drop out for all but vocals, and the song ends with a short piano fill from Billy. This is a three-chord song lasting 5:09 that keeps the listener interested.

The hand clappers are credited on the album under pseudonyms. According to Ed:

The hand clappers were the band members, minus me; I wasn't there that day. Wicker was Ronnie, one of his nicknames. Punnel is Billy Powell; I think Allen Collins was Toby. Kooper was Kooder, Mr. Feedback was our soundman, Kevin Elson, and Gooshie was roadie Joe Barnes. Nixon was a roadie for The Eagles who challenged us at the pinball machine many times. The Eagles were recording *On The Border* in the next room.

Nuthin' Fancy (1975)

Personnel:
Ronnie Van Zant: lead vocals
Gary Rossington: guitar
Allen Collins: guitar
Ed King: guitar
Leon Wilkeson: bass guitar
Artimus Pyle: drums, percussion
Billy Powell: keyboards
Additional musicians:
Barry Harwood: dobro, mandolin
Jimmy Hall: harmonica
David Foster: piano
Bobbye Hall: percussion
Recorded at WEBB IV Studios, Atlanta (except for track 1, Studio One, Doraville, Georgia)
Producer: Al Kooper
Engineer: Al Kooper
Recorded by Rodney Mills (track 1)
Release date: 24 March 1975
Label: MCA
Chart places: US: 9, UK: 43
Running time: 37:34

Bob Burns had made his last recording with Lynyrd Skynyrd. Although considered by Kooper to be the least musical of the band, he left an outstanding musical legacy as the drummer on the first two albums. A combination of factors led to his exit. Burns had been abandoned in childhood, something Mark Ribowsky said he never came to terms with. In *Whiskey Bottles And Brand-New Cars,* he also cites a fatal automotive accident as a contributing factor; Burns had been the driver in a fatal accident on Buckman Bridge in Jacksonville some months earlier. He was a man in decline and was being pushed beyond his limits by relentless touring. Mixing whiskey and codeine apparently didn't help. At one point on tour in Europe, he threw a cat to its death, having seen the devil in its eyes. Perhaps more alarmingly, in Paris, he saw the devil in the eyes of soundman Kevin Elsom and chased him with an axe. Shortly after, the band let him go, and he was hospitalised by his parents. Following a diagnosis of bipolar, he was given a range of medications, finally finding himself 'a free man' after the prescription of Prozac in 1987. Burns never tried to rejoin the band, but he was proud of what he had accomplished. He died aged 64 on 3 April 2015, in a car crash after hitting a mailbox and a tree on a sharp curve in Cartersville, Georgia, shortly after leaving his home.

Thomas Delmer Pyle had already stood in for Bob, at the recommendation of Charlie Daniels, for the 'Saturday Night Special' sessions when Bob had made himself unavailable. He was chosen as the replacement. Pyle was born in Louisville and served in the Marine Corps. He later studied music at Tennessee Technical College, where, due in part to both his appearance and his wild behaviour, he was nicknamed 'Artemis' after the Greek goddess of the hunt and wilderness. It was a nickname he embraced, changing the spelling and legally changing his name to Artimus. Pyle was a good drummer and was difficult to miss; with his long hair and beard, he looked a lot like some representations of Jesus. It is remarkable how well he played, as he was reputedly taking acid before he went on stage.

Ronnie wanted the band to continue its progression and to become a major act. He felt that Alan Walden needed to go. Ed King also believed that Walden didn't have the managerial capacity for a band of their calibre, but believed that Walden recognised this and so was prepared to be bought out. It is possible that Peter Rudge, gaining the confidence of the band, was endearing himself to Ronnie, but he said he wouldn't actively pursue the band. He would, however, manage them if they came to him. Although Pyle later claimed that Rudge was manipulative and shady, he won Ronnie over to the degree that he said, 'I have a Jesus in heaven and on Earth, but in music I've got Peter Rudge.'

Kooper's label deal was up for resigning and MCA wanted to make changes. Kooper and his manager, Stan Polley, attended a meeting and asked for a redrafted contract to be sent to them. The record company, however, stalled. Polley was a hard case entertainment manager, perceptive in his advice to Kooper, but also a fraudster. His handling of Badfinger led to him being named in band leader Pete Ham's suicide note as a 'soulless bastard'. Polley pointed out that Skynyrd were getting five percentage points to Kooper's ten, and it was time to switch this around. The Sounds of the South deal locked Kooper into an exclusive producer contract with MCA, who were withholding royalty payments in an effort to force Kooper into accepting a buyout. Ham predicted it would take MCA a year to realise that Kooper was holding the points they needed to give to Skynyrd. So Kooper played a waiting game, Polley pointing out that they could charge MCA an inflated sum when they eventually came back to them. Almost exactly a year later, MCA came back saying they wanted to buy the ten points and dissolve the deal. Polley put a $1,000,000 non-negotiable price tag on the deal, which was paid, although it included everything they owned of the label and their production royalties for the first two albums.

Then, presumably to MCA's ire, Skynyrd told MCA they wanted Kooper to produce the next album, so they would have to pay him royalties on that album. However, in a move that typifies the music industry, the million-dollar payoff was charged to Skynyrd's account.

Kooper recalled, in his memoir, that the recording of the album was very different to that of the first two. Recording took place at Webb IV Studios in Atlanta, except for 'Saturday Night Special', which was recorded in Studio

One, Doraville. Having toured extensively, the band had not had time to prepare material for the album. There were literally no songs and only a window of a month until they were scheduled to be back out on the road. Al spent the entire first day working on mic placement to get the right drum sound and called it a night at 11 pm, having almost cracked it. On his return the following morning, all the microphones had been pulled back from the kit, and they had begun again. House engineer Dave Evans had told the band he could get a better sound. Evans had overstepped the mark but had the support of the band. Kooper decided at that point to take a step back and let Evans take the engineering decisions. With progress slow, Al took Ronnie to one side and told him that the band had two weeks to write and arrange the songs for the album and that he was going back to New York. Following this, they would have two weeks left to record everything. Quite bizarrely, Kooper recalled that, following the album's completion, the next time he saw Dave Evans was at Ronnie Van Zant's funeral, where Evans was the presiding minister.

When Kooper returned, the band had made good progress with six songs written and only two more required. Sixteen-hour stints were spent in the Studio, ended by Kooper before the band were ready. Skynyrd laced Kooper's drink with speed, unbeknownst to him, on one occasion, which led to a longer session but a sick and angry producer the next day. The final two songs written were 'Cheatin' Woman' and 'Made In The Shade'.

On the last day of recording, the tour bus arrived to pick up the band, and the album was done. The band were to hit the road, and Kooper needed to complete the mixing. Kooper recalls that he told the band it would be their last work together, saying he'd rather be their friend than their producer. In a 1975 interview with *Crawdaddy* magazine, the ever-eloquent Allen Collins shared his perspective:

He tried to tell us what to do, but we wouldn't let him. He once brought up the idea of doing a Grand Funk-like song, but we said we didn't do that shit. There are good and bad parts to everybody, and I'm not saying anything against him, but we ain't gonna use him anymore.

Ed King, on the other hand, felt very positively about Kooper, even if he was asked to remix some of his work:

I really enjoyed working with Al Kooper. I believe, had it not been for Al, no one would've heard of Skynyrd. He was the visionary behind the band and how it should be presented to the world. We didn't always agree with Al, but I certainly enjoyed his presence.

Opinions about the album vary. Some cite a lack of classics as a sign that the band's well was running dry, while *Rolling Stone* were uncharacteristically charitable: '*Nuthin' Fancy* maintains the feel, sonically and stylistically, of (the band)'s first two albums. Tracks such as 'On The Hunt' and 'Cheatin' Woman' are as good as anything the group has put on record. Lynyrd Skynyrd is an important group with a future.' The album went top ten in the US (where it was later certified platinum), and it brought the band international recognition, just missing out on a first top 40 placing on the UK album chart.

'Saturday Night Special' (King, Van Zant) 5:08
Ed King recalled auditioning Artimus Pyle in Atlanta, around June 1974, when Al Kooper called in and said Lynyrd Skynyrd had a spot for a song in a Burt Reynolds film, *The Longest Yard*. Ed had been working on 'Saturday Night Special' with Ronnie, but admitted, 'the version we worked on with Bob Burns wasn't happening.' Ed, Leon and Artimus worked on a new arrangement for the song while Kooper was there, and he was able to make his own contributions to the arrangement. The three musicians went into Studio One in Doraville and recorded their parts. Ed used an Echoplex effect that he had just purchased, but it was never used live. A few days later, Ronnie, Allen and Gary drove up from Jacksonville, came in and added their parts. At this point, Artimus had not officially joined the band, but it was his first recorded contribution.

Ed cites The Who's 'Bargain' (1971) as a major influence on him, and as a source of licks he used in 'Saturday Night Special', noting that 'Townshend is the quintessential rock 'n' roll guitarist. Because he plays rhythm guitar, he gets it.'

Al Kooper's recollections differ slightly in detail but are broadly consistent; it is interesting to note his observations on the song's timing. He recalls the boys counted in the song and came in on beat two of the second bar of the count off, instead of the first beat, so the downbeat fell on the second beat. Therefore, the pulse of the song kept coming on the second beat and not the first. When challenged over this, Ed stated that it all worked out perfectly when they got to the guitar solo before the vocals. Alarmed, Kooper got them to play it again and discovered that Pyle was playing a 7/4 bar between the first two sections. According to Kooper, Ed then claimed you could only have four beats in a bar. In Kooper's autobiography, he states 'That's what I loved about those guys. They had no book knowledge of music – they were just instinctively brilliant.' Kooper backed down in an argument he knew he could not win. It is an interesting perspective, given that Ed knew more theory than Gary and Allen.

'Saturday Night Special' begins with Al Kooper counting in for a strong introduction to the song and album. There is a little solo fill from Ed, doubled guitars and a rolling fill from Artimus, and a short solo from Gary brings the first verse in.

Each verse tells a different story, eschewing the use and proliferation of cheap handguns, the 'Saturday Night Special'. The first verse begins with the story of a man shooting another man in bed with his cheating wife, followed at 1:02 by the chorus telling us 'Handguns ain't good for nuthin' but putting a man 6ft in a hole'.

Another Rossington solo takes us into the second verse, which is a cautionary tale of drinking and gambling, where a man shoots his friend after accusing him of cheating in a poker game. At 2:14, there is a bridge section and a synth drone, unusual in a Lynyrd Skynyrd song, played by Al on a Moog synthesiser. Ed augments this with a few fills, and at 3:00, Rossington takes the main solo. Verse three warns us that we might even shoot ourselves and that handguns should be dumped. At 4:27, there is a galloping outro, with the return of the synth drone. Ronnie can be heard singing, 'And that's the end of this song', and the fadeout begins. Throughout, Leon's bass is tight, and Artimus's drumming is sharp, the two making a formidable rhythm section.

Ronnie may have been unaware of the origin of the phrase in the song title, which was the term 'niggertown Saturday night special', referring to cheap, easily available, often low-quality handguns often used for criminal activity, but by the late 1970s, the phrase was in use in the context he used. Although the message in the song is clear, it wasn't uncommon for members of the band to carry guns. Ronnie owned guns and bought his wife Judy a .38 Special for self-protection. Years later, brother Johnny had to defend 'God & Guns' against the claim that it contradicted the message here.

'Saturday Night Special' was released as a single on 19 May 1975 with 'Made In The Shade' on the B-side. *Billboard* considered that the song was 'ominous sounding' and said that the lyrics contain 'interesting social commentary.' It reached number 27 in the US but did not chart in the UK.

'Cheatin' Woman' (Kooper, Rossington, Van Zant) 4:38
The fact that much of the album was being written in the studio gave Al Kooper more space to contribute, both to arrangements and to co-write this song. With only 14 days left in the studio, a whole day was spent on 'Cheatin' Woman' with both Ed and Al writing the music, according to Al, and Ronnie, naturally, the lyrics. Al claims he played piano and organ on the track, as there simply wasn't time to teach it to Billy. If Al's recollection is entirely correct, it is surprising that Ed doesn't get a songwriting credit, but Rossington does. The assumption must be made that he was mistaken.

The song was possibly chosen to follow 'Saturday Night Special' as it concerns a man betrayed, considering shooting his lover to end his pain, told in the first person. Beginning with a solo guitar playing a blues lick, the song kicks in with bass, drums and organ. Organ and electric piano feature heavily as the song establishes itself as a laid-back 12-bar blues. Ed offers a slide solo from 1:56, tasteful as ever. Allen lays down a simple outro solo, and the song fades out under a repeated mournful bend. It isn't one of Skynyrd's best-known or loved songs, a lesser work in the band's canon, but it would be harsh to call it filler. It remains a good song, but others were great.

'Railroad Song' (King, Van Zant) 4:14
Ed wrote the music in his hotel room and called Ronnie up on his hotel phone. Ed told Ronnie it sounded like a train song, and according to Ed, within half an hour, the song was written, and although Ronnie never wrote his lyrics down, he remembered them perfectly the next day. The lyrics trace the band's country roots and Ronnie's influences. It's a song about riding the boxcar, but we could interpret this as Ronnie feeling like an outsider, searching for a deeper way to express himself through his songs:

> I'm goin' to ride this train Lord until I find out
> What Jimmie Rogers and the Hag was all about
> See I play this rock n roll, and I think that's fine
> But I want to go back a little further in time

Ronnie was clearly influenced by the blues and British rock bands like Free, but he loved country music. In 1992, quoted in Ballinger's *Lynyrd Skynyrd An Oral History*, Judy Van Zant claimed Ronnie owned every Merle Haggard album, whom he references in the song. Following his death, it became apparent that he would have indeed gone a little further back in time. He had expressed an interest in producing records, but he planned to make a country-rock album. He had spoken about recording with both Haggard and Waylon Jennings. Apparently, preliminary talks had begun, and it helped that MCA had recently signed Haggard, so they were interested in the idea. Judy also revealed that when Ronnie came off the road, 'He didn't listen to rock music. He listened to Merle Haggard, Waylon Jennings and stuff like that.'

The song begins with a hypnotic rolling guitar arpeggio and Wet Willie's Jimmy Hall blowing harp beautifully in keeping with the feel of the song. The drums and bass are once again tight and complementary. Ed really liked the drumming in particular: 'This song moves me and moves me bad. I swear, Artimus Pyle did some monster playing on that track. How he remembered all those moves, I'll never know. That tune's got some very cool wrinkles.'

All the guitar is played by Ed except for Allen's solo at 2:08, which is split by 'Choo Choo train' backing vocals from Al and Leon. The same idea is repeated at the end of the song, but the solo resolves and the track slows and stops, like a steam engine drawing to a halt. According to Ed, the slow-down ending wasn't planned, but after hearing how Artimus played it, it seemed a logical way to finish the song. Al plays the organ on the recording, but its contribution is subtle.

'I'm A Country Boy' (Collins, Van Zant) 4:24
Ed King felt that Allen stole the riff going into the verse from Jerry Reed's track 'Amos Moses', from his 1970 album *Georgia Sunshine*. For Al Kooper, it was one of his favourites, which he felt had a great groove and strong lyrics. King always felt Ronnie was a country singer fronting a rock band, and certainly this song wouldn't contradict that.

Ronnie's lyrics are not judgmental but express how he likes things and how he wants them to be. He tells us that 'New York City is a thousand miles away', which he is happy with: 'Big city, hard times don't bother me/I'm a country boy, I'm as happy as I can be'. The three-guitar arrangement once again excels in blending simple, complementary parts. Ed provides tasteful slide, Leon provides bass and backing vocals and Al is credited with percussion. At 1:47, the drum pattern and riff change, providing a bridge into a tasteful Collins solo. A slide refrain from Ed repeats as the song fades out. Once again, maybe this isn't one of the more celebrated songs, but it is well-written and performed.

'On The Hunt' (Collins, Van Zant) 5:25

Ed's recollection was that the band wrote the song in the first week of rehearsal with Artimus, a week where, in his own words, he himself was 'preoccupied with a nervous breakdown! Or close to it. I just didn't show up that week. Bad week, I can tell you. Just stressed out, never fully recovered!'

Lyrically, the song is either about a groupie or a prostitute and hooking up with them, recognising they both want the same thing. He isn't judgmental of her and doesn't care what anybody thinks about the situation. Having said that, there is more than a degree of misogyny in the lyrics as we can see here: 'My daddy told me a long time ago/Said there's two things son/Two things you should know/And in these two things you must take pride/That's a horse and woman, yeah/Well, both of them you ride'.

The song packs a musical punch, and Allen's rhythm guitar work stands out. A short, doubled solo follows the hard-hitting stabs, and the preliminary vocals come in along with the piano, although the verse doesn't begin until 0.30. The song is reminiscent of Free musically and lyrically, the song 'The Hunter' in particular. Ironically, for a song so closely linked to Free, 'The Hunter' was written by Booker T. Jones, C. Wells, Al Jackson Jr., Donald Dunn and Steve Cropper, and found fame when recorded by Albert King on his 1967 Album *Born Under A Bad Sign* and reached the US singles chart in 1969 when covered by Ike and Tina Turner.

Rossington handles the solo and fills, conjuring his inner Kossoff, one of his major influences, from 2:26. The solo leads into a middle eight section and continues until 3:37, where Ronnie delivers his misogynistic final verse. The section at 4:24 has Rossington once again showing his influences, and Ronnie calls for a bit of guitar to lead the song to its fadeout at 5:28. According to Ed, 'Gary's solo on that is one of his finest, but I have to admit I really liked all of the solos he played back then. Well thought-out melodies.' It is difficult to disagree.

Although Ed liked the song, and in his opinion, it was Artimus and Leon at their finest, he also said that Collins had taken his 'Workin' For MCA' riff, slowed it down and made a new tune out of it. He said, 'I was flattered. Until I joined the band, I don't think the band had ever written a song in the key of B before.' Ed didn't think the song needed a third guitar and was unable to think of one, so he didn't record one. When playing live, he doubled Allen's part.

During the last days of recording for the album, Ronnie was cutting the vocals for the song. Al Kooper remembered that the chorus was pitched about half a tone too high for Ronnie's voice. Ronnie was straining and getting angry at himself. He finally hit every note in one take, but Dave Evans had made a recording error, and the vocals distorted in parts of the chorus. Kooper pointed this out to the band, but Ronnie insisted the vocals were kept, feeling it was the best take he could make. This accounts for Ronnie's vocals being buried, to a degree, in the chorus sections in the final mix, as Kooper was trying to hide the distortion. Perhaps Kooper's account of Ronnie's difficulty gives an insight into why Rossington and Collins hadn't written songs in the key of B.

'Am I Losin'' (Rossington, Van Zant) 4:32
This song was one of the last to be written for the album, according to most accounts, although Gene Odum recalled that Gary began working on the song after Elvis had sent each member of the band a dozen roses after breaking his attendance record for Memphis Stadium in March and July 1974. The band went to Graceland to thank him, but he wasn't home. Possibly, then, it was an existing idea that Rossington had that was worked up for the album.

Written in large part as an ode to Bob Burns, Ronnie laments the loss of a good friend. Ronnie extends the notion of losing friends beyond Burns, though, and to friends in general, because of his success, and how people change in their attitude toward him. The acoustic guitar backing from Gary and Ed, panned left and right, sets the tone for what Kooper described as the 'mellowest country thing the band cut.'

Breaking once again with the established Skynyrd ethos of writing solos in advance, Ed improvised the solo. The first part is played on his 1964 SG using the neck pickup, with the tone control rolled off, through a Marshall amplifier. In the first part of the solo, Ed is paying homage to Toy Caldwell of the Marshall Tucker Band. Towards the end of the solo, Ed overdubbed a Strat part that mimics 'Sweet Home Alabama', an idea that Al Kooper had. The solo is great, but Ed was a little more critical of himself, recalling on *ProBoards*:

Unfortunately, you can hear where I switch to the bridge pickup. It was really 'off the cuff' and, to my ears, has quite a few holes. It was a first-taker. It was very spontaneous, so I decided to leave it as is. I should've thought about it more, but I just wanted to get it done and leave it. We were short on time, and I thought what I had was just okay. No one told me to change it. I don't play perfect stuff. I just try and get a good tone and a good vibe. I'm a big supporter of the spontaneous! Be it right or wrong.

For the other guitar parts in the song, Ed played a Fender Strat through a Twin Reverb. A contemporaneous review in *Pop Top* magazine called the song 'an unusually gentle, plaintive ballad that comes right to the threshold of incandescence.'

'Made In The Shade' (Van Zant) 4:40

Ronnie introduces the song by saying, 'When I was young 'un they used to teach me to play music like this here', and then counting in. Allen can be heard coughing in the background. This song is unique in that it is the only song solely credited to Ronnie.

Gary is playing acoustic guitar, accompanied by future Rossington Collins Band guitarist Barry Lee Harwood on mandolin and dobro, Jimmy Hall once again blowing harp, Al on piano and, bizarrely, Ed King on Moog bass and Artimus on tambourine, bass and coke crate percussion. It seems likely the tuba sound is the Moog, and that Artimus is also hitting a marching drum. The band did, at one point, attempt to play this song live, with Gary trying to play a mandolin and Allen the acoustic guitar. There is a recording that can be tracked down, but it is only worth the effort for the genuinely curious!

As has been noted by Gene Odum, Ronnie's tenor is delivered in a Deep South style reminiscent of Leon Redbone and even includes a yodel. Lyrically, it's a tale of a man telling his girlfriend she needs to be careful, or she will lose the opportunities she has been given and what she has: 'Well, when I first met you baby, you was a red-light girl/But I tried to take you to better world/But you would not listen/Still you think I am a fool/Well you had it made in the shade, baby/Don't let that tree fall down on you'. The phrase 'made in the shade' was one that Ronnie got from Shorty Medlocke years earlier and that he adopted. Interestingly, it was the only Skynyrd song that Kooper ever went on to cover himself.

'Whiskey Rock-A-Roller' (King, Powell, Van Zant) 4:15

The song is notable for both the writing credit for Powell and for his absence on the recording. According to Ed, Billy started the idea for 'Whiskey Rock-A-Roller' with a fairly complicated piano part that Ed made usable in the context of the band. However, without Billy's original ideas, the song could not have been written. King recalled, 'Billy complained many times that no one would write with him. I just chalked it up to the fact that Billy's a classically trained musician and it was difficult to write with him.' Billy, despite his significant contributions to the band, didn't get another Skynyrd writing credit. However, he is credited for some works with the other members of the band in the years following the crash but before the reunion tour, specifically with the Rossington Collins Band on the songs 'Opportunity' and 'Getaway' from the 1980 album *Anytime, Anyplace, Anywhere*, the track 'Gotta Get it Straight' from the 1981 album *This Is The*

Way and with the Allen Collins Band for the track 'Hangin' Judge' on the album *Here, There And Back* from 1983.

King recalled doing several takes of many of the songs on *Nuthin' Fancy*, largely because they were being written and arranged on the spot. Recording and writing an album in 28 days was a seriously challenging undertaking. The song isn't deep or philosophical; it's just a barroom boogie telling the tale of life on the road and recognising the nomadic touring life. It also emphasises the availability of whiskey and hard-living women:

> Take me down to Memphis town, bus driver get me there
> I got me a queenie she got long brown curly hair
> She likes to drink old grandad, and her shoes do shuffle around
> And every time I see that gal
> Lord, she wants to take me down

Drinking 'old grandad' is a reference to consuming the traditional American bourbon Old Grand-Dad, known for its high rye content and spicy flavour profile.

The complementary rhythm guitars are typical for Skynyrd in the way they work together, but are worthy of the listener's close attention. Gary provides solo work and Ed provides the fills.

Some criticism has been made that Ronnie's vocal was a little nasal, due to a cold, and that more time should have been taken. The time wasn't available, though. However, Ronnie must have been pleased with the *Circus* magazine review of the song: 'Van Zant's voice rises above a careening wall of guitars and soars high on the melody in a way only Paul Rodgers' vocals can equal.'

Although credited with piano, it seems that there wasn't time for Billy to record it, and Kooper had David Foster add piano when he took the tapes from Atlanta to LA. At this time, Foster was working as a session musician before becoming a 16-time Grammy-winning producer. Although later concert versions of the song missed Ed King's clever rhythm playing, Billy added much to the song by way of compensation.

Associated Tracks
'Cottonmouth Country'

Ed claimed that the original tape of the 'Saturday Night Special' sessions contained not only an extended jam at the end of the track, four minutes with only Ed, Leon and Artimus, but also a partially completed song that was never officially released called 'Cottonmouth Country':

> When everybody was done recording guitars and vocals, Ronnie and I
> started working on this bass riff I had. The band jammed on it, and we had
> something cool going with it, but we had reached a point where we needed

to discuss where to take the arrangement. We never did. Ronnie said 'cut', and we were done for the day.

Beginning with Ronnie saying, 'It's a little swamp song' and warning of the dangers of living 'down south', the song showed much promise and can be found on the internet. Had the original master been found, it had been reported that the band intended to isolate the vocals and re-record the song, which Ed was vehemently against, for the album *God And Guns*. Rodney Mills once again engineered in the studio, and perhaps unsurprisingly, his recollections also differ in detail. He recalls the song being cut in a day and that a couple of songs were recorded to two-track as demos. Only the original tape could settle this one.

'Road Fatigue'

The only known version of this song is a live recording from 9 December 1974 at L'Olympia, Paris, France, although the same recording has been falsely attributed to a concert in Sheffield, England, in 1977. It is a spirited rocker and worth checking out, despite the poor quality of the recording. A finished studio version would have held its own in the Skynyrd catalogue.

Gimme Back My Bullets (1976)

Personnel:
Ronnie Van Zant: lead vocals, lyrics
Gary Rossington: guitars
Allen Collins: guitars
Leon Wilkeson: bass, background vocals
Artimus Pyle: drums, percussion
Billy Powell: keyboards
Additional musicians:
The Honnicutts: background vocals ('Double Trouble', 'Cry For The Bad Man')
Lee Freeman: harp ('I Got The Same Old Blues')
Barry Lee Harwood: dobro, mandolin ('All I Can Do Is Write About It')
Recorded at Record Plant, Los Angeles (tracks 2, 4, 8); Capricorn Studios, Macon, Georgia
Producer: Tom Dowd
Engineer: Gary Ladinsky
Release date: 2 February 1976
Label: MCA
Chart places: US: 20, UK: 34
Running time: 35:16

On 26 May 1975, Ed King left the band. When interviewed by Gary James in 2005, Ed offered this perspective:

Well, I was out of my mind for quitting. But it was the best thing I ever did. We signed with a new manager in New York, and the manager didn't really have a clue as to what the band was about. He was interested in Ronnie only. He was kind of like putting wedges between ... well, he put a wedge between Ronnie and me for sure. Ronnie was drinking a lot. It was just an unpleasant situation. I never drank, but I was into drugs pretty good. I had gotten fed up with, frankly, all the violence. Our new manager used to tell Ronnie, 'Hey, the crazier you are, the better you're gonna be.' And I think he kind of took it to heart. It just got a little too nutty for me. So, in the middle of the night, I just walked out. It had been a bad night the night before. I had good reason to leave. I should never have done it the way I did it.

In 2009, he was more specific when interviewed by Jaan Uhelszki:

Well, yeah, the night before I quit. Actually, two nights before we played in Ann Arbor, Michigan, and Ronnie got thrown in jail along with this guy I knew, John Butler, who took care of my guitars. And it was his job to change my strings every day. Anyway, they didn't show up at Pittsburgh, the next show, until like five minutes before the show. They showed up; they'd gotten out of jail. Got into Pittsburgh, and that night, during 'Free Bird', I broke two strings, which I never did. And by the way, I played a Gibson on 'Free Bird'. I played that Gibson SG every night, which I still have. Anyway, on the limousine ride back to the hotel, Ronnie was just telling me that I didn't amount to a pimple on Allen Collins' ass, which, I wasn't going to argue with any of that, but then Ronnie started, you know, wanting to fight in the limousine and the driver pulled over and got out of the car and said, 'You guys can drive your own car back.' When I got back to the hotel, I said, well, that's it. I just don't need this. You know. I mean, if they want to act crazy and fight amongst themselves, that's one thing. But don't steer it my way.

Ed said he would have come back if Ronnie had asked him, but the call never came. Although there are many who rightly praise the genius of Ronnie, his failings need to be recognised, too. When drunk, he was violent, and he bullied his bandmates. Pyle claims he was the only one who could stand up to Ronnie and once recalled that they came to blows over King's departure. On two separate occasions, Ronnie knocked Billy's teeth out. On the second occasion, he found it funny looking at Billy, who had picked up his six missing teeth and knocked on Ronnie's door to demand that he pay the dentist bill, laughing as he reached for his cheque book. There are many examples of his violence. Gary Rossington recalled 'the bloodbath in Hamburg' for *Classic Rock* in 2019: 'We drank beer and whiskey every night, Scotch or Jack Daniel's, and sometimes champagne,' said Rossington, 'but the guy at the hotel bar gave us cold peppermint schnapps. We'd never seen that, never even heard of schnapps. They had the glass all frozen; it tastes good. So, we were just knocking them back.' Jetlagged and inebriated, the band headed back to their hotel rooms. Unfortunately for everyone else, Ronnie's temper was bubbling over. 'He was so fucking drunk', recalled Rossington. 'He started a fight with somebody, I think it was our road manager. A couple of us were trying to get him off, and then he took this fuckin' bottle and busted it on the head of our tour manager and it broke. You gotta hit somebody hard to break a bottle. And it knocked our tour manager crazy – it was bleeding some.'

That's when Van Zant went for Rossington with the broken bottle. 'He said, 'I'm gonna cut your hands, you're never gonna play guitar again.' And he cut me (indicating slice marks on both hands) here and there and up there.' Things could have been a lot worse if it weren't for Skynyrd drummer Artimus Pyle. 'I remember Artimus coming in really mad', remembered Rossington, whose hands were gushing blood by this time. 'He was an ex-marine and in great shape, and he had a wild streak, too. He was throwing Ronnie around; the first time he ever did that. Artimus finally got him on the bed and was on top of him, cussing him out and yelling. It was crazy.'

With Pyle and the rest of the band restraining their furious singer, Rossington and fellow guitarist Allen Collins headed for the nearest emergency room. The two musicians, neither of whom spoke German, tried to get across the severity of what had happened to the doctors who were attempting to staunch the bleeding and stitch up Rossington's wounds. 'I was trying to say, 'This is important, I play with my hands'', said Rossington. 'Allen was going, 'Hey man, don't fuck this up.' But they did it real good, I guess.'

Peter Rudge recognised the need for an experienced producer, particularly because they needed to have a new album ready for a February release. To his credit, he got one of the most respected of all producers, Tom Dowd. Although Dowd's contract with Warner Communications did not allow him to work with non-company acts, he was given permission by Ahmet Ertegun because he wanted to sign Skynyrd to Atlantic when their contract with MCA expired, and he saw this as an opening. Dowd was massively experienced, and it must have impressed the band that his credits included Clapton's *461 Ocean Boulevard* and *Layla And Other Assorted Love Songs*. They were probably less familiar with the fact that, in an earlier career as a physicist, Dowd had worked on the Manhattan Project, which developed the atomic bomb.

Dowd did not find it easy working with the band; his rigid approach and studio discipline were not always appreciated. Also, his recording time was limited, and he needed to fit in between tour dates in September, October (including 14 dates in Europe) and November.

Recording took place between 7 and 9 September (tracks 2, 4, 8) and between 28 and 30 November 1975 at the Record Plant, Los Angeles (tracks 2, 4, 8), and Capricorn Studios, Macon, Georgia. Ronnie praised Dowd, speaking to *Melody Maker*:

It was our album. We were gonna have to suffer the consequences, so we wanted to do it our way. Tom is more helpful, encourages us and suggests things, but forces nothing. He works with us; we'll say to him, 'We want the snare to sound like Charlie Watts' snare on 'Satisfaction'. We want the bass to sound like something from the Grateful Dead. We want the rhythm to sound like John Fogerty', and he just goes, 'Okay.' He's that good. He's a genius.

The record had some initial success and became the group's fourth gold record. However, Al Kooper hated the album and felt that no one fought over the songs and that he would have thrown half of them out. David McGee, writing for *Rolling Stone*, agreed. He felt the material was weak, the performances uninspired and described Skynyrd as a band in limbo. However, the album has stood the test of time and has become a favourite for some fans. In 2024, writing for *Classic Rock*, Paul Elliott observed: 'There's plenty of grit and grease on the album, not least on its badass title track and the funky 'Double Trouble'. Ronnie was wrong: 'Gimme Back My Bullets' is a Skynyrd classic.'

'Gimme Back My Bullets' (Rossington, Van Zant) 3:28
The title of the track refers to the type of bullet awarded by *Billboard* magazine for fast-rising successful records and reflects the band's desire to

get back to the top. Unfortunately, it was taken a little too literally by some of the band's fans. Although the song was popular on the radio, the band had to stop playing it in concert, as fans were throwing a selection of live bullets at the group on stage.

Reportedly, the last track recorded for the album on 30 November 1975 and based musically around a riff that Rossington had, it begins with a count-in from one of the guitars hitting muted strings, beginning immediately after the third strike. Gary's lead lines are instantly recognisable from the thick tone of his Gibson Les Paul. After a second's silence, the whole band are back in with the first verse, setting the scene and telling us, 'I've seen the hard times/And the pressure's been on me'. Ronnie makes it clear in the lyrics that he has straightened himself out, and he won't see any more damage done to the band. According to Gene Odum, Ronnie's claim was a little premature.

Billy is credited with organ and clavinet, and his understated contribution can be heard, albeit lost in the mix. It is worth taking time to listen closely to the interplay of the rhythm guitars: while one is riffing, we hear percussive moves and long sustained notes subtly blending in the mix. We have a short bridge that takes us into Rossington's solo before another verse. Rossington solos again as the song fades out; his stylistically typical pinched harmonics are clearly audible. Although it is a muscular opener for the album, it lacks the clarity and punch that the earlier Kooper mixed albums had achieved. 'Gimme Back My Bullets' failed to live up to Ronnie's aspirations, failing to chart on its release as a single in 1976 with 'All I Can Do Is Write About It' as the B-side.

'Every Mother's Son' (Collins, Van Zant) 4:56

This is a lyrically simple and effective song that is summed up by the last line, 'Oh, every mother's son will rise and fall someday'. The message is that it doesn't matter what we have; we should never take advantage, and one day it will all be gone – we all die in the end. We are all the same.

Twin acoustic guitars hold down the rhythm, and a beautiful piano roll leads into a short solo that sounds like Gary. Confirmatory evidence comes from the *Old Grey Whistle Test* performance packaged with the Deluxe reissue of the album on DVD. It is already obvious that the tone of this album is different from its predecessors and that Dowd's production is very different from that of Kooper. Jean-Charles Costa, writing for *Hit Parader*, considered the production to be slightly toned down but more focused. Essentially, it lacked impact. Furthermore, the absence of Ed King changes the dynamic, and they missed the power and excitement that his playing brought.

Mid song, another lead guitar, most likely Gary again, takes us into a beautiful Billy Powell solo. This really underlines the extra dimension that he brought to the band, blending classical finesse with honky-tonk to give the band a broader musical range than many other Southern rock bands. Allen takes the lead at the end of the song, which fades out as studio reverb is progressively added for the last few seconds.

'Trust' (Collins, Rossington, Van Zant) 4:25

This is another song recorded on the last day in Macon, Georgia. Although giving a positive review of the album, the writer for *Melody Maker* opined, 'I'm left on occasions with the impression that Skynyrd are strangely trying to manufacture an anthem, bidding to record another 'Free Bird' or 'Sweet Home Alabama'. 'Every Mother's Son' and 'Trust' are the tracks which offend.' It is easy to criticise this comment with the benefit of hindsight; the reviewer would probably have been unaware of the then-unissued Muscle Shoals sessions, which included a version of 'Trust' – the writing of the song predated 'Sweet Home Alabama' by several years.

Perhaps 'Don't tell your woman that you love her because that's when your trouble begins' sounds misogynistic if we ignore the fact that it is preceded by 'Don't talk no stuff to no slicker/Don't tell your feelings to your friends', so the song is basically a warning not to trust anyone. In this instance, the slicker in question is unlikely to be Al Kooper, who was the Yankee slicker referenced in 'Workin' For MCA'. When describing Kooper, the term 'slicker' is used to imply a sophisticated city dweller. Here, though, the term has a more negative connotation and implies someone who is a crook and cannot be trusted.

Once again, this is a solid song, not their greatest, but far from album filler. Artimus is in fine form, and there is another great bassline from Leon, even if it is buried in the mix. Allen and Gary both provide rhythm guitars, with Billy accompanying them. Allen handles the fills and solo. The song ends with a structured finish rather than a fadeout, perhaps an indicator that the song was not written at the last minute.

'I Got The Same Old Blues' (J.J. Cale) 4:08

For the second time, the band decided to cover a J.J. Cale song, this time 'I Got The Same Old Blues', following in the footsteps of Captain Beefheart and the Magic Band, who covered the song on their 1974 album *Blue Jeans & Moonbeams*, the same year that Cale released the song on his *Okie* album, earlier in April 1974. The song was later covered by artists as diverse as Eric Clapton, Bobby Bland and Bryan Ferry. Cale didn't have as much success with his original songs as others did with their covers, but it didn't seem to be a problem for him. As he said himself: 'I knew if I became too well known, my life would change drastically. On the other hand, getting some money doesn't change things too much, except you no longer have to go to work.'

The Lynyrd Skynyrd version stays true to the feel of the original, and once again, the vocal delivery and lyrics suit Ronnie. It could easily be mistaken for his own composition. Recorded in September 1975 at the Record Plant in Los Angeles, the song features Gary on slide and Lee Freeman playing the harp. Interestingly, Freeman had been a fellow member of Strawberry Alarm Clock with Ed King. There is footage available from Skynyrd's concert at Winterland in April 1975, where Freeman joins them on stage to play on their other Cale cover, 'Call Me The Breeze', and plays an extended solo. Ed King left shortly after that concert.

Throughout the song, Allen picks the rhythm, and for the most part, Rossington backs on slide guitar, with occasional picking. Billy is playing a funky rhythm on keyboards. Gary's solo comes at 1:47 – it's typically laid back, melodic, but technically quite simple. Freeman can be heard in the background just before his solo, which he takes at 2:45. Once again, we end with a fadeout to close an enjoyable cover that is true to the original but imbued by Skynyrd's swampy feel.

'Double Trouble' (Collins, Van Zant) 2:49

In the summer of 1975, following an arrest for drunkenness, Ronnie counted his previous arrests and told Gary Rossington, who was in the cell with him, that it was 11 times. Gary turned to him and said, 'You're just double trouble Ronnie.' Typically, Ronnie used the inspiration for a song: 'Eleven times I been busted, eleven times I been to jail/Some of the times I been there, nobody could go my bail'.

Allen's picked riff starts the song, joined by cymbals and then drums, before everyone is in at the ten-second mark. Allen wrote the music, and the song was chosen as the first single from the album with 'Roll Gypsy Roll' as the B-side, but it was never a great hit, stalling at number 80 in the US charts and not charting in the UK. What was inspired, though, was Dowd's decision to bring in female backing singers, credited on the album as the Honnicutts. They add colour and impact to the chorus: 'Double trouble, that's what my friends all call me/Double trouble, I said, double trouble/T-R-O-U-B-L-E'.

In the second verse, Ronnie references both his temper and the peat farm, presumably doing hard labour: 'Well, I was born down in the gutter, With a temper as hot as fire, Spent ninety days on a peat farm, Just doing the county's time'. Ronnie's self-awareness of his temper is interesting, but it didn't change his behaviour. Although Ronnie did say he had been shot at one time, he refused to elaborate: 'Well now, even mama said, 'Son you're bad news/And it won't be too long before someone puts one through you''.

There are a few piano flourishes from Billy, but the song is unusual in that there are no solos, and once again, the song ends with a fadeout. It has been claimed that Ronnie called Dowd from jail, after recording the song, to say they needed to re-record the vocals because it was now 12.

Writer Robert Christgau gave the album a positive review but was disparaging about the backing singers:

Unfortunately, the music could use some Yankee calculation—from Al Kooper of Forest Hills, who I figure was good for two hooks per album, and Ed King of New Jersey, the guitarist turned born-againer whose guitar fills carried a lot more zing than three doo-dooing Honnicutts.

Ronnie liked the expanded sound with the backing singers and later recruited his own singers: Cassie Gaines from Oklahoma, Jo-Jo Billingsley from Mississippi and Leslie Hawkins from Jacksonville, who became integral to the band and became known as the Honkettes, a name given to them by Ronnie. Perhaps we should have little regard for Christgau's opinion, as, in a 1968 piece, he commented:

> I don't know anything about music, which ought to be a damaging admission but isn't. The fact is that pop writers in general shy away from such arcana as key signature and beats to the measure ... I used to confide my worries about this to friends in the record industry, who reassured me. They didn't know anything about music either. The technical stuff didn't matter, I was told. You just gotta dig it.

Although most of the musicians in the band also lacked formal training, they clearly demonstrated their talent for songwriting and performance, and in that sense, were very well musically schooled.

'Roll Gypsy Roll' (Collins, Rossington, Van Zant) 2:50
The song begins with Allen Collins playing a hypnotic rolling ostinato on a 12-string acoustic guitar, joined by bass, piano and Artimus on tambourine as the song eases in. This song likens the lot of a touring musician to that of an itinerant gypsy, always on the road. However, we can see reference to the punishing tour schedules, booked by 'the man with the plan'.

> Ridin' on a greyhound, countin' those white lines
> Destination I don't know and I'm feelin' like I'm dyin'
> Well ten years on this road, might've took its toll
> But the man with the plan says the band has got to go
> I said roll gypsy roll
> Lord just pick up your bags and go

Ronnie reflects on the pressures of life on the road and the choices made. He references women, drugs and implies there is no plan or structure in his life, and the closing lyrics emphasise the lack of control and the part that drugs played.

Subtle organ from Billy adds texture, and Gary delivers well-considered fills and an excellent melodic solo. It is common for people to compare the Skynyrd guitarists, trying to decide who is 'best', but that really misses the point. Gary has the style that is often deemed the most basic, but his tone is exceptionally distinctive, and his control of bends and note choices is exemplary. Here, he resolves his solo with chicken picking from 2:05; very country and possibly a homage to James Burton, who is widely considered to be the pioneer of this percussive hybrid-picking style.

'Searching' (Collins, Van Zant) 3:17
The meaning of the song is clear; a young man is doing well and has lots of money, but he isn't satisfied. The advice he seeks tells him to find his love. The song begins with a Rossington string bend, and then the group all join in to accompany a short solo from Gary. At 18 seconds, the first verse begins. The fills and middle solo are all Gary. Billy does provide some accompaniment, but it is a little lost in the mix. At 2:33, Collins and Rossington trade solos before playing unison lines to take the song to its ending, which sounds very much like a typical Skynyrd live concert ending by building to a frenzied climax. The trading solos are great, but it does seem to be a missed opportunity to develop this section further.

'Cry For The Bad Man' (Collins, Rossington, Van Zant) 4:48
The song reflects the regrets that the song's subject has about their manager, although there is recognition that the bad treatment has made them stronger: 'He knocked me down but I'm on my feet/Now I'm so much wiser'. Although Ronnie wouldn't publicly reveal who the song was about, Gene Odum, in his book *Lynyrd Skynyrd*, claims Ronnie was open with him and that the song was, as many believe, about Skynyrd's previous manager, Alan Walden. At one time, Ronnie was very close to Walden and was the best man at his wedding. Walden was trying to get the band to manage their finances more responsibly, at a time when opening for The Who had exposed them to the influence of the band, and particularly Keith Moon, whose penchant for the destruction of property and the consumption of drugs and alcohol is the stuff of legend. Whether Walden's attempts to rein in the band made him 'the money miser' is unclear, but certainly plausible. It has been said that Ronnie later regretted writing the song, but a primary reference for this is difficult to find. Odum's claim that Ronnie harboured truly harsh feelings would account for the power of the lyrics and their delivery. Perhaps Ronnie had learnt from his deals with the money miser. In his book, *Lynyrd Skynyrd: An Oral History* (1999), author Lee Ballinger quotes Tom Dowd's recollection of visiting Ronnie's home in Jacksonville and finding a large shed in his back garden with a Holiday Inn door and sign. He quotes Ronnie's explanation: 'All the hotels we trash, they keep charging us for the goddamn stuff we trash, so I make them send it to me. I paid for it once; I can do anything I want with it.' Apparently, to let off steam, Ronnie could go down the garden and throw television sets out the window to his heart's content!

The music has an understated but powerful delivery, once again reminiscent of Free. Gary handles the fills and solo. Billy provides organ accompaniment, and this is the second song on the album to feature backing vocals from the Honnicutts, adding emphasis with the 'Cry for the bad man'. The drum delivery from Pyle is sharp and powerful, where necessary. Leon's bassline is locked in with drums and delivers tasteful embellishments and flourishes.

'All I Can Do Is Write About It' (Collins, Van Zant) 4:16

Dowd described 'All I Can Do Is Write About It' as a masterpiece. Essentially, it is a country song and a lament to the loss of countryside and a simpler way of life, acknowledging Ronnie's love of nature and green spaces. Perhaps it's a direct reference to the growth of Jacksonville. Ronnie sings that he 'can see the concrete slowly creepin'/Lord, take me and mine before that comes'. It is interesting to speculate on what he would think of the development of the land where their old rehearsal space, the Hell House, once stood. It is now a gated housing estate. Long gone are the days when one of the band would have to sleep at Hell House to protect the gear from theft by people boating up the river, sleeping with a billy club or a gun to protect from 'gators. Ronnie acknowledges in the song that it is nothing he can change, but sadly, he was taken less than two years after recording the song.

Allen and Gary's acoustic guitars are joined by tasteful dobro and mandolin, skilfully played by Barry Harwood, who had worked with the band on *'Nuthin Fancy* (and would later feature in the Rossington Collins Band). Also of note is the beautiful violin playing. In the album credits, it says the player is unidentified. Listening to the playing, it is easy to make a case for Charlie Daniels. In the album credits, Pyle, on behalf of Lynyrd Skynyrd, acknowledges their kinship to the Marshall Tucker and Charlie Daniels bands. Just four days prior to the recording of this song, Daniels had released his *Nightrider* album on the Kama Sutra label, and in 1976, he signed to Epic for $3,000,000

In addition to the subtly Leslie-affected organ, Billy makes a stunning contribution with his beautiful piano solo from 2:40 to 3:03, augmented by Harwood's mandolin. Throughout, there are touches of electric guitar that add depth and power, without detracting from the delicacy of the song, which closes with a written ending rather than a fade, as the violin plays over an organ chord.

An acoustic version of the song appears on the reissued album and the box set *Lynyrd Skynyrd – The Definitive Lynyrd Skynyrd Collection*.

Street Survivors (1977)

Personnel:
Ronnie Van Zant: lead vocals
Steve Gaines: guitar, backing vocals, lead vocal on 'Ain't No Good Life', co-lead vocals on 'You Got That Right'
Allen Collins: guitar
Gary Rossington: guitar
Leon Wilkeson: bass, backing vocals
Artimus Pyle: drums
Billy Powell: keyboards
Ed King: guitar on 'One More Time'
Greg T. Walker: bass on 'One More Time'
Rickey Medlocke: drums and backing vocals on 'One More Time'
Additional musicians:
The Honkettes (JoJo Billingsley, Cassie Gaines, Leslie Hawkins): backing vocals on 'That Smell' and 'One More Time'
Tim Smith: backing vocals on 'One More Time'
Barry Lee Harwood: dobro on 'Honky Tonk Night Time Man'
Recorded at Criteria Studios, Miami, Florida, in April 1977; Studio One, Doraville, Georgia, between July and August 1977; and Muscle Shoals Sound Studios, Muscle Shoals, Alabama, in 1971
Producer: Tom Dowd; Jimmy Johnson & Tim Smith (track 3)
Engineer: Ken Perry (Capitol Mastering), Dennis Hetzendorfer (Criteria Studios), Jimmy Johnson (Muscle Shoals Sound), Rodney Mills, Tad Bush (Studio One)
Mixed by Rodney Mills
Release date: 17 October 1977
Label: MCA
Chart places: US: 5, UK: 13
Running time: 35:26

Although the band had proved themselves more than capable with only Rossington and Collins on lead and rhythm guitar, they were on the lookout for a replacement for King. In 1977, Rossington explained, 'We were fixing to do a live album and wanted a third guitarist for it because that's the sound we were built on.' John Swenson, who was on the road with Skynyrd, recalled that Leslie West played with the band on stage and wanted to join. However, his style was so distinctive that it wouldn't have been a comfortable fit. Barry Harwood was asked to join by Ronnie, but had other commitments.

Backing singer Cassie Gaines recommended her brother Steve. Although sceptical, the band eventually allowed him to jam Jimmie Rodgers' 'Blue Yodel #1 (T For Texas)' on stage with them. Soundman Kevin Elson listened intently through the headphones and realised that Gaines was outstanding. He was invited back to jam a couple more times and was offered the job, just in time for *One More From The Road*. The first of the three shows recorded was only Gaines's third gig with the band.

Gaines was born on 14 September 1949, in Miami, Oklahoma, sharing his birthdate with Ed King by a strange coincidence. Although Gaines had a number of years of experience, this really was his big break. He had recorded with his band Crawdad at Capricorn studios in Macon, Georgia, in 1975. These recordings were later released by MCA in 1988 as *One In The Sun*, following the reformation of Lynyrd Skynyrd. The album was billed as a solo album at that time.

Gaines's talent was immense. Not only was he a great guitar player, but he also had a superb singing voice. His presence certainly rekindled the band and pushed them to what many consider a new high. Rossington and Collins certainly had to up their game, having become a little too comfortable. Equally, though, the band enabled Gaines to realise his talent. Listening to earlier live versions of the songs he would take to Skynyrd, and the posthumously released *One In The Sun*, it is clear that Gaines owed as much to Skynyrd as they gained from him.

Dowd, once again the producer, had booked the band into Criteria Studios in Miami, but the band were not happy with the sound of the initial recordings. Kevin Elsom had nearly come to blows with Ronnie over his opinion of the recording; however, Gaines stepped in and said he agreed. His support convinced Ronnie. Elsom took a plane to Atlanta with a copy of the multitrack recordings that had been made to that point. Rodney Mills took a listen and tried a mix at Studio One, which Elsom took back to the band. They relocated to Doraville and continued work on the album, recutting several tracks. Accounts at this point differ. Mills recalled Ronnie explaining to Dowd that they appreciated everything that he did, but that the album was so important, they wanted other inputs, too. That night, Dowd checked out.

Dowd recalled that he did follow the band to Doraville, but that his time was tight after getting married and trying to produce Skynyrd and Rod Stewart at the same time. He claims that Leon Wilkeson was incapacitated by an accidental drug exposure that caused production to stop. His claim is that he wasn't told that production had recommenced and that the album was finished without him, and that he only became aware of this when the album was being mixed at Capital. However, Dowd had sent engineer Barry Rudolph as his representative for the recording process at least, so all is not clear. The mixing was completed in Georgia, with Dowd too busy with Rod Stewart to join.

The first printing of the album did not credit Dowd, who, at the time of the plane crash, said the band had instructed MCA to include his name on reprints. The irony of the album's title and the photograph, taken at Universal Studios in California, of the band engulfed in flames, is painful in hindsight. The release of a great album by a band reaching new levels of artistic prowess was overshadowed by the events of 20 October 1977, when

Skynyrd's Convair CV-240 plane ran out of fuel and crashed in a wooded area near Gillsburg, Mississippi, United States.

'What's Your Name' (Rossington, Van Zant) 3:30
As was the case with several of the band's songs, the subject matter is based loosely on real events, in this case, a bar altercation involving roadie Craig Reed. In his biography of the band, Odum recalled that there is some embellishment of the actual event. Ronnie, enjoying a quiet drink in the bar, wanted to be left alone but was being pestered by a drunk making comments. He alleges that Ronnie passed him some money to take care of the situation if the nuisance continued, and he duly obliged, with the Skynyrd entourage being asked to leave. Hence, they couldn't drink in the bar as the lyrics recount.

The song was written by Rossington and Van Zant while at Criteria Studios in Miami, with help from Tom Dowd and Steve Cropper, guitarist with Booker T. & The MG's and featured in the Blues Brothers Band in the movie. The help they gave remains uncredited. From the opening seconds of the song, it is clear we have a revitalised Skynyrd. The sound is crisp, and the rhythm guitars each have their own window in the mix. Leon's bass is clear, and Billy lays down a spritely piano accompaniment throughout, adding fills and flourishes. The addition of horns fattens the sound. Although uncredited on the album, it is widely believed to be Bobby Keys, who had previously contributed to *Second Helping*. The horn overdubs were recorded in August 1977, several months after the track's recording in April. Ultimately, the song is fun and quite commercial-sounding. Between 1:47 and 2:14, Allen lays down a great solo. The revitalised Skynyrd, with the addition of Steve Gaines, now had the Three-Guitar Army back to full strength. This gave the guarantee, with the new competition, that whoever took the lead had to deliver the goods.

As well as referencing drinking and fighting, the song is about groupies, and the lyrics must not have been of much comfort to Ronnie's wife, Judy, at home with their daughter, Melody. The original first line of the song was 'It's 8 o'clock and boys it's time to go', but this was changed when Ronnie found out that .38 Special, fronted by his brother Donnie, were opening their first national tour in Boise. The line became 'It's 8 o'clock in Boise, Idaho'. In 1977, 'What's Your Name' backed with 'I Know A Little' was released as a single and reached number 13 on the *Billboard* Hot 100 in the US, making it the highest charting single to mention Idaho.

'That Smell' (Collins, Van Zant) 5:48
Ronnie wrote 'That Smell', following a serious car accident in which Gary had passed out at the wheel of his brand-new Ford Torino with his foot on the accelerator. The car knocked over a telegraph pole, split an oak tree and did a reported $7,000 dollars of damage to a house, a figure close to $40,000 accounting for inflation. Ronnie made no secret of his anger and berated

Rossington, who was able to recover in time for the *One More From The Road* tour. On the same weekend as Rossington's crash, Allen had preceded him by colliding with a parked Volkswagen Beetle while intoxicated, knocking it across the car park but walking away uninjured.

According to a newspaper report from 27 February 1976, Billy Powell was charged with possession of cannabis, driving while intoxicated under the influence of alcohol and driving on the wrong side of the highway following a collision with the wife of a state trooper, who sustained minor injuries, following an accident on Highway 17, Orange Park, which resulted in the destruction of Billy's 1975 Pontiac Firebird. This is probably the incident Ronnie is referring to when he is quoted in the sleeve notes for the 2008 Deluxe Edition of the album: 'Allen and Billy Powell also were in car accidents, all in the space of six months. I had a creepy feeling things were going against us, so I thought I'd write a morbid song.' Even friend and roadie Dean Kilpatrick drove into the back of a bus and had to have his spleen removed due to internal injuries.

The song begins with a crash, almost sounding like a vehicle impact, but made by the band. A brief solo from Gary ends in sustained feedback and a neat bass fill from Leon. The sombre tone of the lyrics is clear from the outset: 'Whiskey bottles and brand-new cars/Oak tree you're in my way ... The smell of death surrounds you'. A dexterous solo from Steve Gaines leads us to more stark imagery from Ronnie, 'Angel of darkness is upon you, you stuck a needle in your arm', followed by the Honkettes adding emphasis with their vocal line, 'You fool You'. At 1:47, we have a middle eight and more sobering lyrics, directed at Gary, whose nickname was Prince Charming: 'Now they call you Prince charming/Can't speak a word when you're full of 'ludes/ Say you'll be alright come tomorrow/But tomorrow might not be here for you'. The reference to 'ludes is about a favourite drug of Gary's at that time, Quaaludes, a brand name for methaqualone, a hypnotic sedative.

Gaines takes another solo, fierier than the last, at 2:23, at the end of which the lead lines are doubled by Allen. Subsequently, another bridge follows, then, at 3:12, Ronnie whistles us into a Rossington solo, leading us to the next verse. Rossington adds tasty fills to the chorus before he takes another solo. At 4:33, Rossington and Collins both solo before Allen takes the lead. Then at 4:49, Gaines is back and duets with Allen, and at 5:04, they play unison lines before playing call-and-response fast, ascending runs, and then back to doubled lead lines. The song closes with a last Rossington fill and a written ending with twin guitar harmony feedback to the fadeout. This is absolutely staggering guitar orchestration at its finest.

The potential that this lineup had, and what could have been, is painful to contemplate, given the tragedy that was to follow the release of the album. Although the lyrics primarily focus on Gary, we have seen that recklessness was not limited to him, and the future would be a bleak one for Allen Collins. With hindsight, it is clear the song carried a warning he should have heeded.

As a result of speeding, driving under the influence and multiple accidents, Allen's licence was suspended on several occasions. His solution was, at one point, to buy a speedboat and use the St Johns River and its tributaries as a means of travel. This worked perfectly until the night he failed to secure it properly!

'One More Time' (Rossington, Van Zant) 5:03
This is a laid-back ballad about a cheating lover being given another chance. If it sounds a little different musically, it is because the recording actually dates back to the Muscle Shoals recordings in 1971. Rickey Medlocke is playing drums and singing backing vocals, and Greg T. Walker is playing bass and singing backing vocals (both of Blackfoot). Ed King is credited with guitar overdubs, which were recorded in 1975. Before Steve Gaines joined the band, Ronnie had wanted to revisit the Muscle Shoals sessions, with a view to releasing the best and unused material for a new album. Although at this point Ed King was long departed, he was then still a member when overdubbing in 1975. If we compare this version to the one released on *The Complete Muscle Shoals* recordings, we can clearly hear Ed's overdubs in the opening bars, leading into the first verse. Subtle as they are, Ed's additional fills throughout the song, including volume swells, add much to the texture of the song. Interviewed in 2009, Ed downplayed his contribution:

> As far as I recall, it was a volume-pedal type Strat part. There may be more to it, but I can't remember. 'One More Time' is from the Muscle Shoals sessions. I overdubbed guitar and bass on 17 songs in 24 hours. I didn't hear too much in this particular tune that was needed. The main solo is Rossington, and it's pretty sweet indeed.

The main solo is a beautiful Rossington composition, building to Rossington and Collins doubling leads before resolving with Gary. As we head into the last verse, the subject of the song has decided that enough is enough and decides to leave. Doubled guitars from Rossington and Collins lead the song through to the ending fadeout.

'I Know A Little' (Gaines) 3:26
This is the first song on the album with a writing credit for Steve Gaines, credited here as sole composer. Steve had written the song prior to joining Lynyrd Skynyrd when in one of his previous bands, Manalive, a band that preceded Crawdad, who he was a member of before joining Lynyrd Skynyrd. The song opens with percussion and some spirited guitar runs from Steve. In July 1993, Rossington told *Guitar School* magazine that he had never heard anybody, including the then-current members of the band, play the picking right, the way that Steve did. A live version can be found where a pre-Skynyrd Gaines rips through the song with Crawdad.

Artimus and Leon hold down a swinging groove throughout. The rhythm guitar parts mostly sound like Steve, who plays most of the lead and almost certainly the slide solo, although the tone for that section is slightly thicker. It doesn't sound like Gary, and when the song has been played live by the reformed band, Gary doesn't play that section. At 2:20, punctuating rhythmic stabs are answered by guitar licks from Gary, which are then followed by an ascending bass run and a fantastic, dextrous honky tonk solo from Billy. The contribution that Steve made in his short tenure with the band is often lauded, but it should also be recognised how much the band enabled him to shine.

'You Got That Right' (Gaines, Van Zant) 3:44
This is the first opportunity we have, on a Skynyrd studio album, to hear Steve Gaines sing. He has a great voice, and it was an inspired idea to sing this song as a duet. It was released as a single in 1978 with 'Ain't No Good Life' as the B-side, but only reached number 69 in the US. It's an up-tempo song, once again propelled by the tight rhythm section with another great Wilkeson bassline. Leon is often overlooked, but his basslines were always a perfect fit, creating complex counterpoints to the band's triple-guitar attack. Ed King once remarked, years later, that whenever he wrote a bassline, he tried to think what Leon would have done. Horns are present, along with subtle contributions from Billy. Gary handles the slide solos; short solos begin and end the song, with a longer solo coming in at 1.33, following a nice repeated descending guitar run and some notable percussive strokes from Artimus. A similar run-down and a slight pause give the second solo real impact at 2:47. A video of the band performing the song from the Convention Hall in July 1977 has a different solo that is only played by Steve. On this album version, the solo is doubled, and there are slight differences in the phrasing and tone of the guitars. Although often attributed to Steve, this is probably Steve and Allen. Certainly, in a later incarnation of the band, Rickey Medlocke and Hughie Thomasson duetted on this solo, and in terms of guitar duties, Rickey was usually covering Allen's parts and Hughie those of Steve and Ed King. Further confirmation comes from Leon, who is quoted by Marley Brant in *Freebirds, The Lynyrd Skynyrd Story*: 'That's Steve and Allen showing off.'

The lyrics tell another tale of a life of freedom, on the road presumably touring, with no responsibility, living fast and dying young: 'I tried everything in my life/Things I like I'll try 'em twice'. With hindsight, it is uncomfortable to dwell on the duetted lines 'When my time's up, I'll hold my own/You won't find me in an old folks' home', given that three days after the release of the album, Ronnie and Steve would both be dead. Ronnie had, on many occasions, confided that he did not believe he would live to 30. His father, Lacy, went as far as to say Ronnie was gifted with second sight. Whether prophecy or coincidence, he didn't live to reach 30.

This is what Robert Christgau had to say in his review in *Christgau's Record Guide: Rock Albums Of The Seventies:*

Some rock deaths are irrelevant, while others make a kind of sense because the artists involved so obviously long to transcend (or escape) their own mortality. But for Ronnie Van Zant, life and mortality were the same thing. There was no way to embrace one without at least keeping company with the other. So, it makes sense that 'That Smell' is the smell of death, or that in 'You Got That Right', Van Zant boasts that he'll never be found in an old folks' home. As with too many LPs by good road bands, each side here begins with two strong cuts and then winds down. The difference is that the two strong cuts are very strong, and the weak ones gain presence with each listen. I'm not just being sentimental. I know road bands never make their best album the sixth time out, and I know Van Zant had his limits. But I mourn him not least because I suspect that he had more good music left in him than Bing and Elvis put together.

'I Never Dreamed' (Gaines, Van Zant) 5:21
The second and final Gaines/Van Zant writing collaboration is a mid-tempo song about regret, lost love and the pain of realising the value of something once it's gone. The song reflects on a relationship where the narrator took his partner's love for granted, only to deeply regret her departure. The lyrics convey a sense of loneliness and a desperate plea for her return, highlighting the emotional impact of lost love. The lyrics don't come in until 1:16, following some doubled lead lines and then a short slide passage – most likely Gaines and Collins, followed by Gary. Stylistically, it is very laid back, and the arrangement of the melody is fresh, but they hit the groove with a tight rhythm, tasteful organ chords and an acoustic guitar lower in the mix. Steve takes the main solo with some understated melodic picking and pinched harmonics. A more aggressive but melodic solo ends the song; once again, it sounds like Steve, but some of the licks are out of the Allen Collins playbook.

'Honky Tonk Night Time Man' (Merle Haggard) 3:59
Given that Ronnie was such a fan of Merle Haggard, it comes as no surprise that he covered one of his songs. Barry Harwood again makes a guest appearance, this time playing dobro on the solo that is often credited to Steve or Gary by the casual fan.

The song begins with a rolling drum beat and some fine picking from Steve. The dobro slide lines offer colour throughout, as do fills from Steve. At 1:20, Steve takes a country picking solo, and Ronnie can be heard saying 'Sounds Like Roy'. It is often assumed that the reference is to Roy Clarke, but it is more likely to Merle Haggard guitarist Roy Nichols. At 2:29, Ronnie announces Billy Powell on the piano, and he takes a great solo, then at 2:50,

Ronnie invites Barry to take the lead, 'Barry, play me some dobro', and he plays a great picked solo. Ultimately, this is the sound of a talented group of musicians having fun. Prior to the album release, Ronnie called Barry and told him he had got his name on the album. Barry assumed he meant on the credits, which he expected, but was moved when he realised his name was on the recording. It has been suggested that Ronnie wanted Barry Lee Harwood to be one of the guitar players for his proposed country album.

'Ain't No Good Life' (Gaines) 4:36
Like 'I Know A Little', this is a Gaines composition that predates his time with the band. There is a recording available of him performing this song with Crawdad in 1974. The version with Skynyrd is a lot sharper and more focused, and it is apparent how Gaines had grown as a musician.

Stabs begin the song and lead into some trademark Billy Powell honky tonk barroom piano and a short but sweet Rossington solo before Gaines brings in the first verse. Rossington provides another short solo at 1:27 that ends with sustained feedback that carries over into the verse. Billy augments the rhythm with piano, and at 2:40, takes a short solo that leads us into Steve's solo, which continues to the third and final verse. This solo is phrased much more like blues than the country picking we heard from Steve in 'Honkey Tonk Nighttime Man'. Following the last verse, Gary once again solos with his trademark harmonically rich tone and takes us to the song's end.

The song is essentially about feeling the blues and trying to face up to it. Gaines had a great singing voice, and this was the only instance of Ronnie letting someone else take lead vocals (unlike the earlier duet) that was released in his lifetime. 'White Dove' and 'The Seasons' featured Rickey Medlocke on lead vocals and were recorded at an earlier date at the Muscle Shoals sessions, but remained unreleased until after Ronnie's death and the release of *Skynyrd's First And ... Last*.

Ronnie had been having difficulty with his voice, in part due to the way he sang from the throat and not in a trained and disciplined way, but also the extensive touring the band did, and it is reasonable to assume that lifestyle choices would have taken their toll. Some have said that Ronnie intended Steve to take over vocals as he stepped back, perhaps into songwriting or even managing the band. The rumour about Ronnie's plans to step back is difficult to reference as there are scant primary sources. However, there is an audio recording of an interview with Rossington, where he does say Ronnie was going to step back and manage them, and he says they had a singer in Jacksonville, Florida, lined up, but he wouldn't identify him. In the same interview, he claims Van Zant had nodules on his vocal cords. These are small non-malignant swellings that interfere with the normal vibration of the vocal cords, sometimes as a result of excessive singing or poor vocal technique. Randall Hall claimed that Jimmy Dougherty was asked by Ronnie to be the lead singer.

2008 Deluxe Edition Bonus CD

Tracklisting: 'What's Your Name' (Original Version) 3:33, 'That Smell' (Original Version) 5.29, 'You Got That Right' (Original Version) 3:19, 'I Never Dreamed' (Original Version) 5:22, 'Georgia Peaches' 3:14, 'Sweet Little Missy' (Original Version) 5:16, 'Sweet Little Missy' (Demo) 5:11, 'Ain't No Good Life' (Original Version) 5:02, 'That Smell' (Complete Original Version) 7:30, 'Jacksonville Kid' 4:09, 'You Got That Right' (Live) 4:41, 'That Smell' (Live) 6:05, 'Ain't No Good Life' (Live) 5:01, 'What's Your Name' (Live) 3:28, 'Gimme Three Steps' (Live) 5:09

On the bonus CD, the original Criteria Studio versions of 'You Got That Right', 'I Never Dreamed', 'What's Your Name' and 'Ain't No Good Life' (with backing vocals from the Honkettes) are included, along with an additional two versions of 'That Smell', the second of which features extended guitar solos. Additionally, two dropped songs are included, 'Georgia Peaches' and 'Sweet Little Missy'. The latter is included as two versions: the master version and a demo recorded in the band's Jacksonville rehearsal studio on Riverside Avenue. There is also a rewrite of 'Honky Tonk Night Time Man' titled 'Jacksonville Kid', with an autobiographical lyric that is the last ever written and recorded by Ronnie. The lyrics detail his perceived rejection by his hometown and his sense of isolation despite fame and success.

'What's Your Name' is essentially the same as the album release. The vocals sound like they may be double-tracked, and the horns are missing. 'That Smell', although still a good song, suffers from a more distant mix and lacks impact. Similarly, 'You Got That Right' lacks the punch and impact of the original release.

We also have the welcome inclusion of five songs from 1977, the last known recordings of the band in California, and a glimpse of what the *Street Survivors* tour could have sounded like.

'Georgia Peaches' (Gaines, Van Zant) 3:14

The song is an ode to the women of Atlanta and the historic Peachtree Street, around which much of Atlanta grew and which has many historic buildings, including the former home of Margaret Mitchell, where she wrote *Gone With The Wind*. The depiction of the women is not very charitable; the implication is that they will lure you in and take your money, possibly a reference to prostitution. Musically, it is well played and arranged; however, of the songs that Gaines and Van Zant wrote together, this is the weakest, although worthy of inclusion here as a record of the original version of the album. The first release of this song was on 1987's compilation album *Legend*, for which it was a promotional single. At that time, it was great to hear unreleased material a decade after the plane crash, but judged against the songs that did make the final release, the correct decision was made.

'Jacksonville Kid' 4:09

This is discussed in the *Collectybles* album section.

'Sweet Little Missy' (Original Version) (Rossington, Van Zant) 5:16
Starting as if it may develop into a song in the style of Free, it ultimately has a laid-back country feel. Once again, this was first released on *Legend*. The arrangement and feel differ from the demo version, although Gaines takes a solo followed by Billy, as in the demo version. It is a smooth vocal performance from Ronnie, as he narrates a story about a 'sweet little missy' that he has fallen for. Although promising affection, the girl shows reluctance, but the narrator persists: 'Well, I'm the one that wants you forever and a day/ Come on baby, what'd you say?/Just don't be afraid'. It's an enjoyable song, but again, it's difficult to make a case for its inclusion on the original album.

Skynyrd's First And ... Last (1978)

Personnel:
Ronnie Van Zant: lead vocals
Allen Collins: guitar
Gary Rossington: guitar
Ed King: guitar, bass
Leon Wilkeson: bass
Billy Powell: piano
Greg Walker: bass
Bob Burns: drums
Rickey Medlocke: lead vocals, drums, mandolin
Additional musicians:
Gimmer Nichols: acoustic guitar
Cassie Gaines: backing vocals
Jo Billingsley: backing vocals
Leslie Hawkins: backing vocals
Tim Smith: backing vocals
Jimmy Johnson: guitar
Wayne Perkins: guitar
Wayne McCormick: Mellotron
Ronnie Eades: saxophone
Producer: Tim Smith, Jimmy R. Johnson
Engineer: Gregg Hamm, Jerry Masters, Ralph Rhodes, Steve Melton, Jimmy R. Johnson
Release date: 5 September 1978
Label: MCA
Chart places: US: 15, UK: 50
Running time: 36:36

The story of the crash has been told many times, often with subtle differences and contradictions. The accounts of several people who were in the crash even contradicted themselves. What follows, then, is a summary of the key events; their impact on the individuals and their music will follow later.

The band performed at the Greenville Memorial Auditorium in Greenville, South Carolina, on 19 October 1977, two days after the album's release. They boarded their chartered Convair CV-240 to take them to Baton Rouge, Louisiana, where they were due to perform. Towards the end of the flight, it became apparent that the plane had insufficient fuel. Captain McCreary and First Officer William John Gray attempted to reach McComb Airport, which was 16km northeast of where the plane went down in Amite County, Mississippi. Realising the plane would not make their new destination, they attempted an emergency landing in an open field. The plane went down about 270m from the field after skimming along the tree line for approximately 90m before breaking apart after hitting a large tree near

Gillsburg, Mississippi. Gene Odum and road manager Ron Eckerman have written firsthand accounts. Artimus has told the story many times, and a movie was made of Pyle's account, *Street Survivors: The True Story Of The Lynyrd Skynyrd Plane Crash*, the veracity of which is seriously in question. What is indisputable is the horror of the crash. Ronnie Van Zant, Steve Gaines, Cassie Gaines, assistant road manager Dean Kilpatrick, Captain Walter McCreary and First Officer William John Gray all died in the crash, while 20 others survived.

Gary Rossington recalled hearing what sounded like hundreds of baseball bats hitting the plane's fuselage as it began striking trees. Rossington was knocked unconscious and awoke sometime later on the ground with the plane's door on top of him. Gary had both legs, arms, wrists and feet broken, along with a fractured pelvis and several broken ribs. Billy Powell suffered severe facial lacerations, and his nose was nearly torn off in the crash. He also suffered deep lacerations to his leg. Pyle suffered broken ribs, but most accounts say that with two others, he reached a local farm where they were shot at before he convinced them there had been a plane crash, and help was needed. At one time, Rossington claimed that Pyle had run away. Allen Collins suffered two broken vertebrae in his neck and severe damage to his left arm. Amputation was recommended, but his father refused, and he eventually made a recovery. Leon Wilkeson suffered a closed double fracture of his left leg, a severe double compound fracture of his left arm, six broken ribs – including an internal compound fracture that punctured his left lung – upper and lower jaw, nose and facial bone fractures and 15 teeth knocked out. His fretting arm suffered such extensive nerve damage that its amputation was seriously considered. He was left with a greatly reduced range of motion in his arm, which forced him to hold his bass close to his body in an upright fashion.

JoJo Billingsley wasn't on the plane, as she was receiving care for substance misuse, but she had a premonition of a crash and had called Allen Collins, begging him not to travel. Van Zant himself had convinced the reluctant Cassie Gaines to board the flight.

The aircraft had already been rejected by Aerosmith for use in their *Draw The Line* tour, their crew reporting McCreary and Gray drinking from a bottle of Jack Daniels while the Aerosmith team inspected the plane.

According to Nazareth bassist Pete Agnew, his band had made excuses not to travel with Skynyrd on the plane that Agnew described as looking like 'Gaffa Tape Airlines'. Had the band made it to Baton Rouge, they planned on changing planes.

The *First And ... Last* album closed a chapter on the band's first incarnation. In 1978, *Melody Maker*'s review made it clear that it wasn't a cash-in:

Here is a rarity: an album that passes the acid test and honours the memory of a great band, provoking once again the thought of what might have been.

The compilation is certainly carried out with good taste. The band had apparently been planning to release these tapes before *Street Survivors* came out, so there can be no claims of 'cash-in.' The sleeve doesn't even mention that Van Zant and Gaines have died, but presumes them to be still alive. As indeed, on this album, they are.

Indeed, the release of the old demos, as an album, had been planned before *One More From The Road* and *Street Survivors*, but had been delayed due to the arrival of Gaines, who doesn't appear on the album. At least two sessions of overdubs took place, in 1975 and 1976, which accounts for the presence of King, amongst others. It is for this reason that the album is included here, in the main album catalogue, rather than as a compilation. The complete Muscle Shoals sessions would be released in 1998 as *Skynyrd's First: The Complete Muscle Shoals Album*, and this is included as a compilation album, primarily due to its inclusion of all the original material, and not just those originally selected, without overdubs.

'Down South Jukin'' (Rossington, Van Zant) 2:12
The 1978 *Melody Maker* review of the album stated:

> The music on this album, though neither spectacular nor startlingly original, is valuable as a reference point. From here, we can see how the band developed its Southern British-tinged rock sound. There are three tracks that act as definite pointers: 'Down South Jukin'', 'Lend A Helpin' Hand' and 'Wino' touch upon the raunchy style that Skynyrd made their own.

Certainly, the band valued the material, having prepared it for release before *Street Survivors*. Additionally, 'Down South Jukin'' remains a concert favourite of the current band. While the complete review is far from critical, and recognises the album's merits, fans probably hold these songs in higher regard. The song was written by Rossington and Van Zant during a break in rehearsals. Lacking inspiration, Allen, Bob and Leon walked up to the store to cash in collected bottles and get some cold drinks. Ronnie and Gary told them that they would have a complete song, from start to finish, ready for when they got back. He recalled that they just started playing it, off the top of their heads, and Ronnie joined in singing. When Allen, Leon and Bob got back, they played it to them all the way through.

The song begins with two guitars playing countrified licks accompanied by a beating bass drum from Bob Burns. The album credits no less than five guitarists. Joining Rossington and Collins are Ed King, Jimmy Johnson and Wayne Perkins. King's contributions are the 1975 overdubs. The Sheffield, Alabama, native Johnson co-founded the Muscle Shoals Sound Studios in Muscle Shoals, Alabama. Both his contributions and those of Wayne Perkins were recorded in 1976 along with backing vocals from Cassie Gaines, JoJo

Billingsley and Leslie Hawkins, and the saxophone of Ronnie Eades. Perkins, born in Birmingham, Alabama, has an impressive resume, having worked as a session guitarist with artists as diverse as Bob Marley and the Wailers (*Catch A Fire*), The Rolling Stones, Joni Mitchell and other credits for work with Michael Bolton, The Everly Brothers and Billy Ray Cyrus. King's slide is apparent before the laid-back vocals from Ronnie come in at 20 seconds, where he sounds almost drunk, perhaps intentionally, given the theme of the song, which is about letting your hair down on the weekend, getting dressed up, having a drink and chasing women. A close look at the lyrics reveals a point of interest.

Well, Billy Joe told me, well everything's lookin' fine
He got the place all secure, got the icebox full of wine
He said, now hurry on all and don't be late
I got three lovely ladies who just won't wait
We'll do some down south jukin', lookin' for some peace of mind.

Interestingly, the demo version of the song, which was subsequently released, has a slightly different lyric. Published lyrics for the album version of the song have the following line in the second verse, 'I got three fine mamas sittin' all alone'. The line sounds more like 'I got three fat mamas sittin' all alone', but the original demo version, first released on the 1991 collection, *Lynyrd Skynyrd – The Definitive Lynyrd Skynyrd Collection* (box set), has the line 'I got three black mamas sittin' all alone'. Whether the change was a management intervention is uncertain. At 1:20, it sounds like Gary is taking a solo, much shorter than the demo version, and it's augmented by some guitar embellishments low in the mix. What contributions Johnson and Perkins make are unclear, but Eades' saxophone supports the rhythm section. The release as a single in 1978, with 'Wino' as the B-side, did not chart.

'Preacher's Daughter' (Medlocke, Van Zant) 3:39
Although we first heard Ricky Medlocke's contributions to Skynyrd on the *Street Survivors* album, the release of the Muscle Shoals recordings revealed a deeper involvement in the early days. Here we have his first writing credit (measured by release date and track sequence). Rickey is playing drums, and his Blackfoot compadre Greg T. Walker plays bass. By his recollection, Ronnie told him to overdub the parts that Larry Junstrom had played, note for note. Greg is a native American from the Muscogee Creek nation, a woodland tribe from the Southeastern part of the United States, and back in its day, it was probably the largest and most powerful tribe in the entire United States in terms of numbers.

In an interview, published on *Swampland* in 2020 and attributed to Scott Greene, Greg was asked about the early days of Blackfoot and his time with Skynyrd:

Well, we all grew up together, and our paths crossed a lot. In the early days of both bands, we both played the same places. We were up in New Jersey, and we had played ourselves out in the local scene, and Ronnie called Rickey's mom to get our number because they needed a drummer. He was looking for Jakson. Rickey took the call, and he told Ronnie, 'I played the drums', so he and I rehearsed for a week, and he went to Florida to join Skynyrd. I went to Florida and returned to New Jersey, and six months later, Rickey called me and said that Skynyrd needed a bass player. I said, 'Give me 24 hours, and I will be there.' They were about to go into the first recording sessions in Muscle Shoals, so I joined, and we began to record and play some live shows. There are some songs on Skynyrd albums that are basically Blackfoot songs written by Jakson, Rickey and me, but Jakson and I were never given credit for them. I did not stay with them long, as it was not what I felt like I wanted to do. I told Rickey I was going to get Jakson and Charlie and reform Blackfoot, and he could join us or not, without any hard feelings. We played together in different forms off and on. Rickey came back, then rejoined Skynyrd, and we all went our separate ways for a short time. Charlie was playing with a band in North Carolina that needed a drummer, so they called Jakson. Then, they needed a guitar player, so they called Rickey, and it ended up with three of four members of Blackfoot playing in a band, so we decided to just reform, and that's how we got back together.

Rickey has a slightly different version of the events surrounding his recruitment, claiming that he had fallen on hard times with no gigs coming in, so he called Allen Collins to ask him if Skynyrd had any roadie work or similar. Allen said they needed a drummer and asked if he still played drums, and if so, he should call Ronnie. Maybe elements of both versions are correct.

A simple drumbeat is superseded by a descending pick scrape glissando on the guitar, a simple guitar motif and a doubled solo, before Ronnie's reverb-drenched vocals join at 40 seconds, recounting the tale of a preacher's daughter 'Doing what she hadn't ought to'. It is unclear which parts Wayne Perkins overdubbed in 1976, possibly the fast phased-sounding lead lines and fills. They don't sound like Gary, and Allen didn't use effects. Stylistically, the song is reminiscent of very early Blackfoot and is based on a Blackfoot song called 'Keep On Runnin'', to which Ronnie refers, in his new lyrics, in the first line, 'Well, just keep on running mama, until you can't run no more'. The song, a solid rocker, ends by fading out with traded solos panned left and right.

'White Dove' (Medlocke) 2:56

This is a simple but beautiful ballad, penned and sung by Rickie Medlocke in a much higher register than we would come to expect after listening to his work with Blackfoot. According to Gary Rossington, 'Vietnam was goin' on back then and 'White Dove' is kinda like a war song, tired of fightin' and just wanna cool it.' The narrator is 'Tired of fighting for it, gonna lay down my gun' and clearly wants to get back to nature.

The song is driven by the beautiful acoustic guitar of the enigmatic Gimmer Nichols, aka Larry Gimmer Nicholson, whose cult album, *Christopher Idylls*, was recorded in 1968, but remained unreleased for many years. How this collaboration came about remains unclear, but it seems likely that his guitar was recorded at the time, rather than being an overdub. Gary is also credited with guitar, and two acoustic guitars are audible. The Mellotron is credited to Randy McCormick, who was part of the Muscle Shoals Rhythm Section. This is a 1976 overdub, but the bass from Ed King is, however, a 1975 overdub. Despite this, the song is surprisingly coherent. At 1:02, a sustained guitar note brings in a tasteful solo from Gary. Ed's bass playing is sympathetic, and the Mellotron adds subtle ambience without being overpowering.

'Was I Right Or Wrong' (Rossington, Van Zant) 5:21
Author and critic John Swenson recalled being with a group of writers as guests of Al Kooper, who, following the release of the first album, was extolling the virtues of Lynyrd Skynyrd as songwriters. He played them the early recordings, including 'Right And Wrong', which Swenson likened to a John Ford movie in five minutes. In 1978, *Rolling Stone* writer Dave Marsh gave the following synopsis:

> The story of 'Was I Right Or Wrong' is classic. Against his parents' wishes, a young rocker sets out to seek his fortune. His dreams come true, but when he returns home to see his folks (the people he most wanted to convince of his abilities), he learns they are dead. There's an archetypal starkness to this tale that makes it hard to believe the song is only a fantasy. But Van Zant didn't even have a record contract when he wrote it.

Ronnie, despite his father's great pride in his son's achievements, always felt like he let Lacy down and regretted not completing his education. Perhaps the lyrics reflect his feelings, and he is playing out a fantasy, lyrically, of what might happen in the future.

Of the song's genesis, Rossington recalled that Ronnie had gone out and fished for an hour and had then come back and started singing, and they wrote the music. Compositionally, it started mellow and then changed mood to reflect him coming back to show everyone he was right for trying. Reflecting in 1975: 'We went out and learned to play, did everything we tried to do. We tried to be right about what we were doing.'

Leon is playing bass, Bob is on drums and Gary and Allen are on guitars. Ed King's 1975 overdubs sound to be primarily minor fills and embellishments. The following solos are from Rossington and Collins, proving that they had learnt to play. The overdubbed backing vocals from the Honkettes add emphasis at 3:40 before the song mellows once more as the narrator regrets that all he has achieved can't take his father's place. The song once again picks up for the chorus and ends with stabs, similar to those at the beginning, and mournful feedback from Gary fades to the end of the song.

'Lend A Helpin' Hand' (Collins, Rossington, Van Zant) 4:24
In Ballinger's *Lynyrd Skynyrd, An Oral History*, he quotes Gary as feeling that the early unreleased material is some of the band's best, and that although the playing is not as tight, the material is better, in part because he felt it was less biographical than some of Ronnie's later work. The example he cites is 'Lend A Helpin' Hand', which is about helping people out in other countries who don't have as much money to feed themselves.

Writers Collins, Rossington and Van Zant are joined by Rickey Medlocke on drums and Greg Walker on bass, with no 1975/76 overdubs. The intro feels like a slowed-down version of 'The Needle And The Spoon'. When the song hits its stride at 11 seconds, probably due to the rhythm section of Medlocke and Walker, the music has an early Blackfoot feel. A nimble guitar solo takes us into the first verse, where there is a touch too much reverb on Ronnie's voice, making it sound a little distant. Another short solo provides a bridge into the second verse. From 2.07 to 2.33, Allen takes another solo, ending with a creditable drum fill from Medlocke, whose primary instrument was not drums. Another short solo precedes the next verse, and at 3:35, both guitarists solo before the song begins to fade. Although an early recording, the guitarists acquit themselves well.

'Wino' (Collins, Medlocke, Van Zant) 3:15
Here, once again, the lineup is Van Zant, Collins, Rossington, Medlocke and Walker, delivering a dose of proto-Blackfoot. This is a cautionary tale of the dangers of alcohol and the solace that many seek from it: 'Wino, you wasn't born to lose/Sweet wine is making you a fool'. Dual guitar riffing is followed by heavier crashing chords, and at 1:21, Allen hits the wah-wah pedal for a solo, taking us to 1:48 and back to the heavier chords. As Gary mimics a slow police siren, Ronnie warns: 'Yonder come a man to take you downtown/He don't want you hanging around'. Another solo takes us to a tight single-chord crash to end. In his solo, Allen makes great use of the wah, something that he didn't do on record after 'Workin' For MCA'. This recording, of course, predates that.

'Comin' Home' (Collins, Van Zant) 5:30
Unlike in 'Was I Right Or Wrong', where the narrator makes it and then comes home, the narrator has had enough of life on the road – 'Traveling around I've had my fill/Of broken dreams and dirty deals' – and yearns to be back home, questioning why they went in the first place. At the time that the song was written, the band were struggling musicians who hadn't made it and

things were tough financially. Taken literally, the homesick narrator is worn out and missing his mother: 'Coming home to stay/Coming home to your love, mama/I've seen better days'.

A lone guitar picks a classic Allen Collins arpeggio and is joined first by a keyboard, and then at 11 seconds, Greg Walker's bass comes in along with a second guitar and piano, then vocals. Ed King adds a 1975 overdub with a subtle addition of two picked notes. Medlocke keeps his powder dry until 58 seconds, when the drums join. The choruses lift the song and backing vocals are credited to Honkette Leslie Hawkins (also once a Willette, providing backing vocals at one time for Wet Willie) and producer and singer/songwriter Tim Smith. Smith's vocals are from the original recording; those of Hawkins are a 1976 overdub. A short but sweet country solo, more of a fill really, from Ed is a tasty addition at 1:27. Once again, the drums are absent in the verse and back for the chorus. Ed lays some slide down throughout, and there is a short bridge before Allen's solo at 2:41, running through to 3:14. The final solo is a great one from Gary that neatly resolves before the arpeggio returns to fade out, with fills from King.

'The Seasons' (Medlocke) 4:09

Rickey not only wrote the song, but he also sings lead vocals and plays drums and mandolin on the recording. Greg provides the bass, and Gary and Allen are responsible for the guitars, with Ed credited, too, for his 1975 overdubs. The lyrics are poetic and seem to reflect someone's passing, seeing themselves as a reflection in another's eyes, and like the changing of seasons, it is now their time. The song begins with acoustic guitar and mandolin and is beautifully sung by Medlocke, proving himself to be a versatile singer when we consider the contrast between his falsetto on 'White Dove', this delivery and his later work with Blackfoot. Greg's backing vocals complement Rickey, which is to be expected given their familiarity and history. The main solo sounds like Gary and fits the mood of the song perfectly. Ed's fills are subtle and sensitive to the song as always, perhaps a facet of his talent that is not sufficiently lauded.

'Things Goin' On' (Original Version) (Rossington, Van Zant) 5:10

It's interesting that the band went back to 'Things Goin 'On' when they had already re-recorded it for the *Pronounced* album. On that version, Ed King plays bass, but on this earlier version (that is released later), we have Leon on bass, and Ed King's 1975 guitar overdubs. The history of Lynyrd Skynyrd has never been a simple one!

This version is notable for the absence of Billy Powell's piano and the vocal duet Ronnie has with himself. Apparently, to help achieve the effect, Jimmy Johnson used a Cooper Time Cube, one of only a 1000 that were ever made, which funnelled his voice through a tube, not unlike a hose pipe, and then fed it back to sped-up multi-track tape. Surprising as the choice may have been, when unused songs could have been revisited, this version is a worthy addition and has a great groove and feel.

Lynyrd Skynyrd band plane crashes; 6 killed

McCOMB, Miss. (AP) — Six persons, including three members of the Lynyrd Skynyrd rock band, were killed when their twin-engine airplane crashed while attempting an emergency landing.

Twenty others were injured in the Thursday night crash.

The propeller-driven Convair 240 skidded across tree tops for about 100 yards, then slammed nose first into a swampy area and split open about eight miles short of the McComb airport after reporting it was "having fuel trouble or was running low on fuel," an air traffic controller reported.

The dead were lead singer Ronnie Van Zant; guitarist Steve Gaines; his sister, vocalist Cassie Gaines; pilot Walter Wiley McCreary; co-pilot William John Gray, and Dean Kilpatrick, assistant road manager for the group, officials said.

Six other members of the band were injured. Others injured included members of the group's road crew and a television cameraman, officials of Southwest Mississippi Medical Center said.

Officials said 10 of the injured were in critical condition and 10 in stable condition.

The plane "sounded like a car skidding in gravel" as it clipped the trees, said Johnny Mote, who lives near the crash site close to the Mississippi-Louisiana border.

"When it hit ground it was a deep rumble, like it was underground. It sounded like thin wrinkling metal," he said.

The group was en route from a Wednesday night performance in Greenville, S.C., to a Friday night concert at Louisiana State University in Baton Rouge.

Above: An original newspaper report about the tragic plane clash in 1977. (*Authors Collection*)

1991 (1991)

Personnel:
Johnny Van Zant: vocals
Gary Rossington: guitar
Ed King: guitar
Randall Hall: guitar
Leon Wilkeson: bass
Billy Powell: keyboard, piano
Artimus Pyle: drums and percussion (does not appear on album, but is credited)
Kurt Custer: drums
Additional musicians:
Dale Krantz-Rossington: backing vocals
Stephanie Bolton: backing vocals
Susan Marshall: backing vocals
Randall Hall: 'Money Man' voice
Producer: Tom Dowd
Engineer, mixing, overdub engineer, overdubs: Kevin Elson
Engineer: John Hampton
Assistant engineer: Jeff Powell
Reissue producer: Joe Reagoso
Release date: 11 June 1991
Label: Atlantic
Chart places: US: 64, UK: did not chart
Running time: 51:51

Billy was the first to return to music after the crash, guesting on the album *Special Delivery* by .38 Special. Billy and Artimus collaborated with Leon LeBront, while Leslie Hawkins joined Wet Willie as a Willette. Billy, Leon, Artemis, JoJo and Barry Harwood briefly worked with a band called Alias, which included Jimmy Dougherty on vocals and Billy's brother Ricky playing bass. It was Dougherty, several witness accounts claim, that Ronnie had asked to replace him if he stepped aside to focus on production, writing and management. Their sole album, *Contraband,* was released in 1979.

Gary and Allen took a little time, having no wish to cash in on the Skynyrd name. They both walked away from an early involvement in Alias. Gary mentioned that there were some talks about him playing with Allen Collins, Don Nix and Gregg Allman, but it didn't happen. In 1979, the Rossington Collins band was formed, which included Powell, Wilkeson and Barry Harwood. Pyle had agreed to join, but a motorcycle accident prevented this, so the spot was taken by Derek Hess. Former .38 Special backing vocalist Dale Krantz was chosen, thereby ensuring that there could be no comparison to Ronnie. Their debut album, *Anytime, Anyplace, Anywhere,* was released in 1980. Shortly after the release of the album, Allen's pregnant wife, Kathy, suffered a massive haemorrhage and died at the cinema in front of their daughters, Aime and Allison. Allen never recovered from this, withdrawing from friends and family and turning to alcohol. The Rossington Collins Band did record and release a second album, *This Is The Way*, dedicated to Kathy, but it received little acclaim. Pyle claimed that Collins and Rossington were both involved in a relationship with Krantz, but whatever the situation was, the two men found it difficult to work together. Rossington married Krantz, and the couple took a hiatus from touring.

Allen formed the Allen Collins Band, and he was joined by Wilkeson, Powell, Dougherty, Hess, Randall Hall and Harwood. *Here, There And Back* was their only release. The album had poor sales and lacked promotion from MCA, who dropped the band. Allen's deterioration continued, although there were some attempts to keep the band going. In 1984, Collins crashed his Ford Thunderbird, killing his girlfriend, Debra Jean Watts. Allen's injuries were severe, with him being paralysed below the waist and having limited use of his arms. Collins pled guilty to DUI manslaughter. According to Allen's father, Larkin Collins, quoted in Ballinger's *Lynyrd Skynyrd An Oral History*, Allen and Artimus were planning on coming back as Lynyrd Skynyrd II, but the project was cut short by Allen's accident. Larkin recalled that the accident was prior to rehearsals, but a short rehearsal recording has surfaced along with artwork for the band logo. I am unable to confirm the provenance of these.

Pyle formed and recorded with APB, releasing two albums on MCA: *APB* in 1982 and *Nightcaller* in 1983. Rossington and Krantz returned as the band Rossington and released *Returned To The Scene Of The Crime* in 1986. Powell and Wilkeson played and recorded with Christian band Vision. Although Billy was happy playing with Vision, the realisation that people were calling out for Skynyrd, and, according to Gene Odum, the fact that he was broke, led him to consider a reunion. He had asked Rossington, who was not keen, not least because his current band featured his wife on lead vocals. However, despite the surviving Skynyrd members having apparently signed an agreement not to use the Lynyrd Skynyrd name, Powell's manager, Charlie Brusco, had more success convincing Rossington.

Eventually, the remaining members of the band agreed to play a six-week tribute tour, beginning at Charlie Daniels' XIII Annual Volunteer Jam in September 1987. Ronnie's youngest brother, Johnny, born on 27 February 1960, was somewhat reluctantly recruited for the job. He had experience. The Johnny Van Zant band had released *No More Dirty Deals* on Polygram in 1980, where Johnny worked with none other than Al Kooper. Johnny went on to release *Round Two*, produced by Kevin Elsom, and *The Last Of The Wild Ones*, to diminishing returns. He quit to follow in his father's footsteps and drove a truck until he came back and signed with Geffen in 1985, working with John Kalodner and producing the album *Van Zant*. Soon after, he signed for Ahmet Ertegun on Atlantic but put his solo career on hold to sign up for Skynyrd's temporary tour.

Ed King had agreed to come back, and at the insistence of Allen Collins, Randall Hall was brought in on guitar. Pyle, although now living in Jerusalem, also agreed to return. The band rehearsed and played the Volunteer Jam XIII. Due to the success of the Tribute, the band decided to continue but had to fight Judy VanZant and Teresa Gaines over the previously signed agreement that they not use the Skynyrd name. The resulting agreement stipulated that continuation was only possible with the presence of two original members in the band. Gene Odum claimed that Gary Rossington attempted a hostile takeover and extended the tour without consulting Judy. Odum had proof of an existing agreement that was used to settle the court case that went against Rossington. Odum felt that the decision to continue was purely financial, going as far as to say that the Rossington album was a flop and that the Johnny Van Zant Band 'Couldn't draw flies at a manure slinging contest.' Rossington and Krantz, now the Rossington Band, released the album *Love Your Man* in 1988 on MCA, but the future was bleak for Allen Collins. Suffering from pneumonia, Allen was admitted to hospital in September 1989, where he would die on 23 January 1990, aged just 38. He was buried next to his wife, Kathy, in Riverside Memorial Gardens in Jacksonville.

In 1990, Johnny released his solo album *Brickyard Road*, although he continued to front Skynyrd.

It must have been quite daunting to sit down and try to write new material for Lynyrd Skynyrd. King and Rossington – certainly Rossington, who had continued to write songs following the crash for the Rossington Collins Band – must have been confident they could still write the music for songs, but not having Ronnie to bounce ideas off and to write the lyrics must have been a real concern. To many, Ronnie was one of the great songwriters, and he had a natural ability and talent to tell stories in his songs. A pattern of using outside songwriters or accepting their songs and reworking them was established here. King recalled writing some of the lyrics for the album, and he wasn't particularly comfortable with this.

The album was recorded at Ardent Studios in Memphis. Production was handled by Tom Dowd, and in the opinion of Ed King, this wasn't a blessing:

What did I think of the '91 album? It's a good thing Bill Graham's people allowed us to remix it without Tom Dowd there. I have the original mixes and, admittedly, the album isn't a classic, but Dowd's mixes made us look like idiots. I think that was a point he wanted to make. I have a tape of a conference call between all the band members and Dowd after it was remixed. He's actually crying during the phone call and blaming me for doing it all behind his back. He went so far as to claim the added acoustic guitar, by Brent Rowan, on 'Pure & Simple' was out of tune. Like Brent would do such a thing! Graham's people told me beforehand that we could do the needed overdubs and remixing with Dowd's blessing. It turned out he knew nothing about it, fortunately. Until his dying day, Dowd thought I was underhanded about it, but that's not the case at all. As a matter of fact, if I had known of Dowd's displeasure, I wouldn't have messed with it.

His reference to Graham's people refers to manager Bill Graham's team. His association with the band was short-lived as he tragically died in a helicopter crash in 1991.

Although *Guitar Player* magazine felt that the Skynyrd were back with a vengeance, the general reception to the album was more lukewarm. King himself noted: 'The album was outstanding musically. As musicians, we poured our guts into that one. Other than that, it had some strong shortcomings.'

'Smokestack Lightning' (Todd Cerney, King, Rossington, Johnny Van Zant) 4:28

For an album opener, on a release that would clearly be scrutinised by the fans and press alike, you would hope that the band had confidence in the song. This was not the case for Ed King, who made his feelings clear, quoted from *Ed King's ProBoards* forum (2009): 'I hated that song while we were writing it, even more once we recorded it, and the video was the last straw. I think the lyrics to 'Incense And Peppermints' made more sense. For a Skynyrd song, it was just stupid.' Here, he was referring to his 1967 hit for Strawberry Alarm Clock.

Yet, if we look at the subject matter, scrutiny of the lyrics reveals common themes with much of Skynyrd's earlier releases. 'I was sittin' at home all alone when I heard that telephone ring/And there on the line was a friend of mine sayin' he wasn't doin' a thing/So, I'm steppin' out on the town tonight to party where the drinks are free/There's a sweet young thing ready and waitin' on me'. Several earlier Skynyrd songs talk about partying, drinking and women, so it's difficult to see Ed's point of view. Granted, the lyrics are not going to win a Nobel Prize for literature, but nor were Ronnie's. In 'On The Hunt', he said: 'There's two things that you should know/And in these two things baby, oh you must take pride/That's a horse and woman, yeah/Well both of them you ride'. His lyrics for 'Bad Boy Blues' are discussed in the *Collectybles* section. The narrator accepts an invitation to go out and party, meets a 'sweet young thing' but ultimately comes unstuck: 'I said hey sweet thing let me pull your string/Let me take you home/I woke up in an hour with my money and my memory gone'.

Some fans and critics felt the song was a little underwhelming, perhaps inevitable given the weight of expectation, but others quite enjoyed it. The single peaked at number two on the *Billboard* Mainstream Rock chart, which was their best ever showing.

The song does largely capture the zeitgeist of the original band. The song was written in the band's rehearsal studio in St. Augustine, Florida, during the *Tribute/Reunion Tour*. Curiously, Artemis is credited on the album, but Custer played the recorded drums. In the video for the single, both players are present, harking back to the Allman Brothers with two drummers, or when Skynyrd played with both Medlocke and Burns.

Perhaps fittingly, Gary Rossington starts the song accompanied by percussion that sounds like a rattlesnake before a second guitar and piano join. The drums from Custer are straight and powerful, without the idiosyncrasies of Pyle. The guitar arrangement follows the traditional Skynyrd formula, with a place for each guitar and the backing vocals of Dale Krantz Rossington, Stephanie Bolton and Susan Marshall, who evoke the spirit of the Honkettes. At 2:15, Gary takes an instantly recognisable solo, running all the way to 3:02, where we are back into a chorus with heavy backing vocals. The outro solo doesn't sound like Gary or Ed and is probably Randall Hall. Singer, songwriter, composer, guitarist, producer and mixing engineer Todd Cerney has a writing credit, establishing the pattern on later Skynyrd records of outside writers being used.

'Keeping The Faith' (King, Rossington, Danny Tate, J. Van Zant) 5:18
Ed King plays the opening riff on his Pensa-Suhr guitar, subsequently overdubbing lead lines, with accompanying feedback from Gary. The drums then build into an introductory solo from Randall before the first verse starts at 0:52. The narrator is putting his faith in a woman being the right one after negative relationships, but despite previous rejection, he's willing to open up to the special lady and put all of his trust in her.

At 2:45, Gary and Randall take sequential solos, with Randall summoning the spirit of Allen Collins with his whammy bar vibrato to end his solo. At 3:37, the band ease off, and Ed's chords accompany Johnny with subtle cymbal work from Custer before a bridge into the outro, with Rossington once again providing feedback, and a couple of leads take us to the fadeout. This is a solid song that stands up well to scrutiny and that once again has an outside writer. Here, Danny Tate, who has credits for artists as diverse as Jeff Healey, Kenny Wayne Shepherd, Billy Ray Cyrus, Doro (Doro Pesch) and The Fabulous Thunderbirds, joins King, Rossington and Van Zant as writers.

'Southern Women' (King, Dale Krantz-Rossington, Rossington, J. Van Zant) 4:16
The narrative of the song is as simple as the title suggests. From the narrator's perspective, it is a tribute to girls from south of the Dixie line. This song was also written in the rehearsal studio in St. Augustine. Van Zant said of the song, 'It just talks about good ol' Southern girls, how there ain't nothin like them. You can't go wrong singin' about that.' Perhaps the tribute to Southern Women is a little clumsy and focuses a little too heavily on looks and attitude, and fails to celebrate other qualities: 'It's a well-known fact across the Dixie line/And if a man don't agree, I could tell you he's blind/They can drink with the best, and to hell with the rest/And if she takes you home, you ain't getting no rest'.

It's not particularly offensive, and co-writer Dale Krantz-Rossington must have been happy with the message, although she was a Yankee as she noted herself in a 2003 interview with *Swampland*: 'I'll never forget the loveliest compliment someone gave me was when they called me 'The First Lady of Southern Rock'. I felt a little guilty with my Yankee Indiana roots, but my affiliation with Gary and Allen really did put me in a special spot.'

The guitars initially have a feel typical of several old Skynyrd songs, such as their version of 'Same Old Blues' and 'Double Trouble'. The rhythmic picking sounds like Ed, who also layers simple slide guitar into the chorus. At 1:24, we have a middle eight before Ed lays down a slide solo at 1:49 with vocal ad libs from Johnny, ending at 2:16 with a bridge section and stab chords leading into a chorus. Perhaps it is easy to overthink the lyrics, and we should just enjoy a simple song, reminiscent in style of the first incarnation of Lynyrd Skynyrd.

'Pure And Simple' (King, Michael Lunn, J. Van Zant, Robert White Johnson) 3:09

Ed King recalled the writing of the song: 'Johnny and two other guys wrote the chorus. He showed it to me one night. Then I wrote the verses and the bridge. Not much to it.' It is difficult to see how the chorus required the combined talents of Johnny Van Zant, songwriter Michael Lunn and long-term veteran of the Nashville community Robert White Johnson. Johnny had previously collaborated with Lunn and Johnson on his 1990 release *Brickyard Road*.

Another notable contributor to the song is Eric Martin on background vocals. It seems likely that his involvement was a result of his association with producer Kevin Elson, who was credited as engineer for the overdubs and mixing on *1991*. He was the producer for Mr. Big, featuring Eric Martin, for their 1991 release *Lean Into It*, from which their *Billboard* number one single, 'To Be With You', came. He can be heard in the choruses, but he is far from prominent.

Much of the song is based around an acoustic guitar and some nice touches on the piano, but according to King, all is not what we might assume. Ed did not like the first mixes of the album and claimed to have hired Nashville session guitarist Brent Rowan, who 're-did most of the acoustic stuff', and session musician Bill Cuomo to play the keyboard parts, as Billy was in rehab at that point. This recollection is confirmed by Bill on a *Music Business Radio* interview, hosted on Mixcloud.

There was clearly tension between Dowd and King throughout the recording and mixing process. Of the initial recording process for this song, in a 2009 Q&A on his web forum, King said:

I recall that during the recording of the vocal, Tom Dowd eventually threw me out of the studio. He kept needling Johnny about how he sang the words

'Oh – whoa' in the chorus. Dowd correctly says that Johnny has a hard time with the vowel sound 'O', but he was such an asshole about it. He and I got into it, and he threw me out. It was the one time when Dowd wasn't playing his Gameboy machine. He was actually paying attention.

Despite the creative turmoil behind the song, it turned out to be a touching ode to simpler times and a lament to their passing. Ed had written a solo for the song, but after hearing what Gary had written in his hotel room, he thought Gary's idea was better. On the solo, which builds from a volume swell at 1:28, we can hear that Ed does, in fact, play a second lead part which, though understated, is intertwined beautifully with that of Gary.

'I've Seen Enough' (Kurt Custer, Lunn, Rossington, J. Van Zant, White Johnson) 4:22
Lunn and Johson are credited as co-writers with Gary, Johnny and also drummer Kurt Custer. He had received his first big opportunity from Steve Earle, and he can be heard on *Copperhead Road*. In an interview with French journalist John Molet Custer, he recounted how he joined the band:

I met up with Skynyrd through Ed King. He called me one day and said he liked my playing on Steve Earle's Copperhead Road. It took me a year to join because Artimus Pyle was 'freaking out' about not being able to play in time anymore. That was tough, to come in and replace someone who basically saved their lives after the plane crash. But I got through it and became their sole drummer for four years. Very rewarding. I learned a lot! I basically started to arrange the songs from the first rehearsal. I did write with them as well.

The song begins with a couple of excerpts of news reports before a snappy drum beat from Custer brings in the guitars. Two guitars pick the riff in unison, which lacks the creative interplay of their best work, and at 33 seconds, Johnny is in and the riffing stops, leaving vocals and drums until 55 seconds. Ed provides occasional slide fills, and Johnny tells a story that basically reflects a decline in society in terms of poverty and crime. At 2:05, a solo follows a middle eight that includes a return to the news reports and features both Ed and Randall trading and duetting. Billy provides some nice additions on piano, and the backing vocals are strong. Ed plays a slide solo, and Johnny tells us 'I've seen enough' as the song fades. It's a solid song that doesn't retread old ground, and it is well played as you'd expect, but it's difficult to imagine it as anyone's favourite Skynyrd song.

'Good Thing' (G. Rossington, Donnie Van Zant, J. Van Zant) 5:28
This is an original composition and not a cover of the 1989 song by British band Fine Young Cannibals from their *The Raw And The Cooked* album. There

is a writing credit for Donnie Van Zant alongside his brother Johnny and Gary. It is a song about a couple splitting up. He thinks his partner has been cheating and is therefore ending the relationship. However, either out of charity or spite, he adds: 'I'm gonna love ya' just one more time', promising a night that will be remembered for the rest of her life.

Custer's powerful drumming is instantly recognisable. He has a much straighter rock approach than Artimus. It is interesting to think about how different the album would have sounded if the recorded drums were Pyles'. He had been involved in the creative process, as his album credit attests. Rossington's picked riff has us firmly back in familiar Skynyrd territory. Ed's slide and Billy's piano are at once familiar and on point. A brief pause at 1:27 as the backing vocalists take the lead is followed by a short slide solo from Ed. Gary takes the first proper solo at 2:47, followed by Ed's slide solo, taking us into a bridge section, where the level drops and Billy adds atmospheric piano. The song picks right back up, and he takes an instantly recognisable extended solo through to the end of the song, with a little help from the backing vocalists intoning 'Good Thing' and backed by slide licks from Ed. The song tells a familiar story, but the delivery is great. Billy was proud of his contributions to this album and rightfully so.

'Money Man' (King, J. Van Zant) 3:46
'Money Man' revisits the theme of managers ripping off hard-working musicians and recalls the 'money miser' in 'Cry For The Bad Man'. Here, the money man exploits the naive musicians, earning three dollars for their one, reminiscent of the deal the original lineup had with Walden. His deal with Lynyrd Skynyrd was for both management and publishing, plus 30% commission of gross earnings. So, if the band were booked for $500, that would give him $150 dollars. If the band's expenses came to $100, that left the band with $250 to split between the five members they had at the time. So, each member would receive $50, compared to Walden's $150. It is probably no coincidence that this is reflected in the lyrics: 'We play music got families to feed/Ain't good with numbers and he knows we can't read/If we get a dollar, you know he gets three/It ain't hard to figure out it's as simple as can be'.

However, in this song, the moneyman pays the price with a stint in jail and receives a little more than he bargained for, with the lyrics implying sexual abuse by his fellow inmates.

The voice of the moneyman is provided by Randall. Ed King thought that he had a great voice for radio and was impressed by his impressions: 'I've never heard a better Popeye.' The music has a swinging beat, Ed covering slide duties, and Billy covering some of the rhythm on piano. At 1:47, Randall takes the solo and possibly tries a little too hard. Although nimble-fingered, it lacks the idiosyncratic charm that identified the work of Collins, Rossington, King and Gaines.

'Backstreet Crawler' (Randall Hall, King, G. Rossington) 5:31
This seems to be a cautionary tale of a man who had it all, at least materially, with his job on Wall Street making 'the little man bleed', but who lost it all, including friends and family. Now he is the backstreet crawler, living a tough life on the street: 'I threw the first punch that's when he hit the ground/To survive in the street, you gotta win the first round'.

The song begins with a catchy riff and an intro solo with a particularly nasty distorted tone and ending using a whammy bar; the note choices and pinched harmonics sound like Gary, but the tone has Randall's name on it. Billy is all over this song, and Leon creates a great bass-driven bridge at 2:06. At 2:41, Randall takes a solo, leading to a chorus at 3:05, after which the first two lines are sung over a beating bass drum before the band are back in. A short slide solo from Ed precludes a tempo change at 4:37, and Randall closes out the song with some spirited picking before a big crash ending.

King said that to the best of his knowledge, Allen wouldn't have heard any of the songs on *1991*, but Randall Hall had this to say when asked about his time with the Allen Collins Band and with Lynyrd Skynyrd:

We had more songs that were not finished. We were planning on doing a second (Allen Collins Band) album, and when Allen was overcome with his troubles, we just gave it up. One of the songs that we were going to do was one we put on Skynyrd's *1991* record, 'Backstreet Crawler'. We didn't record it with Allen, but had it on a practice tape, that's about it. That would have been 1982, something like that. Allen loved it, and that was one of the very last things I talked to him about before he died. I went to visit him and said we're doing 'Backstreet Crawler'. He couldn't speak, but he gave me a big thumbs up and a smile.

Presumably, the song was altered significantly, as King and Rossington share writing credits with Hall, and neither of them were involved with the Allen Collins Band. Alternatively, it could have been financially motivated.

'It's A Killer' (King, Rossington, D. Van Zant, J. Van Zant) 3:54
This is an anti-drug song telling how drugs ruin lives, lead to murder and violence, ruin neighbourhoods and how innocent people can be affected. According to King, it wasn't without its controversy: "It's A Killer' is about drug dealers. A line in the song seems to go 'A fifty-dollar gram is what the n***** sayin'. Actually, the 'n' word is 'neighbour', but it sure doesn't sound like that. We did get some racist backlash on that.' Presumably, he meant backlash to what was perceived as their racism. It's a more contemporary-sounding Skynyrd song despite Ed's slide and Billy's embellishments. At 1:58, it's Randall taking a solo, followed by Billy, leading into a bridge before the last verse. Again, it's a solid, well-played song, but probably not one destined for many compilations or playlists.

'Mama (Afraid To Say Goodbye)' (King, Rossington, D. Van Zant, J. Van Zant) 6:44
It can be said with confidence that this was not Ed's favourite song. Quoted from *edking.proboards*: 'That song was not well written and totally misguided, as was that whole album.' It is a sentimental tribute to a dying mother. Clearly, this can't be the Van Zant brothers' mother, Marion, as she passed away in 2000, nine years after the album's release. The song begins with piano accompanied by some fills from Ed King. It features some melodic slide from Gary Rossington in both the intro and the main solo. Gary's slide fills and the uncredited mandolin playing add to the country vibe. The background vocals add a gospel feel to the solo and the quiet section of the song at 4:41, singing 'Jesus walked on water, I know it's true' with Johnny. Contrary to Ed's perception, the song is clearly very well written, although some may feel it's a little oversentimental. Leon Wilkeson recalled asking if the song could be played at the funeral of his former mother-in-law. Chaos ensued when the tape was played, as he had put it in backwards and had to bolt to the front of the church, cowboy boots ringing out, to reverse and cue the tape.

Despite his misgivings about the song, Ed's ending solo that runs through the fadeout is an album highlight, and one he was proud of, saying, 'I wish the 'whoa' I screamed was on tape, too. That happened because the whole outro was improvised, and when I played a certain part, I reacted loudly.'

'End Of The Road' (Cerney, King, Rossington, J. Van Zant) 4:34
Far from being about the ending of Lynyrd Skynyrd, the song explains their continuation by acknowledging that, although the legacy is difficult to live up to, it's a family tradition and 'That Freebird keeps on flyin' and it never will come down'. The song is a strong album closer and wouldn't be out of place in a current Skynyrd set, not least because of the message it carries, justifying and celebrating their existence as Lynyrd Skynyrd: 'We still got our music and so many miles to go'. Solos are credited to Rossington and Hall, but from 2:10, the intertwined solos have three voices in some parts all the way through to 3:14. From 3:58, Billy takes a typically lyrical romp through the faded outro.

Associated Tracks

As is often the case, more tracks were prepared for the album than were used. Recordings of demos of songs from the sessions for *1991* are available on the internet.

'Take Me Down Easy' (Randall Hall) 5.50
This is a Randall Hall composition. He had this to say in an interview hosted on *The Ballad Of Curtis Loew* website: 'Bill Graham (the band's manager, not the evangelist) loved it and Geffen and Epic said that's your single hit, but it

didn't have any more writers other than me so … I was all pumped up to get it on the record but didn't even get it into the studio. The powers that be, that's all I'll say.' Randall did recycle the song, with different lyrics and Jimmy Dougherty on vocals. Dougherty was the man whom Randall claimed Ronnie had asked to replace him. The demo song is a little untidy in places, but the arrangement of this gentle midtempo track is fairly well developed. It would have been a good fit on the album.

'Do Unto Others' (Unknown) 5.10
This is a little heavier hitting than 'Take Me Down Easy' and features some solid riffing and soloing. The arrangement and instrumentation sound complete, although the available copy is made from two recordings that have been joined together. This song had a lot of potential.

'My Heart Belongs In Dixie' (Unknown) 5:16
The song is a celebration of the South, and although unreleased, it is worth seeking out. The recording is complete, and the arrangement is fully realised. Billy is a little buried in the mix, but his piano sounds great, and the solos are excellent. There is also an instrumental demo version that includes an additional intro. It's actually still quite catchy and again worth finding.

'Honky Tonk Blues' (Unknown) 4:30
This song is very reminiscent of 'Money Man' in terms of style and feel. The lyrics tell us how hard it is to make a living playing honky tonk blues. The solos are not particularly inspired, and although it's solid enough as a song, there is nothing here that would have added to the album.

'Unfinished Business' (Unknown) 5:38
This is the rawest of the demo songs, backed by an acoustic guitar and a tapped rhythm rather than drums. It is sung as a duet. Johnny is recognisable, but the other singer is less easy to identify. The title is ironic, given the embryonic nature of the recording.

The Last Rebel (1993)

Personnel:
Gary Rossington: guitar
Ed King: guitar
Johnny Van Zant: lead vocals
Leon Wilkeson: bass
Billy Powell: piano, Hammond organ, synthesiser
Randall Hall: guitar
Kurt Custer: drums, percussion
Additional musicians:
Dale Krantz Rossington: background vocals
Tim Lindsey: additional bass
Horns: Jim Horn (arranger), Charles Rose, Denis Solee, Michael Haynes
Producer: Barry Beckett
Reissue producer: Joe Reagoso
Release date: 16 February 1993
Label: Atlantic
Chart places: US: 64, UK: did not chart
Running time: 50:01

At this point in time, the band were still battling many demons, and volatile incidents still dogged them, for example, Johnny having a fight with Ed King on tour in Paris in 1992. In his book *The Gospel According To Abraham*, road manager Paul Abraham recalled that it had been Johnny's birthday, and he was drunk on Jack Daniel's. Between the end of 'Sweet Home Alabama' and the encore of 'Free Bird', Johnny and Randall had words. The fracas that resulted in King's finger getting broken was back at the hotel. According to Abraham, Johnny had no cocaine to counteract the drink. Following this, he trashed his hotel room during an argument with his wife, who had joined him for his birthday. The preceding events closed when Abraham nailed Johnny with a right hand and managed to dissuade the attendant gendarmes from making an arrest, despite Johnny's wife wanting him arrested and Johnny wanting Abraham arrested.

Artimus had not played on the last album, and he was now gone. The account that he left primarily because of everybody else's drug use is contradicted by others. Close band friend Andy Munson remembered this period well in a personal communication:

The trouble with *1991* is that every one of them was all effed up from then through about 1997. I remember hanging out watching .38 Special from the side of the stage with Gary and Johnny during the summer of 1992. Gary was drinking wine and could barely talk, and Johnny was all hyped up. The summer before, they were all messed up, particularly Arti, who was gone a couple of weeks after I'd seen (and attempted) to talk to him. They were really the worst times for the band in terms of substance abuse. 1991 was a night and day difference from 1987-88 for all of them. With that in mind, you can understand why the memories didn't always agree with each other!

Discussing Artimus specifically, he added:

When I first met him in 1987, he was alive, healthy, funny, etc. I spent a bunch of time with them in 1988, and he was still on top of things, riding his bicycle around the runways inside arenas and so forth, but he seemed a bit out of it. I didn't see him again until the summer of 1991. This was less than two weeks before he got fired, and he looked like Charles Manson again, which is fine, but he was so out of it before the show that I had no idea how he'd get through the show! Thank God for Kurt Custer! The two-drummer setup was great, but after a couple of songs, Arti really couldn't keep up. I hated seeing it; it was really sad.

Abraham recalled Pyle's last gig with the band. The two-drummer setup was in place partly to address Pyle's stamina issues following his various injuries. Between soundcheck and the show at Kingswood Amphitheatre, outside of Toronto, Pyle, for reasons best known to himself, was drinking. He was agitated all afternoon, and during the show, he got angrier. Pyle threw his snare behind him and attacked his ride cymbal with a tambourine until it broke. He then threw the remains, nearly hitting Dale. Abraham grabbed him from behind and manhandled him offstage, marking his last performance for the band.

Pyle's troubles continued when his girlfriend of several years, Angela, accused him of sexually assaulting his daughters. Pyle spent all he could fighting the case, but had to plead guilty when the money ran out. He avoided jail but was left very bitter at the lack of support he got from the band.

The album was recorded between September 1992 and January 1993 at Emerald Sound Studios in Nashville, Tennessee. Dowd was no longer producing the album, for which King was glad: 'I liked the record ... a lot better than the *1991* album. It helped that we all got along with the producer, Barry Beckett. Dowd might be the other band members' hero, but Beckett is mine.'

The job of crafting the cover for *1991* had fallen to Atlantic Creative Director Bob Defrin. He had led the design for Johnny Van Zant's solo outing on Atlantic, *Brickyard Road*. Defrin left Atlantic prior to the release of *The Last Rebel*. His successor offered the task of art direction to Larry Freemantle. Talking to *The Ballad Of Curtis Lowe* in 2020, Larry revealed why the image of Gary Rossington, captured by photographer Mike Miller, was chosen for the front cover:

The image of Gary, we shot specifically for that. If we can get one guy, let's go with Gary, who was kind of their leader. Let's shoot one guy up against the tree kind of thing, looking as if he was at the end of his rope, with his horse. It was really funny, the horse was facing one direction, and I was thinking, 'wish that horse would look the other way'. As I said it, the horse looked the other way, and I went 'holy shit!' Wow, that was amazing. The horse was meant to be on that cover, the name, everything.

'Good Lovin's Hard To Find' (Ed King, Gary Rossington, Johnny Van Zant, Robert White Johnson) 3:55
It is possible to look at this song from a couple of different points of view. The most positive interpretation is that the message is about not searching for a perfect partner but accepting the love we find. Or we can interpret the lyrics more negatively and make the conclusion that the message is to accept and take advantage of what we find: 'Can't always get what you want sometimes/So, you're better off just takin' what you can'. We are told that men are interested in looks, looking for a perfect ten, and women in money, trying to find a rich man.

Whatever point of view we take, Skynyrd set out their stall that this is an old time, good time boogie, with slide from Ed, piano backing from Billy, crisp drumming from Custer on his Ludwig drumkit and Zildjian cymbals and horns from Charles Rose, Denis Solee, Michael Haynes and (never did a man have a more appropriate name) Jim Horn, who also arranged the horns. At 1:41, Gary takes a lead break on his 1959 Gibson Les Paul Standard, ending with a pick scrape glissando reminiscent of the one in the intro to 'Preacher's Daughter', followed by Ed on slide, most probably on his Paul Reed Smith Custom guitar. There is nothing innovative here, but they remain true to themselves. The track, released in 1993, could have been from the 1970s, but like AC/DC, you know what to expect, and they are bound to a style.

'One Thing' (Kurt Custer, King, Dale Krantz-Rossington, Rossington, J. Van Zant) 5:13
Howling feedback and backmasked guitar bring in the song before the drums and rhythm guitar join, all augmented by Billy playing organ. The narrator is advocating that we should follow a dream and stay true to ourselves. At 2:25, Gary takes a solo that is not his most creative or imaginative, until 2:55, when the tempo drops and Gary's playing here is simple but haunting. Johnny comes back in, and the tempo picks up again for the last verse. Duelling guitars take the song to the fade out, one predominantly playing an ostinato while the other fires off fast licks. There is nothing wrong with this ending, but it certainly isn't 'Free Bird'. It is fair to say that with a little more work on instrumental (solo) sections, the song could have been better. Most of Gary's licks are predictable, and he was capable of so much more. Whether this is because of time constraints, complacency, or recreational pursuits is unclear.

'Can't Take That Away' (Michael Lunn, J. Van Zant, Robert White Johnson) 4:19

The lyrics to this song explore the themes of holding onto beliefs and faith, even when faced with societal changes and attempts to diminish them, such as the call to remove 'In God We Trust', the official US motto since 1956, from US currency. Hanging onto old values as times change is a theme that runs through several songs in the band's catalogue. This is a country-style song, beginning with acoustic guitar and Ed displaying his subtle mastery of fills, using picked notes and harmonics. The 'one more time chorus' is elevated with the gospel-like backing vocals, matching the religious theme. At 1:14, the line 'Just like my father's father before him/They held on with pride to everything they believed' is maybe a nod to Custer for his contribution to 'Copperhead Road', where Steve Earle sings 'Well, my name's John Lee Pettimore/Same as my daddy and his daddy before'. Pettimore was holding onto the family tradition of making and running moonshine, rather than religious belief. At 2:04, there is a key change, and Johnny ominously sings 'There's a fire that burns forever/Come a day we ain't gonna take no more', leading us to Ed's solo at 2:13, which is understated but a perfect fit. An extended chorus takes the song to its gently faded ending.

'Best Things In Life' (Tom Keifer, Rossington, J. Van Zant) 3:54

Johnny and Gary share songwriting credits with Tom Keifer, frontman, songwriter and guitar player with the band Cinderella. Tom was a Lynyrd Skynyrd fan, and video footage of Zakk Wylde, Bret Michaels, Tom Keifer and Travis Tritt all coming to jam with Lynyrd Skynyrd and open the show at the Fox Theatre in Atlanta in 1993 can easily be found.

The song refutes the notion that the best things in life are free and that, sometimes, despite appearances, you have to work for what you want. In the third verse, the narrator makes it clear: 'You got to get your hands dirty when it's somethin' that you really need/If they ever give you somethin' too easily/Can't be too good, 'cause nothin' good's for free'. Earlier, his resentment was clear, challenging the notion that his achievements weren't built on hard work, and reiterating the Van Zant tradition not to back down from trouble.

The music is classic old-time Skynyrd and, in 1993, very much another anachronism. Gary opens the guitar proceedings with slide guitar, and we have his trademark sound picking notes in the backing, along with familiar but classy piano from Billy. The chorus ends with the line 'That the best things in life don't come so easily', and Johnny is clearly more confident filling his brother's shoes, paying tribute with the way he modulates the last word 'easily' by raising the last syllable an octave and adding vibrato. At 1:56, Randall takes a solo, once again using the whammy bar for emphasis and a tone a little like Gary's but with more gain. It's not a classic, but the solo is serviceable. This is another solid, good-time song

'The Last Rebel' (Lunn, Rossington, J. Van Zant, White Johnson) 6:47
Atmospheric keyboards and crisp military drumming on the snare set the tone early before a guitar arpeggio leads the vocals in for the first verse, and at 1:35, the band are all in. A beautiful bridge at 2:49 brings us to Gary's solo, which resolves back into a gentle section, like the bridge before the rousing 'Last rebel' chorus. There are some simple but haunting slide lines throughout the song, but at 5.00, everything drops out, and a guitar arpeggio is joined by a beautiful slide solo from Ed. This carries on to the song's end at 6:47, backed by atmospheric keyboard chords and an occasional deep, powerful drumbeat.

The song stands as one of the highlights of their post 1977 career. Quoted from *Classic Rock* (March 2023), Rossington said:

This is a very moody song. We had to really get in the mood to record it, then we just cut it live. I wrote the music and named it at my house in Wyoming. The first verse is about a civil war soldier, and the second verse is about me, they say, and the third verse is sort of about us – the last rebels, out on the road, still doing our thing.

The song only seemed to grow in significance as more band members passed away over the years, and surely many fans would happily see this played now in the set as a tribute to Gary. Ed King also felt that it was his legacy piece, and it was probably his greatest contribution to the band since *Nuthin' Fancy*. Sadly, he would only feature on one more studio album, *Endangered Species* (1994), and on the live 1996 release, *Southern Nights*. The last word here goes to Ed:

On 'The Last Rebel', I played a slide solo on a 12-string. That guitar part, I don't mind saying, is a work of art and inspiration. What you hear was done on the original take on the basic track, no overdubs. Actually, the take we did before the one that made it on the record is probably the better solo. Both were quite chilling. I usually don't brag on myself, but that slide solo is the eeriest thing I've ever heard, and it's a 'first-taker', too. Not overdubbed. When I heard that solo played back the next day, I trembled. It was my statement, my obituary. It's that kind of stuff. It's got 'bye bye' written all over it. You can see that last rebel fading into the fog. I want it played at my wake. It's quite unsettling!

'Outta Hell In My Dodge' (Randall Hall, King, J. Van Zant, White Johnson) 3:47
Randall Hall had an old Dodge truck, and, according to King, Randall came up with the tune. However, songwriting credits are shared with Ed King, Johnny Van Zant and Robert White Johnson. The first verse and chorus set the scene, and it's a tale of a man stuck in a rut in a small town, yearning for the

freedom of the open road and his faithful Dodge. Added incentive to leave is given in the second verse, where we find out the narrator has had a run-in with the sheriff, following a drunken tryst with the sheriff's wife the previous evening. The song is a likeable romp and features the familiar roll of Billy Powell's piano, adding a honky tonk feel to the song, with Ed on slide. The backing vocals fill out the chorus, and both Gary and Randall take solos from 2:13 (Gary, Randall, Gary) before Billy shows them both how it's done at 2:40. The track then ends with a final chorus.

'Kiss Your Freedom Goodbye' (King, J. Van Zant) 4:46
Sometime during the writing and recording of the songs for the album, Ed wrote: 'But anything and everything we do in the future hinges totally on how these recording dates go. I think we've got one tune that stands a chance of being the 'Sweet Home Alabama' of the 1990s, but we'll see.' Asked about this, some years later, Ed confessed:

> I must have been crazy at the time. The song I was referring to was 'Kiss Your Freedom Goodbye'. I may have been premature about tooting my own horn. The song didn't turn out like I thought it should. There's a demo version floating around that was done three years before the album version; it's not too bad. The guitar parts are pretty cool.

The theme is one of societal erosion. The narrator is living a simple life in a very small town, but worries about the future. The chorus says that things will change and never be the same. The principal worry seems to be about kids on the street selling drugs, and that the small-town folks will have to change their ways and lose their freedom. The irony seems lost that the members of Lynyrd Skynyrd were long-haired rebels and hellraisers, drinking, doing drugs and crashing cars back in the day, fighting and getting banned from hotel bars. Ronnie had immortalised some of these events in song, proudly recalling the 11 times he had been to jail, for example. These were habits that had never really gone away and were certainly back in evidence in the years that followed the *Tribute Tour*.

It's good to hear Leon holding down the rhythm section, locking nicely in with Custer's powerful drumming. The rhythm guitars are working well together in the arrangement, and the verses are punctuated with sweet fills from guitar and piano. At 2:26, Randall takes one of his best solos before handing the baton to Billy at 2:46, who, as always, delivers the goods. Johnny ad-libs at the end, telling us 'Things just ain't the same' as the outro fades, ending the song at 4:46.

'South Of Heaven' (Lunn, Rossington, J. Van Zant, White Johnson) 5:15
This song is not to be confused with the 1988 song by Slayer! The comeback albums had a few songs that were originals but that shared names with other

artists, notably 'Smokestack Lightning' and 'Good Thing' from *1991*, this song and 'Born To Run' that closes this album.

It can be asked whether it was really a bit anachronistic to be singing about honk-tonk bars and 'a little girl they call the sweet thing' in 1993, when the album was released, but ultimately Skynyrd were trying to recapture the past and give the fans what they wanted. Lyrically, there is some ambiguity. Is the honky-tonk a brothel rather than a bar? Is the 'sweet thing' a prostitute, as we hear 'You'll be one more callin' her name'? It seems to be primarily about struggling to get where you want to be, 'No matter how I try, I'm just south of heaven', but realising that you don't need everything and you can be happy with what you have got.

Beginning with some nice percussion from Custer, a fat, picked guitar riff and organ chords from Billy on his Hammond-B3, the scene is set for Johnny to alternate lines with the picked guitar. Piano and backing vocals are on point for what is at once both a familiar-sounding but nevertheless enjoyable tune. A bridge at 2:24 takes us to an excellent instrumental section at 2:34, where Gary plays slow melodic lines before picking up the pace, and then at 3:06, there is yet more great slide work from Ed, closed out at 3:24 with Billy's B3. Following an extended chorus, there is another slide solo before the vocals return, and the song closes, not fading out this time.

'Love Don't Always Come Easy' (King, J. Van Zant) 4:34
Although Ed never identified as an acoustic guitar player, he was a fan of the Byrds, and here he does play a 12-string acoustic, noting that it doesn't usually have a place in the type of music he played and that 'They're a bitch to re-string!'

This is basically a country song that relates the story of a couple that meet, fall in love and get married, have a child and then find life hard. They have little time together, and the message is that it is easy to walk away or drift apart, but that this is where the effort should be made. Johnny's lyrics are effective, telling a story in very few words. The acoustic guitar, electric guitar with the Leslie cabinet-style tremolo effect and the piano of Billy weave a perfect backdrop to the lyrics. Gary delivers a lovely solo at 1:44. It is far from a technical masterclass, but like many of his solos, it's a perfect fit, and it's like a slow Southern drawl. At 3:12, Gary plays a string-bending motif, followed by another repeated pattern, and the song fades to the end.

'Born To Run' (King, Rossington, Donnie Van Zant, J. Van Zant) 7:25
When asked about 'Born To Run' on his forum, Ed had the following recollections and insight:

> I really like that tune. I don't know the exact inspiration for it, but I can tell you that Lacy Van Zant and one of his truck-driving stories were the inspiration for me to write the bridge. I had sat down with him for an hour

or so – you never sat with Lacy for under an hour – and he was telling me some stories. It was always easy to tell where Ronnie got his storytelling abilities. I was lying in bed one night and had the bridge come to me in a flash. Jumped up, grabbed a pen and paper, and finished it. We'd been working on that tune for a week and just didn't know where to take it musically. When the bridge was inserted, the rest fell into place. The finale to that tune is quite spectacular. Randall's parts are just a fine piece of inspired playing. We originally had that song ready for the *1991* album, but Tom Dowd didn't like it.

The song is a slow burner that picks up just after the midway point with an instrumental section that gives a nod to 'Free Bird'. Ed is on slide, with the bottom string dropped to a D. Randall and Billy both take solos, and there is a writing credit for Donnie Van Zant, alongside Ed, Gary and Johnny. The music begins with drums and heavy rhythm and slide guitar, which drops down to guitar and vocals at 0:21. The rhythm section return for the first verse at 40 seconds. Randall plays a great solo from 0.53 to 1:04.

The song relates the story of an ex-trucker reflecting on his life, as Ed said, inspired by Lacy Van Zant: 'There's an old man sittin' on a front porch now/ Talkin' 'bout how it used to be'. The old man tells us that he drove a tractor and trailer and had six kids and 'a hell of a wife'. The chorus affirms that the truck driving was his life and that he was 'born to run'.

Randall takes another solo at 2:27 and hands over to Ed on slide before everything drops out to a single rhythm guitar and then into a chorus. At 4:14, double-time drums pick up the pace, with guitar licks and feedback. At 4:39, Billy takes an extended solo, over a minute long, with atmospheric slide and feedback notes in the background. From 5:41, twin guitar solos panned left and right with choppy piano from Billy run all the way to the end of the song at 7:23.

Although the song might not fly high like a Free Bird, it certainly has 18 wheels rolling. There are many who dismiss the post-crash band, in all its incarnations, but the loss is theirs. Ronnie paid tribute to his father with 'Truck Drivin' Man', but the writing here, if you compare the songs, is superior. Donnie and Johnny were inspired by their father. Johnny recalled 'He took us out on the road to make runs with him, all three sons, and I think we learned to love the highway doing that. And here we are, still doing it.'

Above: Lynyrd Skynyrd (L-R: Billy Powell, Allen Collins, Leon Wilkeson, Bob Burns, Ronnie Van Zant, Gary Rossington and Ed King) pose for a portrait circa 1974. (*Michael Ochs Archives/Getty Images*)

Left: *Pronounced 'Lĕh-'nérd 'Skin-'nérd* was the first studio album released by the band, although earlier recordings would be released as *Skynyrd's First And Last* and *Skynyrd's First: The Complete Muscle Shoals Album*. (*MCA*)

Right: *Second Helping* opens with 'Sweet Home Alabama'. This enduring masterpiece must be one of the finest songs to open an album. (*MCA*)

Left: *Nuthin' Fancy* was the first album to feature Artimus Pyle, who replaced Bob Burns on drums. Much of the material had to be written in the studio due to the band's relentless touring. (*MCA*)

Right: *Gimme Back My Bullets* was a much more stripped-back album and followed the departure of Ed King on guitar and Al Kooper as producer. (*MCA*)

Left: *Street Survivors* was the only studio album to feature Steve Gaines. His arrival was clearly a catalyst for Allen Collins and Gary Rossington to up their game. (*MCA*)

Right: *Skynyrd's First And Last* featured songs from the Muscle Shoals sessions that had failed to land the band a record deal. (*MCA*)

Left: The band posing on Main Street in Jonesboro, Georgia, at the photo shoot for the *Pronounced 'Lĕh-'nérd 'Skin-'nérd* album cover. L-R: Leon Wilkeson, Billy Powell, Ronnie Van Zant, Gary Rossington, Bob Burns, Allen Collins, Ed King. (*Gems/Redferns*)

Right: Ronnie Van Zant, Gary Rossington and Allen Collins working with producer Al Kooper on *Pronounced 'Lĕh-'nérd 'Skin-'nérd* on 6 May, 1973 in Studio I Doraville-Atlanta, Georgia. (*Tom Hill/ Getty Images*)

Left: The two-guitar version of Lynyrd Skynyrd that recorded *Gimme Back My Bullets*. L-R, back row: Artimus Pyle, Billy Powell, Leon Wilkeson. Front row: Gary Rossington, Allen Collins, Ronnie Van Zant. (*Alamy*)

Right: Allen Collins (left) and Artimus Pyle share their bottle of Jack Daniels with Zip, the roller-skating chimp, at a record company party for Lynyrd Skynyrd in Manhattan, November 1976. (*Richard E. Aaron/ Redferns*)

Left: Allen Collins (left) takes a lead break as Ronnie Van Zant looks on and Gary Rossington plays rhythm. (*Richard McCaffery*)

Right: Ronnie Van Zant backstage with Charlie Watts at Knebworth Music Festival in 1976. Looking on, wearing sunglasses, is Doug 'Cosmo' Clifford, drummer for Creedence Clearwater Revival

Left: Allen Collins and Mike Estes jamming together. Mike's friendship with Allen and his mentoring proved pivotal in his career. (*Estes*)

Right: A promotional picture released by MCA records. From L-R: Cassie Gaines, Leslie Hawkins and JoJo Billingsley, backing vocalists for Lynyrd Skynyrd, collectively known as The Honkettes. (*Getty Images*)

Above: Ronnie Van Zant performing on stage at Hammersmith Odeon, London, 15 February 1976. Despite his small stature and lack of animation, he had a commanding stage presence. (*Ian Dickson/Redferns*)

Below: The triple guitar attack was completed by the addition of Steve Gaines, pictured on the right. His writing, playing and singing reinvigorated the band. He was tragically killed just three days after the release of his only studio album with the band, *Street Survivors*. (*Bert Treep*)

Left: *1991* saw the band reunited in the studio following the successful *Tribute Tour*. Allen Collins had chosen Randall Hall as his successor. (*Atlantic*)

Right: *The Last Rebel* was the final album to feature Randall Hall. With the title, an analogy was being made with Gary Rossington as the last rebel. (*Atlantic/WEA International*)

Left: *Endangered Species* marked the arrival of Mike Estes and was also the last studio release to feature Ed King. This stripped-back acoustic collection proves a worthy addition to the canon. (*Capricorn*)

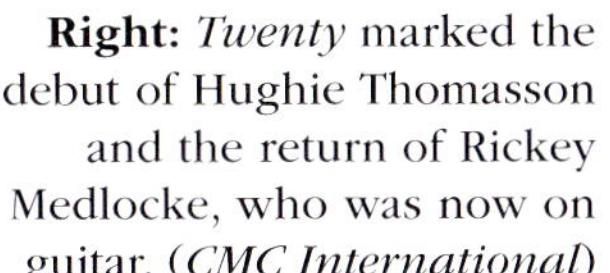

Right: *Twenty* marked the debut of Hughie Thomasson and the return of Rickey Medlocke, who was now on guitar. (*CMC International*)

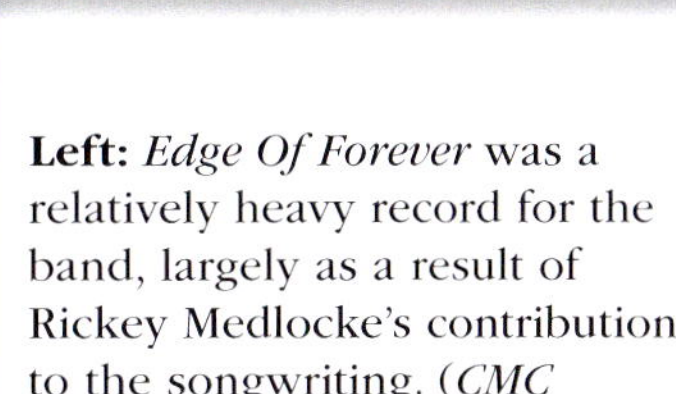

Left: *Edge Of Forever* was a relatively heavy record for the band, largely as a result of Rickey Medlocke's contribution to the songwriting. (*CMC International*)

Right: *Christmas Time Again* was not the band's most lauded release, but it includes contributions from members of .38 Special and the Charlie Daniels Band. (*CMC International, SPV*)

Left: When Lynyrd Skynyrd re-formed for the *Tribute Tour*, it was too painful for Johnny to sing "Free Bird" and it was left to the crowd to sing. Here, Gary Rossington plays the slide guitar introduction. Ronnie's hat was displayed as the song was played in his memory. (*Jon Sievert/Michael Ochs Archives/Getty Images*)

Below: Ronnie Van Zant said that of the three brothers, Johnny (pictured) had the best voice. He was an obvious choice for the 1987 *Tribute Tour*. (*Jon Sievert/Michael Ochs Archives/Getty Images*)

Above: Johnny had fronted his own band, the Johnny Van Zant Band, before joining Lynyrd Skynyrd. He has also performed and recorded with his brother Donnie as Van Zant. Pictured at Shoreline Amphitheatre on 31 August 1991 in Mountain View, California. (*Tim Mosenfelder/Getty Images*)

Right: Lynyrd Skynyrd recorded 'White Knuckle Ride' for a NASCAR-themed album, which provided some great social opportunities. Here they are pictured with road manager Paul Abraham and Dale Earnhardt. (*Estes*)

Left: *Vicious Cycle* features Leon Wilkeson on two tracks, but following his death, he was replaced by former understudy Ean Evans. (*Sanctuary*)

Right: *God And Guns* featured Mark Matejka on guitar, following the departure and passing of Hughie Thomasson. Billy Powell played on the album but passed away during the recording process. (*Roadrunner*)

Left: *Last Of A Dyin' Breed* proved to be Gary Rossington's last studio album with the band, although he didn't pass away until 2023. (*Roadrunner*)

Right: *Best Of The Rest* was released in 1982 and featured two previously unreleased tracks, the origins of which are not entirely clear. (*MCA*)

Left: *FYFTY* was the most comprehensive review of the band's career since 1991's 3CD *The Definitive Lynyrd Skynyrd Collection*. It also included the 2020 digital single 'Last Of The Street Survivors'. (*Geffen Records*)

Right: The 1987 *Tribute Tour* was recorded and released as *Southern By The Grace Of God* as a tenth anniversary tribute to the members of the band who died in the 1977 plane crash. (*MCA*)

Above: Often now tagged as a tribute band, Lynyrd Skynyrd continue to tour and attract large crowds, with a set now focusing almost exclusively on the 1970s material. (*Chris Salisbury*)

Below: Rickey Medlocke salutes Ronnie Van Zant in concert in England, 2025. (*Chris Salisbury*)

Above: Remembering Gary Rossington, who passed away on 5 March 2023. (*Chris Salisbury*)

Below: The legacy of the fallen members of Lynyrd Skynyrd is not forgotten. (*Chris Salisbury*)

Left: A 1976 tour poster. (*Author's Collection*)

Right: Lynyrd Skynyrd supported Black Sabbath, who were touring *Sabotage*, at several venues in what was an unlikely pairing. (*Author's Collection*)

Endangered Species (1994)

Personnel:
Johnny Van Zant: vocals
Gary Rossington: guitar, acoustic guitar
Mike Estes: guitar, acoustic guitar
Leon Wilkeson: bass, background vocals
Billy Powell: piano
Owen Hale: percussion, drums
Ed King: guitar, mandolin, acoustic guitar
Additional musicians:
Dale Krantz-Rossington: background vocals, vocals
Debbie Davis: background vocals
Producer: Barry Beckett
Release date: 9 August 1994
Label: Capricorn
Chart places: US: 115, UK: did not chart
Running time: 43:10

Endangered Species is a studio album, but one recorded acoustically, featuring remakes of eight classic tracks along with four originals and one cover. Randall Hall was no longer a member of the band, and Mike Estes had joined. The songs were cut live in Masterfonics Studios, Nashville, Tennessee. When I asked Mike Estes, in August 2025, about the recording of the album and his involvement, he had the following recollections:

> I was hired by the band to record the pre-production for their upcoming *Endangered Species* album. Gary and Ed had been on an acoustic radio tour with Johnny, and MTV Unplugged was big at the time, so they decided to do an acoustic album. I had been writing with both Ed and Gary by this time, and I was a co-writer on three of the songs they were gonna record. They were without a third guitarist, and Gary and I crashed a rehearsal of a band that his wife knew or was related to somehow. They were so drunk they couldn't play, so Gary and I took over until we were almost too drunk to play. Gary asked me if I wanted to be in the band. I told him to sleep on it, and if he still felt the same the next day, then the answer was yes. The next morning, I was in the band. I went from band runner – airport pickups, luggage, picking up slack wherever on a tour – and writer, to writer engineer, to guitar player/writer in like four or five months. It was a trip.

When interviewed by Michael B. Smith in 1999, Mike recalled being out on the road between 1992 and 1993 and shared his recollections of Randall's exit:

> Randall Hall was still in the band then. Right after that, they fell out with Randall. I don't know what happened. He told me they fired him. They told

me he quit. Only they know the truth, I guess. They had actually asked Greg Martin of The Kentucky Headhunters to take Randall's place, but Greg was undecided or told him he couldn't do it.

Mike, born in Kentucky and raised in Ohio, has had a colourful career. In addition to playing with Skynyrd, he was part of Southern Rock meets NASCAR band Drivin Sideways; has played with The Artimus Pyle Band, The Southern Rock Allstars; recorded with Brave New South and currently records and tours with Skinny Molly. The first music Mike remembers hearing was his father's Hank Williams 45s before he came across Lynyrd Skynyrd and ZZ Top when he was 12. He had found his calling. While a high school student, Mike managed to make a connection to Lynyrd Skynyrd. He found a telephone directory listing for the Rossington-Collins Band and called it up:

So, I called it up, and this guy named Craig Reed answered the phone. I was living in Ohio at the time, and it turned out Craig was from Ohio, so we just got to talking. He was their production manager. I was a junior in high school at the time, so I'm sure I aggravated him to death. I told him I had a band and needed a name for my band. So, he got Allen Collins on a conference call, because Allen was coming up with all these cool names, but Craig couldn't remember 'em. Imagine this. My favourite guitar player. I'm a junior in high school, on the phone with Allen Collins. I said about two words. But he says you can have that name 'Helen Highwater', but you gotta swear to God you'll do something with it. So, I did. I played under that name, and opened for Allen, and he showed me all kinds of stuff. He'd come and sit in when we were playing clubs down in Jacksonville. This was just at the start of The Allen Collins Band. He showed me everything on the guitar and moved me up to the next level. I was lucky; I got to learn from him right there at his house. He had so much patience with me. To this day, I still don't know why he let me hang around, but he did. I was also writing a lot of songs, and he liked those. He just wanted me to get the guitar part together. But I'd stop by, and we'd play for hours. I took an eight-hour guitar lesson from him on Easter Sunday in 1983 that I'll never forget. That's when he showed me how to play 'Free Bird'. It was absolutely unbelievable. That probably had something to do with me getting the Skynyrd gig when I did because I could play all those songs.

Randall was able to clarify his perspective on his departure in his 2001 interview with Michael B. Smith:

Well, I can talk about it now. We had a lawsuit that ended a year ago. It took six and a half years to resolve. But it's public knowledge now. At the time, I couldn't say anything. They were contriving other reasons, saying it was something it wasn't, but in essence, they wanted to cut my money in half.

After being with them almost seven years at the time, they just wanted to take half of my percentage of the gross, and I said, 'No way.' None of them came to see me. They had their manager call my attorney about it. I said, 'Call me and talk to me about this!' My attorney said, 'No. I don't see any reason for you guys to do that. Randall is there. He does his job. I don't see any legitimate reason for you to do that. And it wasn't everybody in the band's decision either. Months later, Johnny called me and said, 'I want you to know I fought for you tooth and nail.' He said, 'If my name wasn't Van Zant, I'd probably be gone, too.' It was about them making more, and me making less. I was an equal shareholder at the time. They tried to say it was because I was late for rehearsal. Bull. I was the one who had to pick up Billy all the time because no driving for Billy. And Billy would want to stop on the way and pick up something. And we'd be late. And they tried to use that as an excuse. It was more than that. I think it was greed, man. It all happened conveniently after Allen was gone. Because if Allen had been around, he would have fought that tooth and nail. I think it was more Ed and Gary, I'm not sure.

This was also the first album to feature Owen Hale on drums and percussion. Born on 15 July 1948, in Louisville, Kentucky, Hale would also go on to perform on the live albums *Southern Knights*, *Lyve From Steel Town* and the studio album *Twenty*. Hale had previously played on the Rossington Band Album *Love Your Man*, where he was credited as an additional musician; his recollection is that Jimmy Johnson had him record the whole album, despite Mitch Rigel having the album credit. Seven years later, Owen got a call from Gary Rossington out of the blue, and he was hired for *Endangered Species*. Midway through the album recording, Owen was offered the Lynyrd Skynyrd drum stool. According to Hale, Gary said they wanted to fire their drummer, Custer, due to his cocaine usage ruining his playing. Hale was busy with studio work, but having thought it through, he decided he would regret not taking the gig. However, his fee took some negotiation before his demands were met. As he was used to studio work, he also realised he had to work on his stamina for live playing.

In 2016, *Ultimate Classic Rock* rated the album as number four in Skynyrd's catalogue, giving this summary:

The best album by the reunited Skynyrd features stripped-down arrangements of some of the band's earlier classics, like 'Saturday Night Special' and 'Sweet Home Alabama'. There are some new songs here, too, plus a down-home casualness lacking in many of the group's latter records. It's a temporary break from the noisy bluster.

'Down South Jukin'' (Gary Rossington, Ronnie Van Zant) 2:38
As Mike said, the MTV unplugged sessions had become a cultural phenomenon at this time, and Eric Clapton released the hugely popular *Unplugged* album in

1992. Some music translated well to the unplugged format, some didn't, although it was seldom exciting even when it worked. It should be no surprise that Lynyrd Skynyrd, given the cultural backdrop, released this album. However, listening back to *Endangered Species* without any weight of expectation, it is clear, and perhaps unsurprising, that the Lynyrd Skynyrd songs do work acoustically. After all, they are strong songs and essentially country-based. Here, a spirited solo from Billy adds a bit of variety to the mix.

'Heartbreak Hotel' (Mae Boren Axton, Tommy Durden, Elvis Presley) 4:01

This is an Elvis song performed as a slow, swinging blues. Gary and Ed prove themselves adept acoustic pickers and play some pleasant chord voicings with Billy adding a little more of his magic. However, it wasn't enough to please everyone. *The Georgia Straight*, on 13 October 1994, opined: 'My only real complaint about *Endangered Species* is its unnecessary inclusion of the mouldy Elvis chestnut 'Heartbreak Hotel'.

'Devil In The Bottle' (Mike Estes, Dale Krantz-Rossington, Rossington, Johnny Van Zant) 3:35

This is a song about battling alcoholism, and the first of the three originals penned in conjunction with Mike Estes. In the *FYFTY* box set notes, the story of Johnny falling down a spiral staircase in Knoxville, Tennessee, as a result of being drunk, is cited as a specific wakeup call that influenced the song. Van Zant says many people who have had problems have thanked him for writing the song, as the message resonated with them: 'There's a devil in the bottle, staring straight at me/Daring me to reach out, but I know he's testing me'. There is acknowledgement that the narrator can't blame the whiskey – 'I can only blame myself' – and that the drinking has had an impact on friends and family, hurting the ones he loves. However, the song is one of redemption: 'I got free on the day I fought the devil in the bottle'. Ed's 00-18 Martin acoustic guitar sounds good here, paired with the darker tones of Rossington's National on which he is playing slide guitar.

Mike discussed the writing of the song:

'Devil In The Bottle' didn't really have a chorus. I wrote the chorus for that one after a pre-production rehearsal. We got to Ed's house, he said to me, 'I wish 'Devil In The Bottle' had a chorus. Don't you think it needs one?' I said, 'I'll see what I can come up with.' I showed it to him the next morning, and he loved it. He called Gary and had me sing it to him over the phone. Gary said, 'That's it!' So, I sang it to Johnny that day at rehearsal, and he latched right on to it.

'Things Goin' On' (Rossington, R. Van Zant) 3:00

There are no real surprises here. Leon's acoustic bass fills the bottom end nicely, and Johnny pays a great homage to his brother Ronnie. The album credits have Leon playing an Ovation acoustic bass on the album, but Mike recalled otherwise: 'Leon's bass was actually an Applause brand, which was a budget line by Ovation. It sounded great and was one of the best bass tones he ever recorded. It was like 200 bucks. He could make any bass sound great, though. Goes to show, it's the picker more than the instrument!'

'Saturday Night Special' (Ed King, R. Van Zant) 3:53
This is possibly not an obvious choice of song for inclusion on an acoustic album, but they make it work. Owen Hale keeps things moving on a stripped-down kit, with Leon locked in.

'Sweet Home Alabama' (King, Rossington, R. Van Zant) 4:01
By way of contrast to the previous song, this is a more obvious inclusion, surely an inevitability, in fact. There are no fingerboard gymnastics attempted during the acoustic solos, but what is there works fine.

'I Ain't The One' (Rossington, R. Van Zant) 3:27
This is quite a laid-back arrangement, another good listen, but not a standout.

'Am I Losin'' (Rossington, R. Van Zant) 4:06
Mike's only performance on the album is here, playing his Gibson J-200. When I asked him about this in August 2025, he said:

Endangered was arranged for two guitars, so I only played on one song, the classic 'Am I Losin'', which was in a higher key than the original. We were all in a fairly small room together, except Johnny was in a booth, and Owen Hale was in his own booth. But Ed, Gary, Leon and I were in a ten-by-six booth. We got it first take; Gary and I each had one tiny fix to do, which we each got on the first go

Mike's presence on guitar allowed Ed to play Mandolin. It is not clear at what point Ed became proficient on the mandolin. Back in 1973, Al Kooper bought a mandolin and taught himself the required chords for 'Mississippi Kid', so clearly Ed hadn't fancied tackling it at that point. I asked Mike to clarify this:

Oh, he could play mando! We used it a lot on songwriting demos, actually. That's one of the reasons it made it onto *Endangered Species*. His chops were up on it, 'cause he and I had already been recording with it. He also played it on the song, 'The Last Rebel'. He had a beautiful Monteleone mando that sounded fantastic. Ed used to get the same suite in the same hotel every time we played in St. Louis, so he could play mando in the bathroom of that hotel room. It was a sound I'll never forget.

The arrangement is spot on, and the mandolin sounds superb.

'All I Have Is A Song' (Rossington, J. Van Zant) 3:21
This is the second of the four original songs on the album. It is an affirmation
of faith, but it is also a reflection on a life spent on the road and the price
that has been paid. There is an acknowledgement that a legacy has been left:
'All I have is a song/A piece of me to live on'. In the case of Lynyrd Skynyrd,
there were many who were lost early, including Johnny's brother, of course,
and in the years that followed this song, there would be many more
premature departures. The music is simple and stripped back with just a
strummed acoustic guitar and more great mandolin from Ed accompanying
Johnny's vocals. There is a solo that must be an overdub, but otherwise this
feels like a highly accomplished first take.

'Poison Whiskey' (King, R. Van Zant) 2:47
There is nothing unexpected here. Leon's bass is understated but pivotal in
filling out the sound. The drums are subdued, in keeping with the tone of the
album; the guitar arrangement is clearly well-honed, presumably from the
touring of the acoustic format, and when Billy steps up, it is always a delight.

'Good Luck, Bad Luck' (Estes, King) 3:23
The narrator is telling us about being on the wrong side of fortune and that
he isn't blessed or cursed, but it's just the way it is. You can work hard, but
luck can still be the determining factor: 'A lot depends on the luck a man has
and the cards that's been dealt to you'. Unfortunately, it seems he gets a little
bit more than his fair share of bad luck.
    The acoustic format and the arrangement of the song really play to the
strengths of Johnny's voice, which is consistently strong throughout the album.
    Mike Estes wrote the song with Ed King and recalled:

'Good Luck, Bad Luck' was a lot of fun to write. Ed and I had a blast cutting
the demo of that song. Johnny got a speeding ticket while he was driving
around St Augustine in his Chevy truck while learning the words from the
demo. Ed actually wrote some of the lyrics. He had crumpled up the paper
he was writing on before letting me see it and pitched it in the garbage. I got
it out of the garbage immediately, changed a couple of minor things and it
was finished.

'The Last Rebel' (Michael Lunn, Rossington, J. Van Zant, Robert White
Johnson) 5:42
Gary and Ed produced a great arrangement, and the exemplary mandolin
work is worthy of particular praise.

'Hillbilly Blues' (Estes, King, Rossington, J. Van Zant) 3:42
'Hillbilly Blues' closes the album. Mike remembered liking the original demo
version of the song more than the finished article, which was significantly

different from what he imagined. Mike recalled it was a completely different story: 'Originally, it was about a guy and his bar band, who were seen by a guy who was gonna make him and his band stars. Without naming names, somebody thought it sounded lyrically as if it was about Johnny Van Zant screwing over his band for his own stardom (it didn't), so I just went with it. I had just got in the band.' The version presented on the album is pure country. Ed is playing mandolin accompanied by Gary on the acoustic guitar. The story told is about the cultural and emotional displacement associated with leaving a familiar, warm community for a much colder, impersonal city. The move is regretted but forced by financial necessity.

Associated Songs
In February 1996, Columbia released the *NASCAR: Hotter Than Asphalt* album, which contained two tracks from Lynyrd Skynyrd. The band lineup was the same as for *Endangered Species*.

'White Knuckle Ride' (Rossington, Van Zant, Estes) 3:19
The track is exactly what you would expect, given the NASCAR theme, with Johnny singing about racing. Mike and Ed trade some sweet licks on the intro and in the bridges. Gary takes the slide and the slide solo while Billy augments the rhythm that is propelled by Owen and Leon. The song went on to be used in the 2006 *Cars* video game. I was able to ask Mike about the track in 2025:

This was a one-off we did for Sony. They were releasing an album to go along with the popularity of NASCAR at the time, songs related to racing with different artists. Skynyrd was a popular band among NASCAR fans, so it was a no-brainer for Sony. It was produced by Blake Chancey. Really good producer. I came up with the title, and Gary, Johnny and I finished it on the bus going down the road somewhere. It was a fun one to write with them and was finished really quickly. We cut it at Blake's studio, done fairly live, actually. That's Ed and me on the intro. Gary played slide. Johnny got the vocal quickly. Johnny, Leon, Billy and I did a bunch of appearances for Sony at Daytona Speedway and elsewhere to promote it. It was a hell of a lot of fun and led to me doing a NASCAR record for Eagle Records in Nashville with my band Drivin' Sideways.

'Save Up' (King, Killer Beaz, Ed King) 3:21
This is a collaboration with Skynyrd backing the comedian Killer Beaz, a long-time Skynyrd fan, who is spinning a racing fantasy tale. Essentially, it's more of a novelty song, but it has a fine country swing. Mike recalled the experience fondly:

'Save Up' was a collaboration with our good friend Killer Beaz. Hilarious comedian from Mississippi. Ed and I are on guitars; I think I played acoustic.

Ed was at the helm producing when I tracked. There was a whole bunch of us in the studio singing on the chorus, including some folks who worked at Sony in the office. It was a whole lot of fun! I later recorded some demos of Killer Beaz and a live record for him for Sony. He's a good friend to this day!

Twenty (1997)

Personnel:
Gary Rossington: lead, rhythm, slide and acoustic guitars
Johnny Van Zant: lead vocals, harmonica
Leon Wilkeson: bass
Ricky Medlocke: lead, rhythm, slide, acoustic and Dobro guitars, background vocals, harmonica
Hughie Thomasson: lead, rhythm, slide and acoustic guitars, background vocals
Billy Powell: piano and Hammond B-3 organ
Owen Hale: drums and percussion
Ronnie Van Zant: vocals on 'Travelin' Man'
Additional musicians:
Carol Chase, Dale Krantz Rossington, Kimberly Fleming*, Vicki Hampton: backing vocals
John Catchings: cello
John Hobbs: electric organ (Wurlitzer), electric organ (B3)
Stuart Duncan: fiddle
'Big Dance' Horns: Denis Solee, Doug Moffet, Vincent Ciesielski, William Fanning
Horns arranged by Chris Dunn
Randy Cutlip: keyboards
Tom Roady: percussion
Bill Cuomo: synthesiser
Josh Leo: acoustic guitar
Producer: Josh Leo
Photography by Mark Weiss
Release date: 29 April 1997
Label: CMC International
Chart places: US: 97, UK: did not chart
Running time: 55:39

Mike Estes and Ed King were now gone. As Mike explained to Michael B. Smith for *Swampland* in 1999:

When Ed got sick with that congestive heart failure, we were finishing a tour up. I had to learn all his parts in one night. I needed a year to learn all of Ed's parts. I got by, but it just wasn't the same without Ed. They hired Hughie Thomasson to come in and play for Ed as a temporary replacement, supposedly. I was a lot happier playing with Ed than with Hughie, and I made it known. Then I was told that Ed wasn't going to be in the band anymore. I went off the deep end. I didn't quit; they fired me. No doubt about it. But it may have been because I was fighting hard to keep Ed in the band. I thought that he was a big part of the sound and the history. Not that Hughie isn't a great guitar player. In his element with The Outlaws, he is wonderful. But it just wasn't the same. It didn't have the same feel. I was just dissatisfied with the whole deal, and maybe the feeling was mutual.

Ed had become seriously ill in 1995; the only treatment for his condition was a transplant, but he was in no hurry to have one. His last gig with the band was on 20 September 1995 in Asheville, North Carolina. Marley Brant, in her band biography, claims Ed asked the band for financial support but was denied. King had agreed to work on the anniversary album, but his management told him he was no longer needed, and Rossington stopped returning his calls. Eventually, King got an out-of-court settlement in 1999. King and Pyle both felt betrayed by their bandmates.

Hughie Thomasson had no hesitation when asked to join the band. Born Hugh Edward Thomasson Jr. in Virginia on 13 August 1952, he was no stranger to Lynyrd Skynyrd and their music, having often joined them onstage prior to 1977 and often playing together with his band, The Outlaws, who were successful in their own right. The Outlaws were the first act signed to Arista Records under Clive Davis. Davis was in the audience at a show in 1974 where the band was opening for Lynyrd Skynyrd in Columbus, Georgia. On the way to the stage for Lynyrd Skynyrd's set, lead vocalist Ronnie Van Zant said to Clive Davis, who was with Charlie Brusco, 'If you don't sign The Outlaws, you're the dumbest music person I've ever met, and I know you're not.' Nicknamed 'The Flame', Thomasson was a formidable guitar player. Perhaps his best-known song and guitar work is on the incendiary track 'Green Grass And High Tides', which, as well as being a Southern rock classic, became a notorious test of skill for players of the video game *Rock Band*.

When interviewed for *Guitar World*, by Andrew Daly, published in September 2024, Rickey Medlocke recalled how his third tenure with the band came about after receiving a call from Gary Rossington: 'When Gary called me in 1996 for the initial audition and wanted me to learn 'Saturday Night Special', 'That Smell' and 'Free Bird', he said, 'If you pass the audition, I'll put you back in the band and give you a buck 50 and a Snickers bar.' That was the exact call I got!'

Medlocke had recorded and toured with the band playing drums, writing and singing back in the early days at Muscle Shoals. He shared influences with Allen Collins and had seen him record early versions of songs like 'Free Bird'. Medlocke played drums on an early recording of 'Free Bird'. It was the Collins role that Rossington wanted Medlocke to fill: 'As far as rhythm and leads, yes. So, that was my role coming back into the band. I promised Gary that I would stick to the integrity of what Allen created. He said, 'Rickey, you've played guitar long enough; if you play those songs with that kind of feel, integrity and recreation … I want you to be happy.' He said, 'If you stray a little bit, that's up to you. You're a guitar player; you've got your own thing.' I said, 'Well, I might stray a little bit, but nothing where anybody can go, 'Wow, he's not even on it.' So that's what I've been doing for nearly 30 years.'

Medlocke, born on 17 February 1950 in Jacksonville, Florida, was raised by his talented multi-instrumentalist grandfather Shorty, himself part inspiration for 'Curtis Loew'. Shorty was on a local television show, *The Toby Dowdy Show*, where Medlocke joined him playing banjo at the age of three. The show ran for several years, with Rickey presumably something of a novelty, albeit one with a precocious talent. By five, he was teaching himself guitar, and was playing drums in Shorty's band by eight. He grew up with the original Skynyrd band members, often crossing paths as their bands played at various venues, Rickey even running lights for The One Percent at the Comic Book Club. Rickey went on to have some success and made several well-respected albums with his band Blackfoot, featuring the formidable talents of guitarist Charlie Hargrett, bassist Greg T. Walker and drummer Jakson Spires.

With Josh Leo producing, the album was recorded at Muscle Shoals Sound Studios, Muscle Shoals, Alabama, which was a return to the band's roots. However, with the new personnel in the band, it was very much a new chapter.

'We Ain't Much Different' (Mike Estes, Rickey Medlocke, Gary Rossington, Hughie Thomasson, Johnny Van Zant) 3:44
Although Mike Estes was no longer a member of the band, he is credited here as a co-writer, with Johnny Van Zant and Gary Rossington, and new recruits and southern rock royalty Rickey Medlocke and Hughie Thomasson. As Estes recalled to me:

> Johnny and I had 'Ain't Much Different' long before they recorded it. We'd become really good friends when I was in the band and were writing together all the time. I really enjoyed working on stuff one-on-one with him. But he and I had that going from the 'With these hands' part. I'm glad he included me in the credits. He is a stand-up guy!

The song encourages the listener to consider that, despite superficial differences, and regardless of backgrounds or lifestyles, we have strong underlying similarities that can unite us all. A mean, gnarly-toned guitar and hi-hat open the album. Bass drum, bass guitar and a second rhythm guitar join with some Hammond B3 organ in the background, and then Gary plays his first hand with a short but instantly recognisable lead line, giving Johnny his cue to state his intent: 'This is a story 'bout livin'/A tale of a long hard road'.

'We Ain't Much Different' is a muscular opener, propelled by the drumming of Owen Hale. A gently building middle eight, from 1:55, provides the springboard for Hughie to unleash some of his trademark lightning Stratocaster picking. Rickey follows with another nimble-fingered offering, reminiscent of his Blackfoot days, and Gary resolves the section with feedback and pinched harmonics. This opener makes it clear that there is a new three-guitar army in Lynyrd Skynyrd that can hold its own with any of the previous incarnations.

'Bring It On' (Medlocke, Rossington, Thomasson, J. Van Zant) 4:56
Lyrically, this is quite straightforward. The narrator's eye has been caught by a girl, but with echoes of cutting a rug with a girl named Linda Lou back in 1973, he runs into trouble. However, unlike in 'Gimme Three Steps', he stands and fights, perhaps because he isn't staring straight down a 44.

There are echoes of 'In The Night' by Blackfoot, where Rickey sang 'She can shake the sheets to a rock 'n' roll beat', when Johnny sings: 'I know you got it in you to shake my sheets/To your rock 'n' roll beat'. The song is a good-time barroom boogie, with guitar and piano sharing solos from 1:54. At 3:34, Gary solos, Hughie follows and then Rickey takes a turn, and this repeats as the three guitarists trade licks four times before a free-for-all during the fadeout. The three-guitar army just made another statement of intent.

'Voodoo Lake' (Bob Britt, Chris Eddy, J. Van Zant) 4:37
Johnny shares writing credits with two others here, Bob Britt – a Nashville-based studio and touring guitarist who appeared and recorded with John Fogerty, Bob Dylon and Leon Russell, among others – and Chris Eddy. Eddy, born in Phoenix, Arizona, is a session singer, guitarist, songwriter and son of Duane Eddy, for whom he played drums. The song is rich in atmosphere, conjuring dark images of the bayou and voodoo, telling the story of a city boy who 'Came looking for the legend of the girl so fine'. He thought the stories about her couldn't be true: 'She's the daughter of the devil, the sister of a snake/The keeper of souls down on Voodoo Lake'. Unfortunately, he realised his mistake too late and became one more soul down on Voodoo Lake. This type of imagery and narrative is unusual for Lynyrd Skynyrd, whose songs are usually rooted in reality. Johnny recalled the song was written about an old, mysterious lady in Louisiana: 'She had this different, kind of haunting thing about her. And the music really brought those melodies and vocal lines out. There was just this haunting feeling to the whole thing.'

Swamp noises are joined by acoustic guitars, and bluegrass musician Stuart Duncan plays the violin. The low keyboard drone is probably Bill Cuomo, and somewhere in the mix is producer Josh Leo, also playing acoustic guitar. Owen Hale does a great job powering the song with some heavy drumming despite the slow tempo. Carol Chase and Dale Krantz Rossington provide more atmosphere in the choruses. Gary plays eerie slide guitar throughout. There is no solo to speak of, but the instrumentation and arrangement are exemplary.

'Home Is Where The Heart Is' (Medlocke, Rossington, Thomasson, J. Van Zant) 5:26
The song returns to the theme of the travelling musician – 'I've always lived my life like a gypsy/I can't imagine myself settlin' down' – and it conveys the

difficulty of maintaining a relationship with a 'music man', a situation that is difficult for both the musician and his love. Billy begins the song with a beautiful piano piece, accompanied by an acoustic guitar and Gary playing some plaintive lines. The minor key verses are quite atmospheric, but the major key choruses have one foot firmly in the country music camp. At 1:13, Hughie fires off a short solo reminiscent of the late Steve Gaines. At 2:05, Hughie plays another solo, doubling his own lines, and then Billy takes over with a solo that's not as quickfire as usual. The final 1:30 is basically an extended chorus of 'Oh, my home is where my heart is' peppered with lead lines from Hughie. Josh Leo again has a credit for acoustic guitar.

'Travelin' Man' (Ronnie Van Zant, Leon Wilkeson) 4:05
Although once a concert staple, 'Travelin' Man' had never had a studio release. It's a song that is propelled by the bassline, and here we have a very rare thing: a songwriting credit for Leon. What makes this release particularly special is the studio trickery that made it possible for Ronnie and Johnny to sing together. The album's sleeve notes briefly recount the process. The music was recorded in Muscle Shoals, Alabama, on 28 January 1997. Ronnie's vocals were originally recorded on 7 and 9 July 1976 at the Fox Theatre in Atlanta, Georgia, and were immortalised on the live album *One More From The Road*. MCA gave the original master tapes to the band, and Joe Gastwirt at Oceanview Digital Recording 'baked' them, and Ronnie's vocals were taken and put into the newly recorded music by Ben Fowler. Baking is a dehydration process that temporarily cures the broken-down, water-absorbing polyurethane magnetic tape binder, allowing the tape to be played and transferred to digital formats without shedding its delicate oxide coating. The idea for the duet came from Rickey, although Johnny was initially reluctant. After some discussion with Josh Leo and Ben Fowler, and jamming the song at rehearsal, Johnny warmed to the idea.

Although, like the previous track 'Home Is Where The Heart Is', the narrator tells us they live their life on the road, this time driving a truck that was passed onto him by his father, they don't share the same sentimentality about maintaining a relationship: 'Travelin' man that's what I am, no woman puts a hold on me/You'll see me once or maybe twice that's all you'll see of me.' The rhythm guitars are handled by Hughie and Rickey, and the slide throughout the song and the solo are handled by Gary. Ronnie's songwriting is more consistent than that we heard on 'Home Is Where The Heart Is', primarily because the verses and choruses are better matched. The live version of the song from 1976 will always be the definitive version, but this song is certainly a special moment, nevertheless.

'Talked Myself Right Into It' (Pat Buchanan, Donnie Van Zant, J. Van Zant, Robert White Johnson) 3:25
Johnny tells a story of someone waking to an early alarm, having spent the night 'raisin' hell'. He is clearly making choices contrary to his better

judgment, although Johnny admitted it's a song about himself, inspired by a phone call from a friend asking him to come round to 'have a good time'.

The lyrics can be viewed as lightweight, telling the familiar Skynyrd trope of drinking, partying and womanising, but given the real addictions many of the band members had faced, perhaps there is an important message here about how hard it is to change: 'I got no one to blame except myself/Said I wasn't gonna do it/Next thing ya know/Here I go again'. Musically, it's another good time Skynyrd foot tapper, complete with horns from the 'Big Dance' horns. It is good to hear Rickey Medlocke take the slide solo, reminding us of songs like 'Rattlesnake Rock 'N' Roller' from his time with Blackfoot.

Pat Buchanan, a Florida native, guitarist, singer and songwriter, is credited as co-writer. His other credits include working with Daryl Hall and John Oates, Cyndi Lauper and Cameo, amongst many others.

'Never Too Late' (Medlocke, Rossington, Thomasson, J. Van Zant) 5:18
Beating bass drum, bass guitar and acoustic guitar open the song, which then builds with a second guitar and, mid-verse, crunch chords before dropping back after the chorus to the acoustic arpeggios. Medlocke's writing influence is evident in the chorus structure and riff. At 2:20, Billy takes the middle eight with strings in the background. At 3:04, there is a heavy solo from Gary, followed by a solo that sounds like Rickey's phrasing, if not his tone. The outro returns to the acoustics, with licks from Gary, before the drums double time at 4:35, and the song fades.

Lyrically, this is one of Skynyrd's wordier songs, basically about it never being too late to change things when we are stuck in a rut, even if we need a little help to do it. It's quite easy to overlook the song, placed as track seven, but it's quite a powerful piece if it's given a careful listen.

'O.R.R.' (Medlocke, Rossington, Thomasson, J. Van Zant) 4:16
'O.R.R.' tells the story of a wild west gunfighter, and for Hughie, there must have been a nod to the outlaw, Sundown, from his 1977 song 'Hurry Sundown'. Johnny tells us 'His only friend was the devil by his side but it caused him so much pain/If his guns could talk, oh, the stories they would tell', quite possibly the same devil that accompanied Sundown, of whom we were told, back in 1977, 'Silver devils in his holsters, stars strapped to his heels/There was fire in his eyes, they say that he was dressed to kill'.

A nice touch in the arrangement has a short instrumental blast of the chorus between the gentler first and second verse, with Gary's slide guitar playing the melody. The title 'O.R.R.' is made up of the first letters of the words 'outlaws, renegades, rebels' from the chorus line: 'They are outlaws, renegades, rebels on the run'. The middle eight reminds us that things haven't changed before Rickey's solo takes us to the final verse, questioning why people are still fighting: 'Brothers and sisters, what are we fightin' for/It's not for the fame or the glory anymore'. The song ends with a riff that is clearly from the Rickey Medlocke songbook.

'Blame It On A Sad Song' (Medlocke, Rossington, Thomasson, J. Van Zant) 5:35
Perhaps unsurprisingly, given the title, this is a lament for a departed lover. The tone is set by Billy's opening piano and a simple but effective solo from Gary. Although Skynyrd had never shied away from sentimentality and country leanings, this type of song left many fans critical of their Nashville inclinations in their post-crash career. As expected, it's well played; Hughie and Gary play nice solos, and the piano is perfectly executed.

'Berneice' (Medlocke, Rossington, Dennis E. Sumner, Thomasson, J. Van Zant) 4:01
Few things are straightforward with Lynyrd Skynyrd. What is clear is that the song is named after Gary's '59 Les Paul that he named in tribute to his deceased mother. What seems likely, based on a variety of accounts, is that Gary bought the guitar from a girl whose boyfriend had left her, leaving it behind. There are rumours that Charlie Daniels had heard about the guitar and was on his way, too. The spelling of the name is unusual but matches the spelling on her memorial in Riverside Memorial Park in Jacksonville, Florida. The guitar, described by Medlocke as 'The Holy Grail of Gibson guitars', was, as of 2023, reported to be in the Rock and Roll Hall of Fame and Museum in Cleveland. The song was written by Medlocke, Rossington, Dennis E. Sumner, Thomasson and Van Zant during writing sessions in Jackson Hole, Wyoming, where Gary lived with Dale.

The lyrics begin 'I can still remember I was eight years old/The first time that I picked her up little did I know', which is rich in poetic licence as he didn't start playing that young and his first guitar was a Sears Silvertone guitar. However, the song is a celebration of his guitar career as much as the instrument itself. The reference to a 'showdown' and 'three against one' is probably a nod to the days when the Three Guitar Army were joined onstage by the Outlaws and their 'Florida Guitar Army'.

Although fittingly driven by Gary playing slide on Berneice, the song is musically predictable and one-paced. There are several traded solos, and some irony perhaps in Hughie now being part of the Three Guitar Army, having defected from the Outlaws. The song did become part of the live set for a while, but there were stronger alternatives.

'None Of Us Are Free' (Barry Mann, Brenda Russell, Cynthia Weil) 5:23
'None Of Us Are Free' was a song written by Barry Mann, Cynthia Weil and Brenda Russell in 1993. Mann and Weil were a formidable songwriting partnership, having co-written many songs, including 'You've Lost That Lovin' Feelin'', co-written with Phil Spector, which was the most played song of the

20th century on American radio and television according to BMI in 1999. Russell enjoyed success as both a writer and performer in her own right.

'None Of Us Are Free' was first recorded by Ray Charles for his 1993 album *My World*, but despite it being a collaboration with Eric Clapton, it received relatively little attention at that time. A review in *Jet* magazine described the song as 'A piece that talks about the need for all people to get to know each other' and quotes Charles: 'Music is powerful. As people listen to it, they can be affected. They respond. But when I was doing this album, I wasn't trying to create an overall message. It just turned out that we got some songs that had something to say.'

It may seem an unusual choice of cover, or indeed superfluous to include a cover song at all, but the song's message of unity and bringing people together is something the band continued to do in concert. Skynyrd handle it well; it is a powerful cover, and Leon and Owen in particular seem to enjoy the groove.

'How Soon We Forget' (Buchanan, D. Van Zant, J. Van Zant, White Johnson) 4:50
This is a bold choice of song title to close an album, and it did give critics the opportunity to make a 'witty' play on words when reviewing the album. The song conveys the message that we should be grateful for what we have and that it is easy to forget that 'So many people have got it worse than me.'

The song has a hillbilly feel reminiscent of 'Made In The Shade', and the instrumentation remains acoustic until 1:30, where electric guitars join the rhythm track. The second verse is perhaps a moment of self-reflection for Johnny, despite singing about a 'friend'. He was no stranger to the challenges of alcohol: 'Got a friend of mine who says he's run all out of luck/But he'll be fine, 'cause he just ain't drunk enough'. At 4:16, there is a guitar lick straight from 'The Ballad Of Curtis Loew', and the song winds down with a single guitar and vocals, closing what is really a very enjoyable album.

Japanese Album Bonus Track
'Sign Of The Times' (Gary Rossington, Hughie Thomasson, Johnny Van Zant, Rickey Medlocke) 3:44
This is an acoustic song and sounds like it could be a demo version that never made full production. It is a little different in style from the rest of the album, with a western/folk feel, but it would have made a great addition to the album. Mandolin and mouth organ both feature in the song. There is a reference to hearing stories a thousand times, and it sounds like this could be from Lacy, if the lyrics are biographical. Additionally, we hear 'People don't care about one another/It's a sign of the times'. Probably then, the song is another reference to the erosion of values. The lyrics printed in the Japanese edition of the CD are not complete. Although not featured on the general album release, Hughie did play a section of this song in concert, during his solo spot.

Edge Of Forever (1999)

Personnel:
Gary Rossington: lead, rhythm, slide and acoustic guitars
Billy Powell: piano, keyboards
Leon Wilkeson: bass
Rickey Medlocke: lead, rhythm, slide and acoustic guitars, vocals, harmonica
Hughie Thomasson: lead, rhythm, slide and acoustic guitars, vocals
Kenny Aronoff: drums
Johnny Van Zant: lead vocals, harmonica
Additional musicians:
Dale Krantz-Rossington: backing vocals
Carol Chase: backing vocals
Michael Cartellone: percussion
Backing vocals: Chris Eddy
Keyboards: Bill Cuomo
Producer, engineer, mixer: Ron Nevison
Release date: 10 August 1999
Label: CMC International
Photography: Chuck Jones, Dan Johnson
Chart places: US: 96, UK: did not chart
Running time: 59:29

Owen Hale was replaced by Bill McCallister in May 1998. McCallister played in Hank Williams Jr.'s band before and after his stint in Lynyrd Skynyrd. Although he toured as a member of the band, he didn't appear on any recordings, and the drums were played on the album by the New York-born Kenny Aronoff, who had played drums with John Mellencamp for 17 years before becoming a go-to session musician. Percussion is credited to Michael Cartellone, who would subsequently join the band. In 2016, *Rolling Stone* ranked Kenny Aronoff number 66 of the 100 greatest drummers of all time. The magazine wrote, 'With a sixth sense for what makes music pop and the patience to take direction, he's ended up as a go-to studio beat smith for The Rolling Stones, Bob Dylan, Bruce Springsteen, Neil Diamond, Eric Clapton, John Fogerty, Sting, The Smashing Pumpkins, Lady Gaga and tons more.' *Modern Drummer* ranked him 'Number one Pop/Rock Drummer and number one Studio Drummer' for five consecutive years.

The album was recorded at Ocean Way Recording Studios, Nashville and The Castle Recording Studios, and was mixed at the Record Plant, Los Angeles. It was produced, engineered and mixed by the very capable Ron Nevison, who had a distinguished career at this point, having engineered Bad Company's *Bad Co*, The Who's *Quadrophenia* and Led Zeppelin's *Physical Graffiti*. His production credits are many and varied and include such diverse acts as Kiss, Ozzy Osbourne, Chicago, Heart, Meat Loaf, Survivor, Jefferson Starship and UFO. Nevison had previously also worked with Hughie

Thomasson on the *Ghost Riders In The Sky* album by the Outlaws. It was Hughie's idea to bring in Nevison, and it was Nevison who brought in Kenny Aronoff. Nevison recorded the drum tracks with Aronoff at Ocean Way Studios before moving to the private Castle Studios for the overdubs.

There are those who feel that Johnny will forever be in his brother's shadow, but after 12 years fronting the band, he was certainly comfortable by this point. On *Edge Of Forever*, the influence of the new blood is clear, particularly that of Rickey Medlocke, whose writing and riffing on the album are very reminiscent of Blackfoot, and he pushed the band into new territory. So, it isn't more of the same, and it is not an attempt to ape the past. Aronoff proves to be a powerhouse, Thomasson and Medlocke work well together, and Johnny is sounding strong and confident. The influence of the remaining originals, other than Medlocke, appears diminished despite a fairly even split of writing credits for Rossington. The album itself has a fairly thick and relatively heavy sound. This must have been Nevison's intention, but whether it was his idea or his brief is less clear.

Ultimate Classic Rock's 2016 overview of the Skynyrd catalogue gave a less than glowing overview: 'Probably the most forgettable Lynyrd Skynyrd album, *Edge Of Forever* seems to have little purpose and less connection to the band's legacy. The dozen songs here are played well enough (even on their worst nights, Skynyrd are one of rock's tightest bands, especially when they steer into blues and country territory as they do here). Just don't ask us to remember any of them.' On the other hand, Christopher Thelen, reviewing the album in 1999, had a different perspective: '*Edge Of Forever* is proof that Lynyrd Skynyrd not only still have some fight in them, but that they carry enough of a punch to create killer music even after over 25 years together. This album rightfully belongs next to the classic work of Lynyrd Skynyrd and could well be the best album of the Johnny Van Zant era.'

As with all the post-crash albums, if they are approached with an open mind and listened to in their own right, there is a lot to like here.

'Workin'' (Medlocke, Rossington, Thomasson, J Van Zant) 4:53
The album opens with a familiar theme: that of the downtrodden working man from a poor background, who works all day and enjoys the free time he has to the fullest: 'I wanna punch the time clock and have some fun'. Perhaps there is an analogy being made about how a hard-working musician is the same as the blue-collar working man: 'I make my livin' by the sweat of my brow/Oh workin' just like you'. There is a lyrical nod to 'Mississippi Kid' – 'I never let no one dog me down' – implying a shared attitude with his elder brother.

After a rattlesnake 'rattle', session drummer Kenny Aranoff makes his presence felt, launching us into a punchy riff and wah wah solo from Rickey. It's a heavy opening with both feet firmly planted in Blackfoot territory. The familiar voices of Carol Chase and Dale Krantz Rossington add body to the

110

chorus, which works well. At 1:44, Gary plays a solo in the middle eight before doubled guitar lines, reminiscent of the pre 1977 era. There is a short solo, and more doubled guitar leads into a chorus at 2:40. The section from 3:18 is reminiscent of Hendrix's version of *All Along The Watchtower* with 'keep on workin'' vocals. Gary solo's again, and it's doubled at the end with a second guitar before all three guitars play simultaneously, building to a crescendo and ending at 4:54. This is a strong opener that sets a heavy tone for the album and is another statement from the new Three Guitar Army.

'Full Moon Night' (Medlocke, Rossington, Thomasson, J Van Zant) 3:44
The song conjures a little mysticism with reference to things appearing from the shadows of the full moon night. The message is cautionary, describing a man who shot his wife and took his own life; the unexpected can happen. To a degree, there is ambiguity about what might happen, but we are reminded to remember our faith: 'Don't forget what the good book says'.

The opening riff and feel are old-school Skynyrd, but with a heavier delivery. The delay used on the intro solo adds a little ambience to match the theme of the song, a theme re-iterated between the chorus and verse. Johnny imitates his brother's vocal inflection at 1:35. At 2:02, Aranoff accents dual-picked guitars that bring us to another guitar statement. There are doubled lines and trade-offs between Rickey and Hughie, finishing with a run alternated between left and right speakers, and some stereo panning in the mix. A final chorus drops to a slow version of the introductory riff, backed with an organ, which could be either Billy or Bill Cuomo, who has album credits for additional keyboards, and some fills from Aranoff that would have sat well in the 'Last Rebel'.

'Preacher Man' (Medlocke, Rossington, Thomasson, J Van Zant) 4:33
A heavy riff joined by the band and a little slide guitar isn't the most original opening to a Skynyrd song, but it is nevertheless a powerful rocker. At face value, the song seems to be about accepting someone for who he is; although he isn't perfect, he is true to himself.

Rickey and Hughie handle the rhythm guitar while Gary adds texture with his slide. The middle eight at 2:29 echoes Blackfoot's 'Fire Of The Dragon', then launches into a wah solo from Rickey with a fiery riposte from Hughie. A brief reprise of the middle eight leads into the fadeout with comping organ.

'Mean Streets' (Medlocke, Rossington, Thomasson, J Van Zant) 4:49
The lyrics are the reflections of someone brought up in a tough neighbourhood. They will always have a mean streak, and they needed it to survive, but their perspective has changed with maturity. They are less willing to fight and recognise that carrying a gun doesn't make you a man. Verse three continues the reflective theme, asking if you ever think about where you are going and where you have been, and if we will ever pass this way again.

This time, a guitar arpeggio and bass start the song, then in come the band and a short lead break precedes the vocals. It is well played, well written and effective, but it is a repeated formula. Like the previous song, Medlocke and Thomasson's guitars complement each other tonally, Hughie's Strat is thinner and compressed by the tube amp he is using, Rickey's a little fatter, and Gary adds feel with occasional lines, slides and feedback. Billy's piano accompaniment works well, playing staccato in the chorus and then adding arpeggiated embellishments. At 2:25, Medlocke plays a nice lead with some melodic note choices as the song drops. At 2:58, Billy offers some incongruous piano, bringing to mind Ed King's comment that Billy didn't always listen to the lyrics when he was reflecting on his contribution to 'Things Goin' On'. Gary precedes Hughie with lead guitar before the three guitars end the song in unison.

'Tomorrow's Goodbye' (Gary Burr, Medlocke, Rossington, Thomasson, J. Van Zant) 5:05

Gary Scott Burr has a writing credit, in addition to Rossington, Medlocke, Thomasson and Van Zant, who wrote most of the album. Rickey came up with the title, and it inspired the writing of the song. Another notable credit is for The Nashville String Machine, a musical collective of session musicians, with the strings arranged and conducted by Dave Campbell, whose credits include Adele, Beyoncé, Johnny Cash, Michael Jackson, Taylor Swift and U2. The notes in the *FYFTY* box set have Medlocke claim that 'Ron Nevison created string arrangements for a 40-piece orchestra in Nashville', but most likely he had the idea for the strings, which were realised by The Nashville String Machine.

Johnny is singing about environmental damage and climate change here, making a clarion call that we need to change, but accepting that there is little he can do, as Ronnie said in 'All I Can Do Is Write About It'. Johnny acknowledged this, singing, 'Like my brother before me/All I can do is write this song'.

An acoustic guitar and strings accompany the vocals before a second acoustic, and then the drums and bass join. It is a very sentimental song and very 'Nashville' in its presentation when all the instruments are in. To some listeners, this may diminish the impact, with the emotion perhaps feeling a little bit contrived. Maybe it is deliberate. 'All I Can Do Is Write About It' was from the perspective of a country boy and was stripped back, whereas the lyrics here begin 'I'm just a city boy/But there's a small-town side to me', so maybe this is the same message from a different perspective, hence the approach taken with the production. Van Zant recalled that it was the longest it ever took him to sing on any song on a record.

'Edge Of Forever' (Medlocke, Jim Peterik, J. Van Zant) 4:23

Heavy riffing starts the song, backing up the feeling that this album is Skynyrd's heaviest offering to date, and it firmly evidences the transition of the band from the legacy sound. Maybe the title recognises this point of transition, reflecting on the new era with the inclusion of new members and a fresh sound, but still drawing on their established legacy. Crucially, though, with a release date in 1999, there is a literal reference to the turning of the millennium: 'At the stroke of midnight/When centuries clash/Some gonna party/Some gonna kneel and pray'. The lyrics recognise that it is a dangerous time, with 'power in the wrong hands/A madman in a foreign land', a thought that resonates today, and that we need to change. For the narrator at least, though, whatever may happen, there is comfort in faith. At 2:32, Rickey, Hughie and Gary have a solo each, with the pace not letting up, and the song ending with each player alternating the final riff.

Notably, James Peterik, who co-wrote several songs with 38 Special, Van Zant and a host of others, is part of the writing team. He is perhaps best known as the founder of the band Survivor and co-writer of 'Eye Of The Tiger', the theme from *Rocky III*. Peterik, in fact, probably saved or made .38 Specials' career. Former A&M Records executive Mark Spector had quit his job to start his own management operation, and .38 Special was his first client. Legendary A&R man John Kalodner, who was working for Atlantic at the time, gave Spector a Peterik song that had been co-written for Survivor. Survivor had intended this song to be on their debut album, but it was axed by producer Ron Nevison. 'Rockin' Into The Night' became a late addition to .38 Special's third album. They were in desperate need of a radio-friendly hit at that point. Donnie didn't like the song, and either would not or could not sing it, so Don Barnes handled the lead vocals. Interestingly, the band recorded the album in Doraville, Georgia, with Rodney Mills as producer. Rodney went on to work with the band for eight albums.

'Gone Fishin'' (Medlocke, Rossington, Thomasson, J Van Zant) 4:22
This song puts us back on familiar ground musically and lyrically. The first half of the song is literally about fishing. There are references to meeting 'my mules', a term Ronnie used for the guitarists in the band as they did the heavy work, and fishing poles and fishing holes. Another reference is to the St. Johns River, the longest river in Florida, which runs through Jacksonville. Halfway through, though, fishing becomes a metaphor for meeting a woman and falling in love: 'Only thing better than settin' a hook/Is settin' my hook in you'. The music has a similar feel to old time Skynyrd and songs like 'Same Old Blues', albeit a little heavier handed in terms of delivery. Gary's slide is evident throughout the song and fits well with the feel and groove.

'Through It All' (Peterik, J. Van Zant, Robert White Johnson) 5.28
With the help of Peterik and Johnson, Johnny tells the story of the band continuing, despite the adversity that they have faced, building it up 'from dust and ashes/To cheat the odds again'. It's a powerful delivery from Johnny, as you'd expect, given the theme of the song. Whatever criticism Johnny faced

for trying to fill his brother's shoes, he has always maintained that the purpose of carrying on is to honour those who went before him and keep the music alive. Hughie follows Gary with a notable solo at 2:51 that resolves beautifully into a short bridge.

'Money Back Guarantee' (Medlocke, Rossington, Thomasson, J Van Zant) 4:01
Johnny's lyrics seem to be about an infatuation with someone who is hard to get. He tells us that he needs her so much but asks her to call his bluff, presumably to show his commitment, promising to buy a house, the use of his car and showering her with diamonds and rings. The hook is that he comes with a 'money back guarantee' and the caveat 'Oh you ain't gonna get my money'.

Billy sets the ball rolling with a great honky tonk piano intro into typical slow, fat Rossington bends on his guitar, Berneice. The song is a good time romp, in contrast to the heavier theme of the previous song. Billy is on top form at 2:00, handing over to Rickey on slide, then Gary and a fiery blast from Fender Hall Of Fame member Hughie.

'G.W.T.G.G' (Medlocke, Rossington, Thomasson, J Van Zant) 4:03
The title comes from the chorus – 'Get it while the gettin's good' – and this makes it clear what the song is about. The lyrics were never going to win an Academy Award, but it's easy to read a set of lyrics and be dismissive. It's another light-hearted Skynyrd tale and, set in the context of the music, the lyrics are fit for purpose if not a little familiar.

Aranoff's drumming in the intro is reminiscent of Blackfoot's Jackson Spires, and the riff at 0:15 sounds a lot like that band's song 'On The Run' from the *Tomcattin'* album. However, the similarity soon ends. Hughie lives up to his nickname of 'The Flame' with his solo, and he lights Rickey's blue touch paper as his reply is equally adept, followed by Billy, whose keys are always up to the mark.

'Rough Around The Edges' (Medlocke, Rossington, Thomasson, J Van Zant) 5:05
Although there is some ambiguity in the lyrics, this emotional ballad is another tribute to Ronnie, viewed from the perspective of his younger brother Johnny. He is acknowledging that Ronnie had his faults, but was a good man at his core. Gary and Hughie both play emotional solos that are very different in approach. Gary's are slow and lyrical, but Hughie lets rip. Ed King and Steve Gaines always get a lot of praise for their contributions to the band, but Hughie's contribution is seldom recognised, and he was also the one, at this point, challenged to cover their parts live. So, it is a powerful and emotional ballad, but probably not strong enough to be on many Skynyrd playlists.

'FLA' (Medlocke, Rossington, Thomasson, J Van Zant) 3:53
This is a light-hearted, good-time rocker that closes the album. Johnny is acknowledging that he is never home; rather, he is out on the road with the band, making a living and earning the money for a mortgage on a house he doesn't spend any time in: 'Wish I could pay for it while I'm in it/Seems like I'm there only for a minute'. 'FLA' is an abbreviation for the state of Florida. While the official postal abbreviation for Florida is 'FL', 'FLA' was historically used as an abbreviation before the standard two-letter abbreviations were adopted, and it is still sometimes used informally, as it is here. Rickey's slide has echoes of 'Rattle Snake Rock 'N' Roller', but they all sound like they are enjoying ripping it up. This type of song would be great fun to play live, and even in the studio, they capture this, but such is the depth of the Skynyrd canon that it wasn't destined to be a concert favourite.

Christmas Time Again (2000)

Personnel:
Johnny Van Zant: lead vocals
Gary Rossington: guitar
Billy Powell: keyboards, piano
Leon Wilkeson: bass, background vocals (credited, but does not appear on the album)
Rickey Medlocke: guitars, background vocals
Hughie Thomasson: guitars, background vocals
Michael Cartellone: drums, percussion
Additional musicians:
Dale Krantz-Rossington: background vocals
Carol Chase: background vocals
Mike Brignardello: bass
Mark Pfaff: harp (track 1)
Bill Cuomo: keyboards (tracks 3, 4 and 9)
Charlie Daniels: guitar, vocals (track 5)
Taz DiGregorio: keyboards (track 5)
Charlie Hayward: bass (track 5)
Pat McDonald: drums, percussion (track 5)
Mark Matejka: guitar, vocals (track 5)
Chris Wormer: guitar, vocals (track 5)
Danny Chauncey (credited as being part of .38 Special, instrument(s) played not noted)
Don Barnes (credited as being part of .38 Special, instrument(s) played not noted)
Donnie Van Zant (credited as being part of .38 Special, instrument(s) played not noted)
Producer: Gary Rossington, Hughie Thomasson, Johnny Van Zant, Rickey Medlocke
Executive producer: Tim Lipsky
Release date: 12 September 2000
Label: CMC International, SPV
Chart places: US: did not chart, UK: did not chart
Running time: 36:54

Perhaps the opening sentence of the *Austin Chronicle* review echoed most people's first thoughts when they saw this album release. 'No, this isn't a joke.' The review itself was very negative and concluded, 'About the only redeeming thing here is some nifty picking by Hughie Thomasson on 'Skynyrd Family'. Otherwise, this thing should be pronounced D.O.A. If I'm Ronnie Van Zandt(sic), I'm kicking these people's asses after they kick the bucket.' One would presume the author will get his ass kicked by Ronnie in the afterlife for not taking the care to spell his name correctly. Even amongst the fans that accepted the post 1977 band, the majority held no truck with this album. Regardless of this, it exists and will be given due diligence.

One notable absence on the recording is that of Leon Wilkeson. Strangely, he is credited as the bass player but does not appear on the album. The bass is played by session player James Michael Brignardello. Michael Cartelone, born in Cleveland, Ohio, is on drums, marking the beginning of his full-time place in the band. Michael knew the band socially from touring with Tommy Shaw in late 1988 and opening for Skynyrd. He had also toured with the band when he played with Ted Nugent in 1994. He had first recorded with Lynyrd Skynyrd on the previous *Edge Of Forever* album. Ron Nevison, also producer for Damn Yankees, was producing that album, and he invited Cartellone down, as he knew Michael knew the band, and hired him to do percussion. During these sessions, he was asked if he would take the role of drummer moving forward, and in November 1998, he agreed. As Cartellone put it, he wasn't the first Yankee in the band, but he was the first 'Damn Yankee'. It is worth noting that although Al Kooper never really rated Bob Burns, Cartellone praises Burns and has spoken of the difficulty of learning some of his parts to play live, particularly 'Swamp Music'.

'Santa's Messin' With The Kid' (Eddie C. Campbell) 3:15
The song is a standard 12-bar blues, opened here by guest Mike Pfaff ably blowing harp. It was written by Eddie C. Campbell (1939-2018), who was born in Duncan, Mississippi. At age ten, he and his family moved to Chicago, where he became part of the local blues scene. Some of the legends who mentored him were Muddy Waters, Otis Rush and Magic Sam. Campbell made his first full album in 1977, *King Of The Jungle*, for the Mr. Blues label. The first song on side one is the Campbell composition 'Santa's Messin' With The Kid' (the title on the back cover; the label calls it 'Santa's Been Messin' With The Kid') According to the liner notes of the album, the song was inspired by Junior Wells' 1960 single 'Messing With The Kid' and written not long after that song was released.

'Rudolph The Red-Nosed Reindeer' (Johnny Marks) 2:31
This familiar Christmas song was written by American songwriter Johnny Marks, who specialised in Christmas songs and wrote many others, including 'Rockin' Around The Christmas Tree' and 'A Holly Jolly Christmas'. Billy Powell and Hughie Thomasson attack the song with gusto, clearly having fun and playing very well.

'Christmas Time Again' (Rickey Medlocke, Dale Krantz Rossington, Gary Rossington, Hughie Thomasson, Johnny Van Zant) 4:34
Two covers into the album, and we have the first of a handful of Skynyrd originals. Long-time collaborator Bill Cuomo handles the keyboards. Johnny and Dale share lead vocals, and their vocals sound good together. It's a

sentimental Christmas song and must be judged as such. It will never be a standard, but worth throwing in the mix if anyone has a Christmas playlist.

'Greensleeves' (Traditional) 2:18
This is credited to Cuomo and Powell, the latter playing the piano presumably and augmented by Cuomo's keyboards. This is a pleasant enough version of the tune.

'Santa Claus Is Coming To Town' (credited on the album as being performed by Charlie Daniels) (Haven Gillespie) 3:08
This is a countryfied version of the Christmas standard, notable here for not including any of the then-current members of Lynyrd Skynyrd but including future member Mark 'Sparky' Matejka on guitar.

'Run Run Rudolph' (Marvin Brodie, Marks) 3:32
Another cover of a song written by Johnny Marks, this time with Marvin Brodie. Vocal credits here are for Johnny, Rickey and Hughie, who each take a verse, and for a children's choir that handle the intro. Billy shows his Christmas spirit again with an enthusiastic solo, Rickey plays slide and Hughie plays some Chuck Berry-inspired licks before rattling off some quick-fire licks of his own. Ed King once said he thought that Rickey's and Hughie's vocals were underutilised in Lynyrd Skynyrd, but I'm not sure this is what he had in mind.

'Mama's Song' (Medlocke, G. Rossington, Thomasson, J. Van Zant) 3:52
This is another original. It is very sentimental and without doubt a song for Marion Zan Zant, mother of Ronnie, Johnny and Donnie, who passed away in April 2000, the year that the album was recorded and released. 'Joy to the world' backing vocals by Carol Chase and Dale Krantz Rossington ring out the last ounce of emotion to close the song.

'Santa Claus Wants Some Lovin' (Mack Rice) 3:39
This is another cover, this time written by the prolific songwriter Mack Rice, whose most famous song is 'Mustang Sally', which he wrote and released a year before it was covered by Wilson Pickett. Skynyrd's interpretation of 'Santa Claus Wants Some Lovin'' is quite different from the funky feel of the Albert King version, but they pay homage with the tasty blues licks that punctuate the song. Medlocke had shown his blues prowess before, having tackled Albert's 'Wrapped Up In Love, Again' on the album *Fit For A King (L.A. Blues Authority Volume IV)* in 1993. Gary played on a couple of blues-based Skynyrd demos, which were eventually released on *Collectybles* and *Thyrty*. Hughie just does what he does best and takes a less pure approach to his phrasing as the three take it in turns to end the song. Had Leon been present, he would have had fun with the bassline.

'Classical Christmas' (Medlocke, J. Van Zant) 2:09
Rickey's acoustic guitar is the focus and shows another facet of his playing. It showcases clean fingerpicking and crystal-clear articulation of the notes. The fretless bass from Mike Brignardello fits well, and Bill Cuomo's synth lines are unobtrusive and atmospheric. Presumably, Johnny's contribution to the writing was the vocals sung by the children's choir.

'Hallelujah, It's Christmas' (credited on the album as being performed by .38 Special) (Don Barnes, Danny Chauncey, Donnie Van Zant) 4:01
This is credited to .38 Special and was written by Donnie Van Zant, in collaboration with .38 Special alumni Don Barnes and Danny Chauncy. Of particular interest to Skynyrd fans is the mixing and mastering by former collaborator Rodney Mills. It is a harmless country romp with a nod to 'the wild-eyed boys'. *Wild Eyed Southern Boys* was the title of their 1981 studio album, which featured a track of the same name.

'Skynyrd Family' (Medlocke, G. Rossington, Thomasson, J. Van Zant) 3:00
The song references .38 Special and the CDB (Charlie Daniels Band) in the lyrics – the Skynyrd family. It is a short blast of foot-tapping country music with solos from Charlie, Billy and, most impressively, Hughie. There are also references to 'big wheels keep on turning', from 'Sweet Home Alabama', 11 months on the road and going home for Christmas. Despite the scepticism of some fans and listeners, they sound like they are having fun, and their kids probably loved the album.

Vicious Cycle (2003)

Personnel:
Gary Rossington: guitars
Billy Powell: keyboards
Ean Evans: bass guitar
Michael Cartellone: drums
Rickey Medlocke: guitars and vocals, co-lead vocals on 'Pick 'Em Up'
Hughie Thomasson: guitars and background vocals
Leon Wilkeson: bass guitar on 'The Way' and 'Lucky Man'
Johnny Van Zant: lead vocals
Additional musicians:
Carol Chase: background vocals
Perry Coleman: backing vocals
Melody Crittendon: backing vocals
Eric Darken: percussion
Chris Dunn: trombone
Tom Hambridge: backing vocals
John Hobbs: organ, piano
Jim Horn: baritone saxophone
Dale Krantz-Rossington: background vocals
Sam Levine: tenor saxophone
Greg Morrow: drums
Gordon Mote: organ
Nashville String Machine: strings
Steve Patrick: trumpet
Kid Rock: co-lead vocals on 'Gimme Back My Bullets'
Brent Rowan: tiple
Brad Warren: backing vocals
Brett Warren: backing vocals
Biff Watson: bouzouki, acoustic guitar
Producer: Ben Fowler and Lynyrd Skynyrd, except track 15 produced by Rickey
Medlocke, Rob Robinson
Release date: 20 May 2003
Label: Sanctuary
Chart places: US: 30, UK: did not chart
Running time: 70:40

With the exception of track 15, the album was recorded between November
2002 and January 2003 at Cartee Day Studios in Nashville and produced by
Ben Fowler and the band. The facility is now closed but saw recordings by
artists as diverse as Kenny Rogers, Willie Nelson and Zakk Wylde's Black
Label Society.

Gary shared his thoughts about the album and the presence of Leon
Wilkeson, who died during its creation, with Michael B. Smith in 2003:

I think on this particular album, we just tried real hard. We took three years to do it. Not intentionally, but we were touring and doing projects. We were always writing and working on it. As a matter of fact, Leon is on it. He had started the record with us, and after he passed away, we decided we needed to use at least a couple of songs with Leon on 'em. Because it was him, and there are a million reasons. We just redid 'The Way' and 'Lucky Man' and kept his bass parts and played to them. The writing was different. We wrote with a few different people to get a fresh feeling and have a little bit of newness. We tried to make the songs more – I can't say 'like Skynyrd' because we are Skynyrd – but just more our style. We tried real hard, and I think it shows.

The passing of Leon was yet another blow for the band. Wilkeson was born on 2 April 1952 in Newport, Rhode Island, but he was raised in Jacksonville, Florida. Leon had a brief association with Ronnie, as bass player for his band, the Collegiates, but had to leave due to plummeting grades. His initial on-off relationship with the band was long a thing of the past; Leon left a significant legacy with his contributions to the recordings and live shows. Leon's health issues, including liver function problems and emphysema, meant that there were occasions when the band had to use a stand-in. Leon married several times, and he was always on the move, but he was a very sociable person. Apparently, his days of truly excessive drinking were behind him, but he was taking a variety of prescription drugs. It was the conclusion of the coroner that Leon died from complications of emphysema, with drug intoxication and cirrhosis as contributing factors. It was the belief of the medical examiner that too much oxycodone combined with diazepam caused him to fall asleep face down on his pillow. With his breathing problems, this proved to be fatal. He was found dead on 27 July 2001, in a Ponte Vedra Beach, FL hotel room, aged just 49. His life was relatively short but colourful. He had survived the plane crash in 1977 and having his throat cut on the tour bus in 1995, but years of excess took their toll. Always a religious man and very knowledgeable of the bible, it is perhaps fitting that his favourite psalm, 33, has a line in The King James Version, which was the name of his band back in the days with Dru Lombar, which says 'Sing unto him a new song; play skilfully with a loud noise'.

Bassist Ean Evans, who was born on 16 September 1960 in Atlanta, had understudied Leon when he was incapacitated. Following Leon's death, he became the full-time bass player and played most of the basslines on the album.

'That's How I Like It' (Blair Daly, Rickey Medlocke, Gary Rossington, Hughie Thomasson, Johnny Van Zant) 4:33
Lyrically, we are back on familiar ground, with Johnny affirming his faith and admitting his faults: 'I am no saint sometimes a sinner and I can't tell you why/

But I get up every morning and thank the man above'. The song is a celebration of being a simple Southern man, living a no-frills life and 'Working with my hands for hours'. It echoes the themes of 'We Ain't Much Different' and 'Workin', which opened the *Twenty* and *Edge Of Forever* records, respectively. There are references to cold beers, hot women, dirt roads, American flags and the 'sound of a crowd', which acknowledges his trade.

A scratchy guitar, sounding like a dobro, begins the song, complete with a tapping foot and the added crackle simulating a worn vinyl record. An ominous organ swell leads to thumping guitar chords, with heavy drums and Ean Evans's bass making their presence felt. The thumping chords are augmented by a lightly picked, ringing Strat, the type of move that Ed King would have added, but here it's Hughie. Gary adds occasional slide, and Rickey adds colour with the wah pedal, notably mimicking the 'that's how I like it' melody. There is some nice heavy riffing in the bridge at 2:36. Rickey takes the first lead break, resolving with licks typical of his style. Next up is Hughie, also with a touch of wah, and as Rickey adds a wah fill, we have a rare moment: two guitars with wah at the same time. The bridge riffing returns to lead the song to a fade out with atmospheric noises and organ, and a rather abrupt fadeout. Brothers Brad and Brett Warren are credited for harmony vocals, but their contribution is not prominent. Eric Daily, American songwriter and producer, has a writing credit.

'Pick 'Em Up' (Tom Hambridge, Medlocke, J. Van Zant) 4:20
The first surprise here is that the first line is sung by Rickey Medlocke, a fine singer in his own right, as his early contributions to Skynyrd like 'White Dove', 'The Seasons' and his work fronting Blackfoot attest. 'Pick 'Em Up' is a duet; Rickey and Johnny trade lines in a style reminiscent of his elder brother and Steve Gaines on 'You Got That Right', from *Street Survivors*. Although Medlocke explained that the song is about when the band come on stage, they 'Pick 'em up and lay the song down', the lyrical theme sounds more like one of a man who likes his freedom, women and whiskey, who is sexually promiscuous and proud of his sexual prowess. We are told: 'Jim Beam (And women), they treat me right/I make my own rules, like it or not' and that 'I pick 'em up/And lay 'em all down'. The song is being sung to a partner, of sorts, who is given the following reassurance, 'Yeah, well, it's tough love honey/I'll leave you with a smile', and attempts some justification with 'I wouldn't tell you no lies/And just like me, you're a wild one/Won't you take me for a ride?'

The drums and bass are locked in and Billy's piano comping gives the song a great groove, augmented by horns and saxophone. It is another good time romp in the Skynyrd tradition and doesn't deserve overthinking. The solo section ends with two guitars played in unison, reminiscent of the early days of the band. Vocal adlibs and some nimble keys from Billy end proceedings. Tom Hambridge, who has written songs for Susan Tedeschi, Buddy Guy,

Johnny Winter and Quinn Sullivan, amongst others, is a co-writer and contributes harmony vocals.

'Dead Man Walkin'' (Kevin Bowe, Medlocke, Rossington, Thomasson, J. Van Zant) 4:30
The narrative here is of a man sentenced to death for taking the life of another man 'who done his daughter wrong', and the question is asked whether you'd do the same thing. Having let the wrong man go, the subject of the song took the law into his own hands. Presumably, the execution is by electrocution, but the convicted man is still 'standin' tall', and there are other people who will fight injustice.

A thumping bass drum and nifty percussion with the sticks propel the Country acoustic instrumentation, which is joined by Hughie picking a neat riff, and Johnny says, 'Let me tell you a story'. Taking turns to solo has become the established modus operandi, and here it is no exception, with Gary playing slide before handing over to Hughie, who resists the temptation to open up. 2:43 brings the middle eight, which references the introduction to the song, and the pace then picks up for Gary to take another slide solo, and Johnny asks, 'So if I ask you that question, would you tell the truth?/Dead man walkin'', before the song winds down and fades with acoustic guitar.

Kevin Bowe is a co-author of this song. His first break came when his song 'Riverside' for the Revelators, a band he fronted, was covered by Kenny Wayne Shepherd on his album *Ledbetter Heights*, which went on to become platinum-selling. This led to a songwriting contract with Jerry Leiber and Mike Stoller in 1997.

'The Way' (Medlocke, Rossington, Thomasson, J. Van Zant) 5:32
This is the first of the two songs on this album that feature Leon. After his death, during the making of the album, the band decided to use two of Leon's basslines, re-recording the other parts from the preproduction demos and playing along to Leon.

Although written with a degree of ambiguity, the lyrics reference changes in America and, as has become a recurrent theme, changes not for the better. The narrator appears to be looking for clarity or meaning to their life, reflecting that 'Life is like an open door we're all walkin' through'. The words imply that life is challenging, but what is less clear is whether they suggest there is an afterlife, reincarnation or whether we just pass the torch to the next generation: 'When my life is over and done/Finally made my way through it/Another life has just begun/Is this the way you do it/Oh the way'.

A picked arpeggio and a backmasked guitar, panned left and right, begin the music backed by strings from The Nashville String Machine. Careful listening reveals what sounds like a mandolin, but is presumably a bouzouki, for which country producer and guitarist Biff Watson has an album credit. At 55 seconds, a heavier guitar riff begins the second verse. Gary's slide and feedback are understated, but without them, the song would sound very different. In fact, at times, it is the last discernible link to the sound of the original band. Medlocke is breathing fire, but Hughie fires back, raising the bar and leaving Gary to bring it back down with a simple melodic contribution. The song rocks to a close at 5:32, and it is a strong offering.

'Red, White & Blue' (Donnie Van Zant, J. Van Zant, Brad Warren, Brett Warren) 5:31
Following – and indeed before – the album's release, 'Red, White & Blue' proved popular and became successful as a single. According to this report, dated 9 April 2003, and reproduced from *top40-charts.com*:

The early groundswell of support at radio for Lynyrd Skynyrd's new poignant and moving single 'Red, White & Blue' has urged Sanctuary Records to move up the release date of *Vicious Cycle*, the group's first new studio material in four years, to 20 May. A week before its official release date, 'Red, White & Blue' is already receiving overwhelming radio activity, jumping to number 15 (from number 40) on the Mainstream Rock chart, and debuting at number 30 on the R&R Rock chart with over 50 stations across the country proudly playing it.

When asked about the song receiving radio airplay, in a 2003 interview for *Swampland* with Michael Smith, Gary had this to say:

Oh, it's a great feeling. We haven't had a song on the charts in a long, long time. 'Sweet Home Alabama' and all of those get played a lot on the classic rock stations, but we haven't had a new song played in a while. And the song, to me, is just about us and our fans. It's all about what's happening. It's been 30 years since our first album, and we're all getting more grey or white hair, we're all working and most of our fans down South have a little bit of a red neck, whether they admit it or not. And a lot of them will admit it right out, too! But we just wanted to say we're proud to be Americans. After 9/11, everybody started writing about it, but the song is really about us and our fans, you know.

Johnny and Donnie co-wrote the song with the Warren brothers, who also provide harmony backing vocals. Johnny and Donnie would later cover this song and name their 2016 live album after the song. That concert was originally recorded in 2006 but was not released until ten years later.

The song is a big ballad, both powerful and sentimental, but it met its criticism from those who felt it was overly sentimental and derivative. *Rolling Stone* slated the album in their 2003 review:

An echo of the Skynyrd sound is present on *Vicious Cycle*, but the soul is sure gone on these smug songs, offering endless praise to Mama, flag-waving and drinking. But nothing can forgive the shameful, pandering 'Red, White & Blue', a Toby Keith-style piece of jingoism with a guitar solo nicked from 'Free Bird'.

In fact, there is one lick in the ending solo that comes from 'Free Bird', and it is referenced deliberately, as is the bird song slide as the song closes. What is not in doubt, though, is that it was a big fan favourite in the live set, and a song that Johnny and Donnie were clearly proud of. This was the song that gave Lynyrd Skynyrd their last top 30 placement on *Billboard's* Mainstream Rock Tracks chart.

'Sweet Mama' (Hambridge, D. Van Zant, Robert White Johnson) 3:59
It is interesting to note that no Skynyrd members are credited with writing this song, although Donnie was credited. In 2005, the Van Zant brothers included the song on their successful *Get Right With The Man* album, which was released in 2005 on Columbia Records. It peaked at number two on the Top Country Albums chart and was certified Gold by the RIAA.

'Sweet Mama' is at least party biographical, referencing the part of Jacksonville where the boys were raised on the west side Shanty Town, and although it talks about a tough upbringing and learning how to 'duck and swing', it celebrates the 'hot Florida sunshine/Good lookin' women, backwoods and moonshine'. There is no note of regret, but rather a celebration of the upbringing where 'Sweet Mama didn't raise no fool'. It became a criticism of the band's post-crash output that there were repeating themes and too many references to 'mama', Southern living, faith and even their resented societal change, and in that sense, they were easy targets. However, this is what they were all about.

The song is a high-energy boogie, and Hughie and Billy are clearly enjoying themselves for all 3:59 of the song. Rickey's short slide solo hands over to Hughie, who gives the song a country feel with both the lead work and his rhythm guitar. Billy's accompaniment and extended solo at the end of the song are great, with Hughie changing up his rhythm playing and riffing.

'All Funked Up' (Medlocke, Jim Peterik, Rossington, Thomasson, J. Van Zant) 3:33
The song begins with some heavy modern riffing, in contrast to 'Sweet Mama'. It quickly drops down for the first verse, which builds back up for the 'Situation normal/All funked up chorus' and stays heavy for the second verse. Having established that we have been let down by our leaders, there is a muted call to arms asking us to stand up and be counted. A heavy bridge with a few solo licks briefly drops back down, but the riffing remains heavy, driven along by powerful drums. The song juxtaposes heavy riffing with the more familiar old school Skynyrd sections; maybe this deliberately has the

music referencing the theme of the song, the simple man in the modern, dysfunctional world.

Survivor alumnus Jim Peterik is the co-writer of this song and no less than three others on the album, having previously co-authored *Edge Of Forever*, the title track from their earlier 1999 album.

'Hell Or Heaven' (Medlocke, Peterik, Rossington, Thomasson, J. Van Zant) 5:14

The song opens with Billy playing a beautiful piano piece, accompanied by strings, that would not be out of place at the beginning of a hymn. The theme is reminiscent of 'Simple Man' – 'Mama used to say to me/You can make your destiny' – and is a message to live a good life, and if you do, 'you'll find Heaven right here'. Gary plays well-considered solos and fills, clearly more at home away from the heavier riffing, warning against greed, reminiscent of 'Backstreet Crawler' from *1991*: 'Saw a man the other day/Had it made in every way/'Til his greed brought him down/He was blinded by the city lights/ Now he shivers in the cold tonight'.

Gary's second solo is followed by Billy, echoing his opening motif. Billy and Gary adlib after the last chorus, taking a final bow. So, to the chagrin of the critics, the song is sentimental, moralistic, references faith and 'mama' again, but to some fans, it's a warm, familiar blanket, with the references *Rolling Stone* detested being exactly what they want to hear.

'Mad Hatter' (Rossington, J. Van Zant, Medlocke, Thomasson, Hambridge) 5:38

The song is a tribute to Leon Wilkeson, who passed away on 27 July 2001 during the making of the album. The writing credits differ on the compilation album *FYFTY*, where there is also a writing credit for Mike Estes. When I asked Mike, he was unaware of this. When interviewed for *Swampland*, this is what Gary had to say:

Leon. He was just such a nice guy. So down to earth. Leon was just Leon. He did so many funny things. We used to call him 'Leon Spillkerson' because he always spilt his coffee or his Coke or his drink. He was always doing so many things at one time; it caused him to spill things. And every time he came in or out of a room, something would get knocked over. He was so funny. Out on the road, one of us would hear something fall, and we'd say, 'There's Leon!' He used to always press the alarm or bell buttons on the elevator; they're emergency alarms, really, you're not supposed to touch them, but every elevator he'd ever get into, he'd push those buttons. So, you could always tell Leon was coming by the bells ringing. Now, sometimes elevators would stop when you did that. He'd do that, and we'd get mad at him. But he was just a great guy. He was amazing. I really miss him a lot. His loss is still fresh in our hearts, you know.

The lyrics acknowledge how he will be missed, along with his practical jokes, and how the Cat in the Hat had nine lives: 'You had nine lives/I can't believe they're all gone'. There are also two lyrical references to other songs: 'taking three steps with you' and 'Travelin' man, the spirits never gone', Leon having co-written 'Travellin' Man' with Ronnie. Fittingly, it is a dominant, slippery bassline that drives the song, which has a slow, grinding, bluesy feel. Rossington is in fine form throughout, his playing suitably melodic and heartfelt.

'Rockin' Little Town' (Hambridge, Medlocke, Rossington, Thomasson, J. Van Zant) 3:36
This is another celebration of touring and playing shows, with big wheels that keep on turning, kicking out the lights, letting the party begin and every night being a Saturday night. There are no musical surprises, but it's difficult not to tap your foot. The middle eight serves to launch Gary's solo. Billy just had to take the end solo, having provided some great backing earlier in the song.

'Crawl' (Medlocke, Peterik, Rossington, Thomasson, J. Van Zant) 5:09
The drums are crisp, with a prominent ambient snare drum. Ean Evans does a great job when he joins the mix at 0:34, capturing Leon's feel with his bassline. Whether he is playing Leon's line from a preproduction version or whether it is his own contribution is not clear. The song is a spacious, atmospheric ballad augmented by strings and Rossington's slow licks. Hughie's fills are on point, too. The story is a heartfelt admission from the protagonist, who is infatuated with the subject but is losing her, which is breaking him. Perhaps the chorus may be a bit overdone for some, but this type of ballad was by now part of the established Skynyrd oeuvre.

'Jake (When The Smoke Clears)' (Hambridge, Medlocke, Rossington, Thomasson, J. Van Zant) 3:41
Bass guitar and drums start the song as an organ swells into a growl. In the verses, a heavy guitar riff answers the vocal 'call'. There is a lighter chorus with Medlocke's still heavier chords accompanied by Hughie's picked riffing. The second chorus introduces some variety, with fills from Gary in the 'answer' section. Medlocke and Thomasson trade two-bar solos, both tonally and stylistically distinct. In a way, the song juxtaposes the new and old Skynyrd sound with the contrasting approaches taken to the verses and choruses. The verses feature heavy riffing, and the choruses feature cleaner-picked guitars and an old-school Skynyrd feel.

Rotgut whiskey and homemade wine have turned Jake crazy, with no fear of consequence. It's not the first time Skynyrd have warned us about rotgut whiskey: 'Poison Whiskey' told us that 'Twenty years of rotgut whiskey done killed the poor man dead'. Jake catches his daughter, Betty, in the back of a car with Bobby, and the lyrics euphemistically tell us why Jake 'blew a fuse and went for his gun'. Apparently, 'Bobby got caught with his hand in the cookie jar'. He catches up with them and puts a 'dead end to all of Bobby's fun' with his gun. The final verse tells us he got away with it and is hiding in plain sight, 'Sippin' on an ice-cold beer'.

'Life's Lessons' (Medlocke, Peterik, Rossington, Thomasson, J. Van Zant) 5:59

Clean guitars and strings on the verses contrast with heavier choruses. Johnny's singing is impassioned and far removed from his first tentative steps with the band in 1987, on the *Tribute Tour*. There is some deliberate ambiguity in the lyrics, which seem to consider mistakes at both the individual and the species level: 'We're all caught up with winnin' losin' time and space' can be interpreted as us not valuing the simple things that really matter, and maybe the space we are losing is 'the concrete slowly creeping' that Ronnie sang about in 1976. The notion that this is also a societal commentary is supported by these lines: 'Will we realise we all share one fate/Is this another life's lesson ... Too late'. At the individual level, the material goals we chase are at the expense of our time and space, and as a species, our misguided actions will lead us to a common, doomed fate.

The difficulty for latter-day Skynyrd is illustrated here. They were pilloried if they stuck to familiar stylistic tropes and criticised when they did something a little different. So, it's another well-played and well-written song, but the AOR stylings won't be for everyone. Peterik's influence is apparent in the songwriting, and this song would sit comfortably in the .38 Special catalogue.

'Lucky Man' (Medlocke, Rossington, Thomasson, J. Van Zant) 5:35

Johnny starts the song with a vocal 'Mmmm', which is fine, but it must be noted that nine of the 14 new tracks here begin with an 'Oooh' or a 'Mmmm' or both. Individually, none are out of place, but by track 14, it has been overused.

Relatively clean electric guitar, which sounds like Hughie, is accompanied by what sounds like a mandolin, but this is most probably guest Brent Rowan playing a tiple. Rowan's first contribution to the band dates back to the *1991* album, where Ed King claimed to have hired him to replace or play the acoustic guitar parts. In a way, this is a song to cherish as it's the last contribution from Leon that we would hear. It's a relatively slow, laid-back, reflective song and has a nice lead section from Gary after the first chorus. Gary also takes the main solo and is followed by Billy, who also makes subtle piano embellishments throughout. Perhaps unsurprisingly, Johnny's final contribution is 'Mmmm, I'm a lucky man, woooo just a lucky man'. The tiple is present throughout, but is more prominent during the outro, where Hughie adds some classy lead work. This, other than a songwriting credit for 'Still

Unbroken' on the 2009 release *God & Guns,* would be Hughie's swansong with Lynyrd Skynyrd, and it is a very tasteful, if overlooked, way to bow out.

Bonus Track
'Gimme Back My Bullets' (Bonus Track featuring Kid Rock)
(Rossington, Ronnie Van Zant) 3:41
In a 2008 interview with Jen Kajzer for *The Aquarian*, Rickey explained his association with Kid Rock and how he came to appear on this re-recorded version of the song.

We met each other back in 1999. ZZ Top and ourselves were out touring together. We played the Palace in Auburn Hills (Michigan), and he actually came out to visit and meet everybody, being that we were right near Detroit. We met him like that and kinda struck up a relationship and had a cool kinda bond with each other right off. On the *Vicious Cycle* record, we did a remake of 'Gimme Back My Bullets' that he sang on, and that came about right after we had met him. I had approached him and asked if he'd consider doing that, and he said he'd love to.

For his part, Kid Rock has acknowledged Lynyrd Skynyrd as an influence, and in 2007 released 'All Summer Long', which was, musically, an amalgam of 'Werewolves Of London' and 'Sweet Home Alabama' and featured a guest appearance by Billy Powell.

Only Rossington, Van Zant and Medlocke represented Skynyrd on the recording; the drums were programmed, Rob Robison was credited with guitar and percussion and Chris Rollo was credited with guitar. Although this must have seemed like a good idea at the time, it wasn't. The then-modern production style, incorporating hybrid textures, precision editing and heavy compression, coupled with Rock's shouted vocals are incongruous at best. However, Rossington clearly respected Kid Rock and said this of him and his involvement with the song to *Swampland:*

He ain't as crazy as everybody thinks. He puts on a little front there. And sitting in a hotel room with a guitar, we just sat around and played a bunch of old Merle Haggard tunes, and Hank, Jr., and Hank Williams, we played a lot of country tunes. We talked about old-style music and what it's all come around to, including rap. What he's doing. But he does it all. He does rap, rock, blah, blah. He just puts it all together in one song. He's a good guy. On that particular song, Ricky Medlocke just thought of a song that we could do that would have a little bit of a rap feel and a new kind of energy. Ricky put it together and sent it up to Kid Rock, who has a studio at his house in Detroit. He just sang it a few times and sent it back to us to mix it. So, it's Johnny singing and Kid Rock. And at the very end, some of the ad-libs are Ronnie. So, it's Ronnie, Johnny and Kid Rock on it. It's pretty cool, you know.

Associated Track
'Born To Boogie' (Hank Williams Jr) 3:53
The original version of this song was the title track from Hank Williams Jr's 14th studio album, which was released in July 1987. Lynyrd Skynyrd recorded a version for the 2003 album *The Songs Of Hank Williams Jr (A Bocephus Celebration)*. Bocephus was a nickname that was given to Hank by his father, Hank Williams Sr. The name came from a ventriloquist's dummy from one of Hank Sr's favourite acts. The version cut by Skynyrd is a little longer than the original, and the guitars, riffing and production are much heavier. The performance is energetic and the guitars and piano all trade solos. A live version of the track, featuring Hank Williams Jr., appears on Skynyrd's 2018 *Live In Atlantic City* CD/DVD release.

God & Guns (2009)

Personnel:
Johnny Van Zant: lead vocals, harmonica
Gary Rossington: guitars
Rickey Medlocke: guitars, backing vocals, co-lead vocals on 'Skynyrd Nation', harmonica
Mark Matejka: guitars, backing vocals
Ean Evans: bass, backing vocals
Michael Cartellone: drums
Billy Powell: keyboards
Additional musicians:
John 5: guitars
Rob Zombie: vocals on 'Floyd'
Michael Rhodes: bass
Greg Morrow: drums
Perry Coleman: background vocals
Jerry Douglas: dobro
Bob Marlette: piano
The Honkettes (Dale Krantz-Rossington & Carol Chase): backing vocals
Strings on 'Unwrite That Song' and 'Gifted Hands' arranged by Lisa Parade
Producer, engineer: Bob Marlette
Additional producer: Trey Bruce
Release date: 29 September 2009
Label: Roadrunner
Chart places: US: 18, UK: 36
Running time: 49:32

Hughie Thomasson made the decision to leave Lynyrd Skynyrd over a contractual disagreement that seems to have been about the four-way split on the writing credits with Van Zant, Rossington and Medlocke. The details are not clear, but Hughie was on record as saying that despite the split and the circumstances around it, there were no hard feelings. He reformed the Outlaws, continuing to tour and record. Sadly, aged just 55, Thomasson died in his sleep on 9 September 2007, of a heart attack in his home in Brooksville, Florida.

Mark 'Sparky' Matejka was recruited to complete the guitar lineup. Born in Houston on 2 January 1967, Sparky was brought in to play the Ed King and Steve Gaines parts as well as to add his own very capable contributions. His guitar credentials were established at the University of North Texas College of Music in Denton, and he gained experience in the country music band Hot Apple Pie. He also played for the Charlie Daniels Band and Sons of the Desert. Matejka had already appeared on the Skynyrd album *Christmas Time Again* as part of the Charlie Daniels Band. When interviewed in 2016, Rossington shared his opinion on Matejka's ability: 'I'd say he's one of the best guitar players I've ever seen. We actually have to kind of tell him to slow down here and there, but he's a freak. He plays every style, and he's a really good picker.'

On 28 January 2009, at his Orange Park home, Billy Powell died following a heart attack. Billy was only 56. Perhaps unwisely, he had skipped a doctor's appointment the day before. He had already laid down some piano work for the album, and so he is featured on the album.

Recording took place in 2008 and 2009 in Blackbird Studios, Nashville, Tennessee, Studio Sea, Fort Myers, Florida and Sound Kitchen, Franklin, Tennessee, with Bob Marlette as producer. His production, writing and mixing credits include a substantial and diverse collection of artists. Those credits include Rob Zombie and John 5, who appear on the album. John 5, real name John Lowerey, is a songwriter and guitarist who has worked with Ricky Martin and K.D. Lang, although he is better known for his association with Rob Zombie, Marilyn Manson and Mötley Crüe. His publishing deal with Chrysalis Records helped connect him to artists looking for a collaborator, including Lynyrd Skynyrd. During an interview with Lipps Service, John 5, having co-written six of the album's 12 tracks, explained his contribution to this album:

Chrysalis flew me over to Nashville to go write with Skynyrd, and I came in, and I looked crazy. I mean, I looked crazy. It was cold, and I had this big black fur coat on, high heels. But I would play, and there's this delay thing that a lot of the country guys would do. I would do all this country stuff, too. And they were like, 'Oh, rad.' And they would name off country songs, and I would just play them. So, we got along great. I ended up writing a shit ton of songs on the record. Great songs that I'm so proud of to be a part of this Lynyrd Skynyrd history, just because I loved Lynyrd Skynyrd so much. And what they were so great at was, it was like a country rock type of thing, but they also had this blues feel to them. So, we got along great, and I just stayed in touch with the guys. And it is such an honour to be a part of that Skynyrd history. They were such an important band for me.

The band had a new home with Loud & Proud/Roadrunner Records, and as Johnny said, 'They're a heavier record label, too, with Nickelback and Slipknot and Black Stone Cherry. They got a lot of heavy stuff on there, and we don't mind that at all. We finally found us a home that we thought would fit us.'

'Still Unbroken' (Rickey Medlocke, Gary Rossington, Hughie Thomasson, Johnny Van Zant) 5:06
'Still Unbroken' was the first single from the album, and it was used as the official Theme Song of the WWE Breaking Point Pay-Per-View event on 13 September 2009. The song was written after the death of Leon Wilkeson in 2001. Gary, in an interview with *AntiMUSIC*, recalled:

It's kind of about us and me, and what we've been through and done. Anybody who's been through a lot and had a life go on can relate to it. A lot of stuff happens. Huey Thomasson wrote that song with us; Johnny, Rickey and he passed away a couple of years ago, so that shows you how long we were writing for this album. That is kind of our story, but you can find a lot of people in life who are still unbroken. You go through stuff, and you keep going.

So, although it has been said that this song was written as a tribute to Leon, it is more about the remaining members reflecting on their continued survival through the lens of his passing. The song was started prior to Hughie Thomasson's death, in December 2007, at Rickey's home in Fort Myers, Florida. Johnny recalled Gary bringing the song back to their attention, 'We wrote that before *Vicious Circle*. Gary always keeps a cassette of stuff. He brought it in while we were in the studio, said, 'Ya'll need to listen to this, man; we can do something with this."

The song is a great opener, with chunky chords giving way to an open, atmospheric verse, and it hits hard again in the chorus. Gary's slide adds ambience in the quieter sections. Rickey takes the first aggressive lead at 3:13, followed by Mark 'Sparky' Matejka at 3:35, making his first appearance with the band as a member. This section ends with a melodic dual guitar harmony, and as an opening song, it works well and sets a high bar, albeit in the heavier modern Skynyrd vein.

'Simple Life' (Medlocke, Rossington, Jeffrey Steele, J. Van Zant, Hughie Thomasson) 3:17
The country feel of this song could be attributed to the presence of multiple Country *Grammy* nominee Jeffrey Steele. Steele, born Jeffrey LeVasseur, has had a successful career in the band Boy Howdy, as a solo recording artist and as a songwriter. He has co-written more than 60 hit songs for such artists as Tim McGraw, Faith Hill, LeAnn Rimes, Billy Ray Cyrus and many others. Around the time this song was written, Steele also co-wrote the song 'I Thought I Lost You' with Miley Cyrus for the 2008 Disney animated film *Bolt*, which Cyrus sings as a duet with John Travolta.

From the title alone, we can see we are returning to a familiar theme, and in that respect, there are no surprises. The lyrics are a lament for times past. The opening verse has an additional message, though, and it's an admonition to the listeners to reflect on their priorities: 'Hey, when is the last time you sat down and had dinner with your kids?/Talked about what's going on in their lives?/Hey, when is the last time you just stopped and helped somebody out?/I bet you can't remember'. Despite the familiarity of the theme, many fans will relate to the sentiments expressed, although the country feel of the song drew criticism. Steve Newton, reviewing the album in 2009, was damning:

Gary Rossington is the only member still breathing from the band's 'Free Bird' heyday. The current group, which has been fronted since its 1987 reformation by Ronnie Van Zant's little brother Johnny, is proficient enough, but the shit-kicking Southern zeal of old has now been withered by a mainstream vibe that veers toward the artistic no-man's-land of commercial country. How the mighty have fallen.

To be fair, Gary himself felt that the album had more of a country sound than they had expected. As for the recurrent theme, Johnny may have said it best in a 2009 interview with Brittney McKenna for *American Songwriter*, 'We're doing what we do and singing what we know about. I can tell you it's great and there's a lot of good stuff on there, but the fans will tell us if we did the job right.'

Rossington's perspective is shared in the *FYFTY* album track notes: 'We're Southern. Everything stays the same down here, a little bit. People don't go for all the new, politically correct things. We don't want to change anybody's opinion or mind. We believe how we believe, and we're not scared to say it or show it or vote it. We don't want the change. We just want the way things used to be, just good ol' America like it was years ago.'

'Little Thing Called You' (John Lowery, Medlocke, Rossington, J. Van Zant) 3:58

John Lowery, better known as John 5, is a surprising contributor. Having left Dave Lee Roth's solo band to join Marilyn Manson in 1998, his stage name was given to him by Manson and refers to both the Bible chapter and him being the fifth member of Manson's band.

Relatively heavy chords and riffing, accompanied by Rossington's slide, give the song a similar feel to the album opener. Lowery is credited as a performer on the album, but what contributions he makes and to which songs are difficult to pick out. The 'Little thing' referenced in the song's title is a woman who has cheated and has been caught out, her lover having previously ignored the warnings from his friends. A descending riff forms the middle eight, leading, as expected, into the solos. Harmony guitar parts were never a Skynyrd staple; historically, they favoured doubled lines unlike the Allman Brothers Band and the Outlaws, but they are used to good effect here.

'Southern Ways' (Lowery, Bob Marlette, Medlocke) 3:48

Speaking about the album in 2009, Johnny told *Billboard*: 'The old saying is if it ain't broke, don't fix it, so we didn't step out too far', and that comment certainly resonates through this song. 'Southern Ways' sounds like Lynyrd Skynyrd have listened to Kid Rock's 2007 release 'All Summer Long' and reverse-engineered 'Sweet Home Alabama'. 'All Summer Long' had been heavily influenced by 'Sweet Home Alabama'. John 5 contributes to the writing, as does the album's producer, engineer and mixer Bob Marlette.

There are lyrical references to the early days of Lynyrd Skynyrd – 'Me and my boys started a band/Practiced everyday out on the Hell House land' – and it is about leaving to see the world, but missing home. The nostalgia is clear, with further references to the early days and their legacy. The musical referencing of 'Sweet Home Alabama' is clearly deliberate and relates to the lyrical content. Although it is bright and breezy easy listening, it really is Skynyrd lite.

'Skynyrd Nation' (Lowery, Marlette, Medlocke, J. Van Zant) 3:52
Things pick up again with 'Skynyrd Nation'. Just like 'Southern Ways', Lowery, Marlette and Medlocke are credited for the writing, but with the addition of Johnny here. Johnny Van Zant told *Billboard*, following the passing of Billy Powell, 'I was on the computer right after Billy passed away and was just seeing the messages that people were posting. Somebody said, 'Will the Skynyrd nation go on?' I thought, 'Wow, I never thought of it as being a nation, but it really is." So, although not a tribute to Billy as such, his passing proved to be the inspiration for the song. Rossington noted: 'There are three generations of Skynyrd fans at some of these gigs, it's really cool to see that. It is like our nation.'

Crisp drumming drives the big chords and riffing guitars, and Medlocke and Van Zant perform a rare duet. It is hard not to think of Medlocke's vocals as being underutilised since he rejoined the band in 1996. Rickey possesses one of the finest voices of all the Southern Rock singers. The song is a celebration of playing to the crowd, playing 'that sweet soul Southern music' and bringing three generations together as the Skynyrd Nation. Sparky shows his class here with two rapid country-inspired, Thomasson-like solos, both answered by Rossington on slide. What sounds like a guitar with a tremolo effect ends the song, and its sound is reminiscent of the keyboards on The Who's 'Won't Get Fooled Again'.

'Unwrite That Song' (Medlocke, Tony Mullins, Rossington, Steele, J. Van Zant) 3:50
In terms of song sequencing, the album has thus far alternated between more rock-oriented songs and more country-oriented songs. It is therefore not a surprise that following 'Skynyrd Nation', the pace drops. Jeffrey Steele once again has a writing credit along with country songwriter Tony Mullins, so the country feel is perhaps no surprise. Mullins had previously written for the duo Van Zant, having co-written 'Nobody Gonna Tell Me What To Do', which was the second single from the album *Get Right With The Man*. He also has contributed to songs for LeAnn Rimes, Tim McGraw and other country artists.

The song is written from two perspectives, one male and one female. Both are listening to a song, the first on the radio, presumably on the road trucking, the second watching the music video on TV in the early hours of the morning. Both are upset by the lyrics, 'They were talkin' about love/I do and forever/And how two people ought to stay together', which we can assume is because it reflects their failed relationships. Both want the message in the song to change, 'Un-sing them lines about those happy times'. It's not clear if the two are strangers or were a couple, but their feelings are the same. Musically, it is obviously well played, but it lacks the raw feeling and impact of the early band and the rockier numbers from the later incarnations. Pedal steel guitar adds to the country flavour, as does the short slide solo, which is probably the work of Jerry Douglas, who has an album credit but whose contribution is not specifically identified.

'Floyd' (Lowery, Medlocke, Rossington, J. Van Zant) 4:03
'Floyd' opens with a swampy feel, leading into acoustic guitars, with slide guitar low in the mix, before Johnny joins along with drums and bass. The chorus is heavier and drops back down for the verses. The middle eight references souls crying and the creeper creeping, and it's followed by a third verse with Rob Zombie intoning the last lines, echoing Johnny, 'how, how, how, how'.

'Floyd' tells the story of a trapper and moonshiner who appears to have dealt with 'two law dogs' who got in his way. The G-men came to track him down and failed, and when 'Sheriff Boudreaux came to talk to his neighbours/All they could say is he was eaten by a gator/The legend lives on but Floyd he's at home singin'/How how how how how'. 'Floyd' is a solid rocking song that is stylistically far removed from the pre-77 material.

Blabbermouth.net, from September 2009, quotes the following recollection, from Johnny Van Zant, regarding how the collaboration came about:

Rob Zombie, we met through John 5 out at the Greek Theatre in Los Angeles. We were out there playing and just became friends. We had this crazy song called 'Floyd' that's on the album. We said, 'Man, that's kind of dark and mysterious; would Rob like to sing on the chorus?' Of course, he said yes. He just directed the new *Halloween* movie. For him to take his time out of that was cool. Of course, he got paid a lot more for directing than singing on the Lynyrd Skynyrd album. But it was quite an honour.

'That Ain't My America' (Medlocke, Rossington, J. Van Zant, Brad Warren, Brett Warren) 3:44
Following the album's established pattern, the rockier 'Floyd' is followed by a country song, and one that, lyrically, flies the American flag proudly. The theme of unwanted change and longing for times gone by is a familiar one in the years following the *Tribute* reunion. This song, along with 'God & Guns', received its share of criticism. At its simplest, Johnny is not accepting of the changes he sees. He doesn't want to be told where to smoke, he wants the soldiers in the armed forces to be thanked, he wants kids to be able to pray in school and he resents the $100 dollar tanks of gas.

Longtime Lynyrd Skynyrd friend Andy Munson offered the following perspective to me in 2025:

During the 2008 campaign, the soon-to-be President Obama was speaking about Republicans. He said that they just stick to their Bibles and their guns. At around the same time, he said that the Constitution was a good document, 'for its time.' These two statements, but especially the first, caused a lot of outrage in conservative circles. Then, as energy prices surged to levels never before seen, the president and a very willing media worked in unison to get the message to conservatives that virtually everything they thought and felt was flat out wrong. Essentially, they were belittling just about half of the country and thinking that it would lead to a liberal utopia of some kind. Now that is why Donald Trump was elected in 2016.

So, lyrically, the message polarises people, and the same can be said for the music. To some, it is 'commercial country' and lacks the punch and outlaw swagger of the pre-1977 band. Andy offered this perspective:

People did say things about the country flavour of 'My America', but they weren't thinking, in my opinion. No matter what Skynyrd album you look at, there are country influences or flat-out country music on it. 'Made In The Shade', 'Every Mother's Son', 'Honky Tonk Night Time Man', etc. I think that 'I Never Dreamed' could climb the country charts today. The three Van Zant brothers never hid from their love of country or Country, for that matter. When you think about it, 'That Ain't My America' has a lot in common with 'All I Can Do Is Write About It', message-wise.

'Comin' Back For More' (Blair Daly, Medlocke, Rossington, J. Van Zant) 3:28
A heavy picked riff starts the song and quickly sets the tone. This isn't deep and introspective, but it is a rocky foot tapper and an ode to a man who likes his carnal pleasures: 'It's like a drug – gotta have the feeling'. It would seem that he has tried to move on but can't help 'comin back for more'. The middle eight at 2:06 is led by bass and leads into a short organ and guitar solo and a final verse and chorus. While it would be churlish to describe the song as an album filler, it is certainly an album track.

'God & Guns' (Mark Stephen Jones, Travis Meadows, Bud Tower) 5:44
The title track of the album doesn't credit any of the band as a songwriter. This is ironic given the lengths that Johnny had to go to defend the song and its message. The song title is a reference to a speech President Obama gave in San Francisco, where he referred to Americans who 'cling to guns or religion.' Vocalist Johnny Van Zant admitted to *Billboard* magazine that this track is likely to strike people as politically incorrect. He said:

We were just in Europe, and (with) everybody, that was the first question: 'What is the meaning of this 'God & Guns?' We believe in God, and I think that Rickey says it best: 'Any religion that you believe in, you should be able to pray to it.' For me, personally, it is Jesus Christ and the Lord above. It is a scary world out there, and believe me, if someone were to try to come into my house, I want to be able to protect myself. We are not saying that every idiot out there should own a gun, and there should be better background checks on guns. Not everybody should have the right.

Interviewed for *Classic Rock*, by Dave Ling in 2014, Johnny said: 'I don't own any pistols. It's like Ronnie's lyric to 'Saturday Night Special': 'Handguns are made for killing. They ain't no good for nothing else'. As far as shotguns go, I've got an old Winchester that I love. I keep a single-barrel shotgun next to my bed.' When asked if that was for protection, he replied, 'Yeah, but not necessarily against intruders. I live in the country, and there are snakes and all sorts of dangerous animals.'

Despite this, the song does reference handguns: 'So you say your prayers, and you thank the Lord/For that Peacemaker, oh, in the dresser drawer'. However, it is also fair to say that Ronnie recognised the role of the handgun in self-defence, having bought one for his wife Judy. Furthermore, critics would do well to remember the rehearsal years earlier in the Hell House, when Bob Burns refused to play a song, and Ronnie pointed a handgun at his head and said, 'You play the motherfucking song, or I'm gonna blow your brains all over the room.' Steve Newton, reviewing the album in 2009, was harsh and perhaps unaware of this and Johnny's perspective when he said:

The worst thing about today's Lynyrd Skynyrd is embodied by the CD's NRA-approved title. If these guys are so entrenched in their redneck ways that they still believe, in the scorched-earth aftermath of George W. Bush, that religion and weaponry are the way to go, then that's just plain sad. I'm sure Johnny Van Zant thinks he's on the righteous path when he sings, in the anti-Obama title track: 'Out here in my neck of the woods, where God is great and guns are good, you really can't know that much about 'em, if you think we're better off without 'em'. Maybe someone should explain to him that when his bro penned the lyrics to the deathless 'Saturday Night Special' back in '74, he was condemning handguns, not praising them. The line 'Why don't we dump 'em, people, to the bottom of the sea' is a dead giveaway.

The song, written by Mark Stephen Jones, Bud Tower and Travis Meadows, who went on to contribute material for the band Blackberry Smoke, was covered by Hank Williams Jr. on his 2016 album *It's About Time*. It was first presented to the band as a rough demo, recorded live with just guitar and vocals. Gary and Johnny loved the song. By that time, religion had become a huge part of Gary and Johnny's lives, and the message resonated with them.

The music starts acoustically, with sparse bass. There are two acoustic guitars and some slide lines that sound more like the work of Jerry Douglas, and they differ from the lines Gary played on the song live. Although Gary was a competent and melodic slide player, it is a speciality for Douglas, who has a lighter and more dextrous touch, evident in the subtler nuances of his phrasing. At 2:56, the band shift gear with hard power chords and a bridge leading to Rossington's slide solo. Doubled guitar follows before Rickey plays a solo, resolving with a familiar lick; it is one he used around 2:57 in the song 'That's How I Like It' from the *Vicious Cycle* album. It's not plagiarism if you copy your own ideas! Unexpectedly, the song picks up again for the last chorus, which features some lead lines and acoustic slide, sounding once again like Jerry Douglas. A reprise of the intro brings the song to a close. Musically, it is great, it is sung with passion, and it is an enjoyable listen, whether you take umbrage with the theme of the song or not.

'Storm' (Lowery, Marlette, Medlocke, Rossington, J. Van Zant) 3:15
According to *Songfacts*, the song is a tribute to Ean Evans, who had died during the recording of the album. Evans passed away after a battle with lung cancer, but was able to make his final appearance with the band from a chair on 19 April 2009 at the Mississippi Kid Festival, organised in support of him. The music begins with a catchy riff, which is low down and dirty, but the choruses are uplifting and speak of salvation, in contrast to the verses, which reflect suffering: 'There's a light at the end for you my friend/Oh, take it from me/The Storm will someday end'. The middle eight has great backing vocals and is reminiscent of Blackfoot. It's a good song and a fitting tribute to a man who had difficult shoes to fill following Leon Wilkeson.

'Gifted Hands' (Lowery, Marlette, Medlocke, Rossington, J. Van Zant) 5:22
The closing song is a tribute to Billy Powell, who had also passed away during the recording of the album. The lyrics begin in a biographical fashion and recall how he joined the band: 'Just an old friend that hung with the band/A drinkin' man he had no plan/But he played the 'Bird/Played it for free'. Here, the lyrics also acknowledge Billy's demons, which surely contributed to his early death at 56, but they also show Johnny's faith, who thanks the lord for 'these gifted hands'.

The song is topped and tailed with acoustic guitars. There is a subdued backing piano on the track, presumably played by producer and engineer Bob Marlette. There is also a superb string arrangement from Lisa Parade that fills out the energetic solo sections, which resolve back to the acoustic guitar. The solo section starts in a laid-back fashion with slide guitar and the building strings before some rapid-fire soloing reminiscent of 'Free Bird'.

Associated Tracks
Special Edition Disc 2

The Special Edition of *God & Guns* came with a second disc, which featured three new studio songs and three live cuts. All three originals were written by Trey Bruce, Medlocke, Rossington and J. Van Zant. Bruce is a successful American songwriter and has written ten *Billboard* number-one singles and co-written with many other artists, notably ZZ Top, Black Stone Cherry, Leane Rhymes and Duff McKagan's Loaded.

The three originals are followed by the live tracks from Freedom Hall, Louisville, 15 June 2007: 'Red, White, & Blue', 'Call Me The Breeze' and 'Sweet Home Alabama'.

'Bang Bang' (Trey Bruce, Medlocke, Rossington, J. Van Zant) 3:10
This is a wholesome story of picking up a girl in the desert, riding to an illegal bar called the Broken Wheel, running out of money and, at the girl's instigation, robbing the joint, with the narrator being the getaway driver and lamenting, 'Oh, blue lights in my eyes/Oh, I must've been outta my mind'. 'Bang Bang' has a great rocking opening riff, maintains its tempo and makes a great bonus track.

'Raining In My Heartland' (Bruce, Medlocke, Rossington, J. Van Zant) 3:54
The song is a lament for a hometown that has changed beyond recognition, with factories that burned down and schools demolished: 'Main Street's still there but the stores are all empty/The car lot where my daddy worked is dirt and stone/The only thing that comes through here/Is stormy weather/With nothing there, it is time to move on'. 'Raining In My Heartland' is a breezy country song that is certainly a worthwhile addition to the bonus disc. The reference to Main Street is Jacksonville's Main Street. Jaxtoday.org carried an article by Ennis Davis, from May 2025, discussing how the once vibrant commercial corridor has been forgotten and lost to time:

Main Street's prominence extended to the Downtown waterfront, where the majority of the city's 78 wharves and port terminals were located, particularly near the intersection of Main and Bay streets. In this mid-century heyday, Main Street was also Jacksonville's primary shopping street, home to major national chains. However, in the 1960s through the 1980s, Main Street's role as a retail destination began to fade. The construction of Interstate 95 and the migration of commerce to suburban shopping malls contributed to its decline. By the end of the 20th century, what had once been a vibrant urban streetscape, lined with diverse architecture and a rich mix of uses, was transformed into a one-way arterial 'freeway'. The pedestrian-friendly corridor gave way to wide lanes, synchronised traffic lights, surface parking lots and garages, reflecting a broader shift in priorities from walkability to automobile convenience.

'Hobo Kinda Man' (Bruce, Medlocke, Rossington, J. Van Zant) 3:53
Train noises start the song, which is an old school hillbilly country blues until the 57-second mark, when it takes more of a 'Same Old Blues' feel. Unusually, there is a brief trade off with electric and acoustic slide. The first verse talks about hobos after the Second World War and says that Mr. Roosevelt understands. This is a reference to the Itinerant workers who played an integral part in a growing America. Millions of men led the hobo life through the early 20th century, hopping on trains to take seasonal jobs around the country in lumber, mining, agriculture and more. Without their underpaid labour, America would look quite different. Roosevelt's New Deal was a series of social, economic and political reforms that benefited the poor. The second verse draws a parallel between the hobo of yesteryear and a modern-day itinerant musician living out of a suitcase, leaving his loved ones behind. This is the 'modern day hobo kind of man' who has swapped the 'train to a Silver Eagle' (which is a type of coach, and one that was often used as a tour bus).

Last Of A Dyin' Breed (2012)

Personnel:
Johnny Van Zant: lead vocals
Gary Rossington: lead guitar
Rickey Medlocke: lead guitar
Mark Matejka: lead guitar
Peter Keys: keyboards
Michael Cartellone: drums (credited, but does not appear on the album)
Johnny Colt: bass (credited, but does not appear on the album)
Additional musicians:
Dale Krantz-Rossington: backing vocals (credited, but does not appear on the album)
Carol Chase: backing vocals (credited, but does not appear on the album)
Greg Morrow: drums
Mike Brignardello: bass guitar
John 5: lead guitar
Jerry Douglas: dobro
Stacey Michelle Plunk: backing vocals
Chip Davis: backing vocals
Lisa Parade: string arrangement and horns
Producer, engineer: Bob Marlette
Release date: 21 August 2012
Label: Roadrunner/Loud and Proud Records
Chart places: US: 14, UK: 83
Running time: 45:01

In a 2012 interview with Joe Bosso on *musicradar.com*, Gary discussed the approach taken during the recording process and the instruments that were used:

We just wanted to do it like we did in the old days. In the 1970s, we kept it simple. We picked the material, everybody came up with their parts, and then we'd play live in the studio. We made sure the band feel was there. Sure, we've tried stacking things and building songs from the drums on up, but that's not how you get the real band feel. We've learned some things over time, and we know how to make a great Lynyrd Skynyrd record. It's all about making the fans happy and keeping the band name alive, you know? I always use my Les Paul. That's what I use on every song. It's a reissue of my '59, and I just love it to death. I use that, Rickey uses his Explorer or Firebird, and Sparky plays a Stratocaster. We try to have three different sounds going on.

The use of effects was limited, and Gary was still using a Peavey Mace amplifier, which is the type of amplifier he had been using for decades. They are very loud amplifiers with a solid-state pre-amplifier and tube output stage. He also made it clear that it was a deliberate decision to make a less political or 'preachy' album.

Once again, Bob Marlette handled production, and John 5, who had made a great impression on the band during the writing and recording of *God & Guns*, co-wrote some material. Discussing the songwriting with Matt Wardlaw in 2012 for *Ultimate Classic Rock*, Johnny said the band had moved away from deliberately trying to write songs that sounded like Lynyrd Skynyrd:

> Nowadays, man, we just go 'hey, let's write songs'. Let's write songs, and if it sounds like a Skynyrd song, that's great. If it doesn't sound like a Skynyrd song, that's great, because this is what we're writing. And it seems to have worked out with us. It started on the *God & Guns* album, and now we're into the *Last Of The Dyin' Breed* album, and we're just writing what we feel instead of going 'okay, well we might need to write something in this vein or whatever.' We're having fun with it, and Gary's playing better than he's ever played in his life, to me. I love doing it, so hopefully we can do many more.

Sadly, bass player Ean Evans had passed away. Former Black Crowes bassist Johnny Colt had been recruited as his replacement, but not in time to record the album. Bass duties were handled by Mike Brignardello, who had worked with the band previously. The drums were played by Greg Morrow, who was standing in for the absent Cartellone. He had also previously played in the studio with the band.

'Last Of A Dyin' Breed' (Gary Rossington, Johnny Van Zant, Rickey Medlocke, Mark Matejka, Dan Serafini, Bob Marlette) 3:51
This was the title track and first single from the album. Explaining the title, Gary told online music and entertainment service *Spinner*, 'All the Southern bands that were popular in the 1970s are all either gone and died, God bless them, or else they're not playing anymore, and the music or their names kind of faded away, so we're one of the last of a dying breed.' When interviewed for *Classic Rock*, he discussed the naming of the track and album: 'When we were writing that song, we had about 100 different names for it. I just thought of that line, as a last resort, and it ended up really fitting the band and what we're doing now.'

There is a little nostalgia in the lyrics, 'A barefoot brother who gave me hell/I learned from the best who taught me well' and 'Just like my daddy – I'm a Traveling Man', referencing Ronnie and his music but also drawing a parallel between their father's truck driving profession and their own life out on the road, which is an analogy they have made on several occasions.

Gary's drawling slide quickly gives way to a punchy rocking song, with some effective picked rhythm guitar, slide and piano all driven by Morrow's drums and the bass guitar. Johnny Colt, having replaced Robert Kearns, was a recent recruit, *Billboard* reporting that founding Black Crowes bass player Colt had joined up with the band for the album in 2012, where he served with the band until 2017. However, as Johnny Van Zant recalled, 'Johnny just joined the band, so Johnny actually did not play on the CD. I wish he had. But we had Mike Brignardello, who's a good friend of ours, who played on the CD.' Peter Keys was already established in the band, having joined in 2009, following the passing of Billy Powell. At 2:20, the guitar is reminiscent of the Allman Brothers Band, possibly a passing tribute echoing the theme of the song. Doubled lead and slide guitar, which is unusual, take the opener to its ending. When originally written, the song had more of a country feel, but was rocked up for the album.

'One Day At A Time' (Gary Rossington, Johnny Van Zant, Marlon Young, Rickey Medlocke) 3:46

The idea for the song came from Marlon Young, guitarist with Kid Rock and a friend of Lynyrd Skynyrd. Gary Rossington discussed writing the song with *Classic Rock* in 2012: 'We co-wrote some of the lyrics, and they were a little different from what he had in mind, but he liked it. It really reminded us of an old type Skynyrd song, or an old Rossington Collins Band song. It was just kind of us, so we jumped on it.'

The introduction is stylistically typical, with chords and a picked riff. The chords carry the verse, and there is a lift for the chorus and a melodic Rossington solo, before a return to the opening chords and riff. The lyrics are more poetic than those penned by Ronnie, and cover the themes of life, mortality and the passage of time. In the opening stanza, where 'Angels sing and buzzards fly/Kingdoms fall and rivers rise', 'angels' represent heaven and 'buzzards' death. The second line relates to power and nature in flux; nothing is permanent. We are encouraged, in the chorus, to slow down and enjoy the simple things in life. The wheel turning is the inevitable passage of time. The message is to accept our fate and live a meaningful life. 'Money burns and good gold shines' contrasts false value and true worth, whilst 'World keeps spinnin' round and round/Save our souls before it all comes down' places emphasis on the passage of time and offers a plea for salvation before everything ends. There is a powerful message in the song, and there are clear references to faith with 'angels', 'the sin' and saving our souls.

The song was played in the live set following the release of the album.

'Homegrown' (Blair Daly, Gary Rossington, Johnny Van Zant, Rickey Medlock) 3:41

This is the first of three contributions to the album from Blair Daly. Rossington told *Classic Rock* that the song is 'about a crazy girl, but it also has that double meaning of weed.' A heavy riff starts the ball rolling for the song, which fits well in the rockier side of the latter-day Skynyrd catalogue. The vocals in the first part of the choruses are heavily effected in the studio, backed with tremolo-affected instrumentation. This provides a contrast to the otherwise heavy guitars. Rossington trades his slower solos with the nimble-fingered Matejka before Rickey takes a longer solo that resolves to the final chorus and the finale. It is good to hear a return to form in terms of the guitar trade-offs. When asked about the song by *Ultimate Classic Rock* in 2012, Johnny had this to say about 'Homegrown':

When we got down to that song, the little effect on the voice, it was kind of like 'hey, that's cool, that sounds current, let's do it, let's step out.' So, there's a line (with that effect) – 'I can't forget how she tastes on my lips, she's as good as it gets' – and you know, we're having fun with it. And again, we're in touch with a lot of the newer bands. Two of my favourite bands, Blackberry Smoke and Black Stone Cherry, I just think both of those bands are a good new progressive kind of Southern Rock, a little different than us, but still with a rootsy thing going on. So, we're pretty much in touch with a lot of different things.

'Ready To Fly' (Audley Freed, Gary Rossington, Johnny Van Zant, Rickey Medlock) 5:26
This is reminiscent of 'Mama (Afraid To Say Goodbye)', insofar as it is talking about the imminent passing of 'Mama'. Again, maybe this is a fictitious person or an amalgam. The lyric 'Hard times it was '69, The war was raging on, That's the reason my daddy left, And never made it back home' clearly relates to the Vietnam War. Gary's father, Robert, had passed away in 1962, but not a casualty of war, although the family did suffer hard times as a result. Marion Van Zant died in 2000 and was survived by Lacy. In 'Mama', the lyrics affirm that 'Papa' was alive. So, it is not the same person.

Starting with a sensitive piano accompaniment from Keys, now established in the Powell role, the song builds with guitar and strings once again arranged (and composed) by Lisa Parade. Keys plays his part perfectly, and the guitars are well arranged with careful attention to detail. Although shamelessly sentimental, the song is powerful, and four songs into the album, it is clear that there has been a lot of attention to detail in the arrangement.

Co-writer Audley Freed is an accomplished musician himself, having released two albums with Cry Of Love, and one studio and one live album with the Black Crowes. The live album was *Live At The Greek* in 2000, and featured Jimmy Page. Freed went on to be part of the backing band for the live concert, and DVD/Blu-ray *One More For The Fans*, released in 2015.

'Mississippi Blood' (Gary Rossington, Jaren Johnston, Johnny Van Zant, Rickey Medlocke) 2:57
Rossington substantiated the earlier claim that the album had an approach reminiscent of earlier days, telling *Classic Rock*:

That song has a lot of guitars that interlock with each other and play different parts; that's what we used to do. Allen would have a part, I would have a part and Ed King, or Steve Gaines, would have a part, and when we put them all together, they would just have that sound. Ronnie would put lyrics to it, and his voice would make the song. We started doing that again with this album. We decided to do that once again, instead of all of us just playing the same thing, over and over.

Johnny and Rickey tell us the story of 'a dirty little thing, crazy as hell', who has broken her daddy's heart. He is a man who, we are told, will 'blow you away' with the gun in his boot. The story is being told 'Before they be carvin' my name in stone', presumably reflecting the potentially fatal consequence of a relationship with the girl. Whether she is just wild or a prostitute isn't entirely clear. The line 'Her mama was a looker from New Orleans' could be a tenuous reference to her virtue, given the city's historical reputation for prostitution, particularly through its infamous red-light district, Storyville. Perhaps the line 'Work all day and I'm going again' substantiates the assertion. Either way, the narrators are smitten and can't get her out of their mind, singing, 'Like an old blues song stuck in my head'.

Jerry Douglas plays a tasty acoustic slide intro before he is joined by a banjo. Johnny and Rickey's entrance then heralds the crunchy guitars. The two men have complementary voices, and it's good to hear another duet, and as Gary said, there is thought in the guitar arrangements. The individual guitarists' lines interlock and become greater than the sum of the parts. The title is a tribute to bassist Ean Evans, who died from lung cancer in 2009, aged just 48. Future Cadillac Three member, country musician, rock singer, drummer and songwriter Jaren Johnston contributed to the writing in partnership with Rossington, Van Zant and Medlocke.

'Good Teacher' (Blair Daly, Donnie Van Zant, Johnny Van Zant, Tom Hambridge) 3:07

Blair's second contribution to this album, this time co-authoring with Donnie, Johnny and Tom Hambridge, gives two examples of a 'Good Teacher'. First comes the reference to Ronnie: 'He was 5 foot 7/Strong as an Oak tree/Yeah he had a good reason/For every lick he gave me'. The first chorus is about him, too. However, in the second verse, we encounter the second teacher, who it would appear taught him things his brother didn't: 'She was 6 foot 1/Shaking that money thing/I was high school dumb/When I had my first tall one'.

The song is a heavy offering, beginning with wah wah and distorted chords with chugging guitars driving the verse. The wah continues throughout the song and takes the first of the solos and the outro. According to Johnny, interviewed for *Ultimate Classic Rock* in 2012, this one was a lot of fun to play live, and one of three songs from this album initially in the live set.

'Something To Live For' (Bob Marlette, Gary Rossington, John 5, Johnny Van Zant, Rickey Medlock) 4:29
This song is another social commentary, a lament for a society that has lost its shared purpose, and it longs for something meaningful in which to believe. The lyrics speak of helping foreign countries but forgetting their own and not supporting veterans. The blame is clearly put on the politicians, or the people who voted them in, noting that they took a left when they should have taken a right. However, Johnny shows his resilience through his hope and faith: 'I'll keep my faith, no I'll never change'. Lyrically, it is a theme the band have explored on several occasions, and musically it doesn't break new ground. It is arranged as a ballad, well played and with plenty of space in the instrumentation, sung with intent, and is undoubtedly another one to polarise those with strong views on the American political system.

'Life's Twisted' (Blair Daly, Chris Robertson, Jon Lawhon) 4:34
Chris Robertson and Jon Lawhon, from Black Stone Cherry, have known Lynyrd Skynyrd since 2009, when they toured with them and Kid Rock. Chris, interviewed for Roadrunner Records, spoke about how they came to write the song and its presence on the album:

Well, what happened was, we had some time off, and Jon (Lawhon) went down to write a song with a guy named Blair Daly, whom we wrote with for *Between The Devil & The Deep Blue Sea*. None of the songs we wrote with him ended up making the cut, but Blair's a great guy, and we wrote some great songs with him. Jon went down and wrote the song with him, and they wanted me to play the guitar solo on it, and have Jon record it at my house, since I've got a small studio. When Jon brought me the song, he was like, 'Man, is there anything else you want to add?' I said, 'I'll tell you what, if you'll split it with me, we'll make it however you wanna make it.' So, we went in and rearranged and restructured the song a little bit. It's funny because you spend all this money doing demos, but we ended up doing it in GarageBand on a Mac, just to make it quicker. We made it a little heavier, changed the vocal melody here and there. And then out of the blue, we got a phone call and an email from Blair saying Skynyrd's cutting 'Life's Twisted', and I'm like, 'Holy shit.' My favourite band of all time, hands down, is Lynyrd Skynyrd, and the fact that from now until the end of time one of their records is gonna have my name on it as a songwriter – that just blows my mind.

When the song was originally written, they were thinking about the modern contemporary country artists that dabble in rock 'n' roll, like Eric Church or Jason Aldean. A lot of the modern country is very Skynyrd-esque, with the distorted guitars, and so it ended up working for them. After hearing the song was being used, Chris called Bob Marlette, who was a good friend, and he said it was funny because Skynyrd were fans of Black Stone Cherry. Marlette had recognised Chris's voice on the demo, but Skynyrd didn't believe him at first, as the song had come from Blair Daly. However, when they checked the writing credits, they saw Jon and Chris's names. Chris concluded, 'So, for us, the band that people say are the new wave of Southern rock, or whatever they wanna say, the fact that we got the band that started it all to cut a song that a couple of us wrote on, it's pretty fuckin' miraculous, in my opinion.'

The song starts gently enough, builds at 0:43 and hits the heavier chorus at 0:48. The middle eight precludes the solos, which include a short 'Outlaws' style harmony. Sparky and Rickey take the outro solos, which are more dynamic than those earlier. This was clearly a good fit for Skynyrd and a good choice of song.

'Nothing Comes Easy' (Gary Rossington, Johnny Van Zant, Rickey Medlock, Tom Hambridge) 4:13
Although approached in a very different way, 'Nothing Comes Easy' carries the same message as 'Something To Live For', and other themes that have been raised before, such as inflation and the price 'to fill my pick-up truck' and 'Politicians preachin'. Again, Johnny is stating his working man credentials, getting up to work because people depend on him, and he is trying to keep his faith in the American dream.

Although the one-note basslines of the intro and verses and the chord delivery are less subtle in approach, this is still recognisable as Skynyrd. At 2:24, the picking is similar to the intro of The Eagles' 'Life In The Fast Lane', but this is dispelled by Medlocke's solo. The bass on the album is basically session work from Mike Brignardello, and it would have been interesting to see what approach the new recruit Johnny Colt would have had. Leon's basslines would certainly have been a worthy alternative.

'Honey Hole' (Gary Rossington, Johnny Van Zant, Rickey Medlock, Tom Hambridge) 4:35
Although there is a fairly transparent double entendre, the little place in Jackson County referred to in the song is a favoured fishing spot. An almost psychedelic-sounding backmasked introduction builds slowly into a dreamy open arrangement with well-placed instrumentation. Gary is at home providing the fills and slide guitar in the verses. The chorus is a contrast, with heavier distorted guitars. The middle eight riffs into the solos before dropping back down for a verse and a 'Free Bird' bird noise from Gary, which he reprises in the gentle outro. Although the song itself has a fresh sound, it has the attention to detail of a classic Lynyrd Skynyrd tune.

'Start Livin' Life Again' (Bob Marlette, Donnie Van Zant, John 5, Johnny Van Zant) 4:23
This is the closing track of the album, although there were other versions of the album carrying bonus tracks. The message conveyed in the song is an

encouraging one. Essentially, it is about making a positive shift from past troubles to a positive future, shaking off drink, drugs and the shackles of wealth to embrace the recognition that 'Time with your family is precious'. There are clear references to embracing religion, such as in the first verse: 'So, you better get down on your knees/And ask the good lord to take it away'. The second verse asks a question: 'Don't you think it's time to get help?/Let your spirit fly and you won't need to get high anymore/Ask him into your life/'Cause he can open up any door!'. Johnny is suggesting that turning to God will deliver the help you need to beat addiction and free your spirit. The chorus carries the same Christian message, asking us to let the good lord be with us. Johnny had explored substance abuse before in his writing and said 'Sometimes when you get on things, man, it's hard. But I think there's an obligation as songwriters to write songs that help people get through things.'

The introductory slide playing should not be confused with that of Gary or Rickey. It is clear that it is the slide master, Jerry Douglas. His playing is a beautiful and integral part of the song. The second slide guitar accompanying the song sounds like Gary; however, in a 2012 interview with *Guitar World*, Gary claimed that John 5 and Jerry were the only two guitar players on the track. The drums are minimal, and the bass is simple. Once again, the arrangement is first class, but it would be interesting to hear this stripped back to acoustic slide and vocals. If we did, it would evoke memories of the 'Four Walls Of Raiford', another deceptively simple country blues.

Digipack Release
'Poor Man's Dream' (Bob Marlette, Gary Rossington, John 5, Johnny Van Zant, Rickey Medlocke) 4:08
There are nods to corruption in the lyrics, which warn us that we shouldn't trust a politician's promise, as it won't be kept. However, the message seems to be that if you work hard, you can get 'a piece of that American Pie', but nothing comes easy; in reality, 'that's a poor man's dream'. The solos trade and intertwine. Elements of the song do sound familiar – there are echoes of 'Southern Ways', for instance – but as a bonus track, it certainly cuts the mustard.

'Do It Up Right' (Gary Rossington, Johnny Van Zant, Rickey Medlocke, Tom Hambridge) 3:57
This is instantly recognisable as a Skynyrd boogie, with keys, horns and big female backing vocals on the choruses. Keys summons his inner Billy Powell and does a fair job, especially trading with the slide guitar. This is one of those songs where the lyrics work far better in the context of the song than they do in isolation. The narrator is running late for a date and is sidetracked by helping Rickey out of a jam. However, he plans to make it up to her, and

despite the fact she has heard it all before, he appears to get away with it, and it is left to the imagination how he is going to 'do it up right!'. It's a good-time, tongue-in-cheek slice of fun. Lisa Parade composed the horns, which sit well in the mix.

'Sad Song' (Bob Marlette, Gary Rossington, John 5, Johnny Van Zant, Rickey Medlocke, Shaun Morgan) 4:01
The song is about the end of a relationship and someone reflecting on how things went wrong. It is also a powerful musical statement, and Johnny was right in saying this was 'pretty kick ass'.

When *Ultimate Classic Rock* caught up with Johnny in 2012, ahead of their set in South Dakota at the annual Sturgis Rally, he discussed 'Sad Song'. Initially, he was prompted by a comment that 'Homegrown', although sounding like Lynyrd Skynyrd, had 'current elements' to it, reminding the questioner of Seether or Theory Of A Deadman:

You know, man, it's ironic that you said Seether because we actually wrote with Shaun (Seether lead singer and guitarist Shaun Morgan), and we've got a song called 'Sad Song' (which was recorded during the sessions for the new album). The thing about Lynyrd Skynyrd is that we go over to Europe and we play these heavy metal festivals; we just did Hellfest in France, and to be honest with you, I didn't even know the band before us, but the guy was like (Van Zant imitates 'Cookie Monster' heavy metal vocals of the singer). And I'm looking at the audience going, 'how the hell are we going to fit into this?' It's not on the regular album; we're doing it as a bonus track because we wanted to, really. A lot of times, people give shitty songs as bonus tracks. And the tracks that we have to do for different corporations like Wal-Mart, Target, Best Buy, or whatever, each one of them wants a bonus track and something that's not on the actual CD. We think our bonus tracks are pretty kick ass, so we said, 'Hey, let's give 'Sad Song' as one of the bonus tracks.' Shaun's just a great guy, man. We sat down and wrote with him, and he's a very intelligent guy, if you ever really talk to him. He's very intellectual and a very cool guy. I really enjoyed writing with him, and I hope to do it again.

'Low Down Dirty' (Blair Daly, Gary Rossington, Johnny Van Zant, Rickey Medlocke) 3:14
This is the modern heavy riffing Lynyrd Skynyrd, telling a story of irresponsibility, sin, drinking and giving in to primal urges with no regard for the consequences. This is certainly one of the punchiest and heaviest songs Skynyrd recorded. It is interesting to wonder whether Skynyrd could have returned the earlier favour from Blackstone Cherry and offered this song to them, in return for 'Life's Twisted'. It is certainly a worthy addition as a bonus track, but it is easy to see how it wouldn't have been the best fit as a main album track.

Classic Rock Fan Pack
The Classic Rock Fan Pack was a specially curated bundle produced by *Classic Rock Magazine* that included the album, with different bonus tracks, and an artist-approved magazine featuring interviews and track guides. It included 'Poor Man's Dream', 'Do It Up Right', 'Skynyrd Nation' (Live) and 'Gimme Three Steps' (Live).

Associated Track
'Winning Isn't Everything' (Unknown) 3.31
Self-confessed fans of the *Pawn Stars* show, Lynyrd Skynyrd were more than happy to contribute a theme tune in 2013. The result was a hard-hitting, heavy riffing, 3.34-minute blast of heavy Southern rock. The band released the track as a single on Spotify, where it was titled 'Pawn Stars Theme (Winning Isn't Everything)'.

Compilation Albums

Although not quite innumerable, there are too many Lynyrd Skynyrd compilations to include. These are the most significant releases.

Gold & Platinum (1979)

Tracklisting: 'Down South Jukin'', 'Saturday Night Special', 'Gimme Three Steps' (Live), 'What's Your Name', 'You Got That Right', 'Gimme Back My Bullets', 'Sweet Home Alabama', 'Free Bird' (Live), 'That Smell, On The Hunt', 'I Ain't The One' (Live), 'Whiskey Rock-A Roller', 'Simple Man', 'I Know A Little', 'Tuesday's Gone', 'Comin' Home'

Best Of The Rest (1982)

Tracklisting: 'I've Been Your Fool', 'Gotta Go', 'I'm A Country Boy', 'Double Trouble', 'Workin' For MCA', 'Call Me The Breeze', 'I Never Dreamed', 'T For Texas'

'I've Been Your Fool' (Allen Collins, Gary Rossington, Ronnie Van Zant) 3:49

The origins of the first two songs on this album are a bit of a mystery. The album credits list Jimmy Johnson and Tim Smith as producers for Muscle Shoals Sound Productions. If this is the case, the songs should have been included on the *Complete Muscle Shoals* album, but weren't. Also, Billy is playing the piano, and Ed is playing the slide. So, for this to be the case, these would have to be overdubs. We know Ed did overdub some of the Muscle Shoals recordings. Some say this song, which contains two slide guitars, is the only recording of Allen playing slide. In reality, it sounds like King and Rossington. Another possibility is that these songs are from the Al Kooper demo session prior to the first album. King overdubbed slide on 'Take Your Time', so this is a possibility, and the tracks do have a similar sound to the demo recordings. When Andy Munson was researching for his uncompleted book, he investigated these two songs, and this was his perspective:

In 1982, Leon Tsilis began putting together what became *Best Of The Rest*. Less than a month before he died, Leon and I discussed it, as I wanted to know why they bothered with only two new songs. The short answer is that lawyers messed it up. I asked about 'Gotta' Go' and 'Fool'. Leon told me that Alan Walden had offered them to MCA for one million dollars, and MCA paid it! As close as he could tell, these were the first two songs recorded in Muscle Shoals. Alan had them mixed to two-track and unsuccessfully shopped them around. He said he didn't have the multi-track tapes, but I doubt that. Jimmy Johnson didn't have them, so...

Regardless of origin, and despite being a little rough around the edges, this sub-four-minute romp, about being taken for a ride by a lover, was a good find and an unexpected bonus five years after the crash.

'Gotta Go' (Allen Collins, Gary Rossington, Ronnie Van Zant) 4:35
Giving credence to the Kooper demo theory is the fact that Allen's solo at 2:02 is buried in the mix until the engineer turns up the channel partway through the solo, implying that it was mixed on the fly on a two-track recording. The song is a solid rocker, albeit one that contains one of Ronnie's less politically correct lines: 'You can tell your big sister thanks a lot for the hole'.

Legend (1987)

Tracklisting: 'Georgia Peaches', 'When You Got Good Friends', 'Sweet Little Missy', 'Four Walls Of Raiford', 'Simple Man', 'Truck Drivin' Man', 'One In The Sun', 'Mr. Banker', 'Take Your Time'
'Georgia Peaches' and 'Sweet Little Missy' are discussed as bonus tracks with the expanded edition of *Street Survivors*.

'When You Got Good Friends' (Allen Collins, Ronnie Van Zant) 3:03
As has been stated, Ronnie wanted to do some country music and something different from Lynyrd Skynyrd. Jeff Carlisi recalled that Ronnie wanted to put a band together, for which he already had a name. By Carlisi's recollection, it 'was something like' Arthur Wills And The Swamp Critters (a play on Bob Wills And The Playboys). He planned on doing shows with the band, but it was not to be. One night, the boys in .38 Special got a call to go down to Skynyrd's studio, and they cut a song with Ronnie. The song they recorded, 'When You Got Good Friends', was written by Allen and Ronnie and performed by them with the help of Billy Powell on piano, Larry Junstrom on bass, Don Barnes on guitar and Steve Brookins on guitar. Gary Rossington is also credited as a performer, and Carlisi played pedal steel on the session. By his own admission, he was learning the instrument, and his part was left out, being slightly out of tune. The song namechecks Merle Haggard, Waylon Jennings, Willie Nelson and Charlie Daniels and, along with 'No One Can Take Your Place', is as pure a country song as Skynyrd ever recorded. Perhaps this song should be borne in mind before criticisms are levelled at some of the post-crash band's more country offerings.

'Four Walls Of Raiford' (Jeff Carlisi, Ronnie Van Zant) 4:15
Ronnie wrote 'Four Walls Of Raiford' with .38 Special's Jeff Carlisi. This version took the original recording by Ronnie and Jeff and was overdubbed by Powell, Rossington and Wilkeson for this release. This was Tom Dowd's idea, and the definitive version is the original demo cut on the same night as 'When You Got Good Friends', which was released on the 1991 *Lynyrd Skynyrd – The Definitive Lynyrd Skynyrd Collection* box set. The song is discussed further there. On this version, the overdubs are sympathetic and fill out the mix, but the raw country blues version is a case of less is more.

'Truck Drivin' Man' (Ed King, Ronnie Van Zant) 5:17
According to Tom Dowd, this song was like a tribute to Ronnie's father, his way of being proud of what his father did. In early 1973, the band cut demo songs for the first album, from which the material for the first album was to be selected. Ed King, who has a writing credit, is playing bass, having replaced Leon at this point. Although well performed, the recording is rough and ready. You can hear the solo being turned up live on the mixing desk as the song was recorded. Billy's playing is particularly spirited throughout. The 1987 single release, with 'When You Got Good Friends' on the B-side, did not chart despite strong radio play in the US.

'One In The Sun' (Steve Gaines) 5:19
This track is a Gaines composition and was the title track for the only solo album he is credited for, which was released in 1988. The original master tape (original recording 14 April 1975 Church Studio, Tulsa, Oklahoma) has been overdubbed to include Powell, Rossington and Wilkeson. Gary's guitar becomes fairly dominant, and the necessity for the overdubs is questionable at best, now that we have the original version available for comparison. The drum track is the original, played by Ron Brooks.

'Mr. Banker' (Gary Rossington, Ronnie Van Zant) 5:18
This is another of the demos cut with Al Kooper. It is a basic stripped-back blues. Rossington handles the rhythm guitar while Ed plays some fiery slide in an early demonstration of his skill. Gary demonstrated his sense of melody on slide in songs like 'Free Bird', but he was never as competent as King. Possibly slightly tongue-in-cheek, the lyrics are a plea from a poverty-stricken man to the banker to provide money to bury his father.

'Take Your Time' (Ed King, Ronnie Van Zant) 7:31
This also appeared as a bonus track on the reissue of *Second Helping*. Ronnie is singing about the fact that although 'ladies like their diamonds/They like their brand-new clothes', he 'was blessed with plenty of other things they love the most'. What is of some interest here is that this is also one of the Kooper demo tracks that has Ed on bass, and yet his slide is also prominent. So, at some point, there must have been an overdub, probably when the song was chosen as the B-side for the 'Sweet Home Alabama' single. Although it is always great to hear the work of Billy and Ed, the song is a little overlong. It's a fairly standard, blues-based song, easily recognisable as Skynyrd, but not an essential track.

Skynyrd's Innyrds (1989)
Tracklisting: 'Sweet Home Alabama', 'Swamp Music', 'I Ain't The One', 'Gimme Three Steps', 'Double Trouble' (Outtake/Alternate Version), 'Free Bird' (Outtake/Extended Version), 'Truck Drivin' Man' (Demo Version), 'Saturday Night

Special', 'Workin' For MCA', 'What's Your Name', 'That Smell', 'Don't Ask Me No Questions', 'Call Me The Breeze'

Lynyrd Skynyrd – The Definitive Lynyrd Skynyrd Collection (1991)
CD1: 'Free Bird' (Demo), 'Junkie' (Demo), 'He's Alive' (Demo), 'One More Time' (Original Version), 'Gimme, Three Steps' (Original Version), 'Trust' (Original Version), 'Comin' Home', 'Mr. Banker' (Demo), 'Down South Jukin'' (Demo), 'Truck Drivin' Man' (Demo), 'I Ain't The One' (Demo), 'Poison Whiskey' (Demo), 'Tuesday's Gone', 'Things Goin' On', 'Free Bird'
CD2: 'Sweet Home Alabama', 'Was I Right Or Wrong?', 'Workin' For MCA', 'Don't Ask Me No Questions', 'Swamp Music', 'The Ballad Of Curtis Lowe', 'The Needle And The Spoon', 'Call Me The Breeze', 'Saturday Night Special', 'Made In The Shade', 'Am I Losin'', 'On The Hunt', '(I Got The) Same Old Blues', 'Double Trouble' (Live), 'Roll Gypsy Roll', 'All I Can Do Is Write About It' (Acoustic), 'Four Walls Of Raiford' (Undubbed Demo)
CD3: 'Gimme Back My Bullets' (Live), 'Searchin'' (Live), 'Simple Man' (Live), 'Crossroads' (Live), 'T For Texas' (Live), 'Whiskey Rock-A-Roller' (Live), 'Ain't No Good Life', 'What's Your Name' (Alternate Mix), 'Georgia Peaches', 'What's Your Name', 'I Never Dreamed', 'I Know A Little', 'Honky Tonk Night Time Man', 'That Smell', 'You Got That Right'

'Junkie' (Demo) (Allen Collins, Ronnie Van Zant) 3:48
Miranda Ray made the following observation about 'Junkie' for *Country Rebel* in 2016:

'Junkie' was written by lead singer Ronnie Van Zant and guitarist Allen Collins. The 3:48 song tells the story of a man who feels lonely and sad all the time, as he sings, 'Disillusions fillin' my head, Never happy, I wished I was dead'. Despite its mournful message, the tune has a bit of a groovy feel, which especially comes out during a large instrumental break in the middle of the song. Those who never purchased the Lynyrd Skynyrd box set were missing out on a lot because 'Junkie' was just one of the many gems featured in the collection.

'Junkie' is also noteworthy for featuring Allen using his wah-wah pedal on one of only a handful of occasions. Here, he uses it in both the chorus and the solo, at one point employing it as a notch filter.

'He's Alive' (Demo) (Allen Collins, Ronnie Van Zant) 3:09
This is a song about a man remembering his late father, with whom he had a strong bond, but it also carries the meaning that his father gave him faith. It is another Collins/Van Zant collaboration and features some nice rhythm guitar, particularly from Allen, who also takes the main solo. It's a decent song, and once again Allen makes use of his wah, but only for the rhythm in the outro.

Perhaps this song was worthy of further development. Following these demos, Allen made very little use of wah, other than his great solo in 'The Needle And The Spoon'.

'Four Walls Of Raiford' (Undubbed Demo) (Jeff Carlisi, Ronnie Van Zant)

This song was previously released on *Legend*, although the version there contained overdubs of guitar, bass and keys from Gary, Bill and Leon. After the session for 'When You Got Good Friends' (see *Legend*), everyone was leaving, and Ronnie asked Jeff Carlisi if he had some time to help him with a song that he was working on. Ronnie started to sing the verses of 'Four Walls Of Raiford', and Jeff picked up Gary Rossington's dobro, took out a slide and started playing a traditional arrangement, very much a back porch kind of blues. Jeff recalled that the song was finished in 30 to 45 minutes. After a few hits off a bottle of Jack Daniels, and with the time past two in the morning, they rolled the tape. After several takes, they realised that making it 'perfect' would detract from the quality and ambience of the song.

Raiford is a real penitentiary, and the song tells the story of an unemployed Vietnam veteran who goes to prison for a crime he did not commit. Lyrically, it is powerful, and the performance captured by Jeff and Ronnie in the stripped-back form is excellent. As a footnote, Donnie Van Zant and Jeff Carlisi performed the song at the premiere of the *Freebird* movie, which, according to Jeff, is the only time it has been performed live.

Skynyrd's First: The Complete Muscle Shoals Album (1998)

Tracklisting: 'Free Bird' (Muscle Shoals demo), 'One More Time' (Original Version), 'Gimme Three Steps' (Original Version), 'Was I Right Or Wrong?', 'Preacher's Daughter', 'White Dove', 'Down South Jukin'', 'Wino' (Original Version), 'Simple Man' (Original Version), 'Trust' (Original Version) (Collins, Van Zant), 'Comin' Home' (Original Version), 'The Seasons' (Medlocke), 'Lend A Helpin' Hand', 'Things Goin' On' (Original Version), 'I Ain't The One' (Original Version), 'You Run Around' (Medlocke), 'Ain't Too Proud To Pray' (Medlocke)

'You Run Around' (Medlocke) 5:39

This was one of a number of Blackfoot songs brought in by Medlocke. Greg Walker has stated that both he and Jackson Spires should have had writing credits for some of the songs, although he has not identified which ones. Here, what is essentially a Blackfoot/Lynyrd Skynyrd hybrid rip through a spirited rocker with Medlocke on vocals and drums and Allen and Gary on guitars. The bridge at 1:35 wouldn't have been out of place on Blackfoot's *No Reservations*. Greg's bassline is propulsive and tight with Medlocke's drumming. There are some good solos here, too – portents of things to come. At 3:49, things change drastically, with a rhythm reminiscent of Hendrix's version of Dylan's 'All Along The Watchtower', accompanied by more enthusiastic soloing. The two sections are very different, giving the song a bit of a jam feel, but there are some good ideas. Miranda Raye, writing for *Country Rebel* in 2017, had this to say: "You Run Around' is an upbeat, peppy tune akin to other Skynyrd tracks such as 'Call Me The Breeze'. The song features an extensive guitar jam that is sure to have you grooving along in your seat.'

Interestingly, there is a live version of the song recorded live at the Beach Coliseum in Jacksonville Beach, FL, in late 1971 or early 1972. The band that night was Ronnie Van Zant on vocals, Allen Collins and Gary Rossington on guitar, Larry Junstrom on bass and Rickey Medlocke on drums and backing vocals. The fact that Ronnie is singing one of Rickey's songs live gives some affirmation to his status as 'an original member', a subject that remains controversial to this day. The live recording hasn't been officially released and, unsurprisingly, as a live bootleg, the fidelity is not the best.

'Ain't Too Proud To Pray' (Medlocke) 5:26
The same Skynyrd/Blackfoot hybrid performs this Medlocke composition. Although there are similarities in style to 'The Seasons' and 'White Dove', 'Ain't Too Proud To Pray' is an interesting listen. Allen and Gary play acoustic guitars, and Rickey sings and drums while Greg holds down the bottom end. It's a difficult song to categorise. It has a folk tinge and an unusual vocal melody line, but sounds a little dated. The extended guitar strumming sections could have done with either an edit or a solo, but perhaps this was a work in progress to which they did not return. Miranda Raye, again writing for *Country Rebel* in 2017, summarised the song's meaning: 'The song is told from the perspective of a man who was able to escape all his troubles through the power of prayer. As the song progresses, the man proclaims how he will never be 'too proud to pray' when 'Mr. Trouble' visits him again.'

Collectybles (2000)
Shade Tree Recording (1968-1970): 'Free Bird', 'Need All My Friends', 'Michelle', 'If I'm Wrong', 'No One Can Take Your Place'
Quinvy Recordings (1970): 'Hide Your Face', 'Bad Boy Blues'
Second Helping Outtake (1974): 'Memphis'
Live On WMC – FM (1973): 'I Ain't The One', 'Call Me The Breeze', 'Sweet Home Alabama', 'Woman Of Mine', 'Workin' For MCA', 'Free Bird'
Quinvy Recordings (1970): 'Need All My Friends' (Complete Version), 'Michelle' (Complete Version)
Live At The Fox Theatre (1976): 'Saturday Night Special', 'Whiskey Rock-A-Roller', 'Gimme Three Steps', 'Call Me The Breeze'
Street Survivors Outtakes (1977): 'I Never Dreamed' (Alternate Version), 'You Got That Right' (Alternate Master)
Live At The Fox Theater (1976): 'T For Texas', 'Crossroads'

Street Survivors Outtake (1977): 'Jacksonville Kid'
Live At The Fox Theater (1976): 'Free Bird'

Shade Tree Recording (1968-1970)

'Need All My Friends' and 'Michelle' were recorded, edited for airplay and 300 promotional monaural copies released as a single in 1968. This was sent out to radio stations but was met with no interest. A year later, 8-track recordings were made of 'If I'm Wrong' and 'No One Can Take Your Place'. The final track recorded by Tom Markham and Jim Sutton was 'Free Bird'. Shortly after, they released the band.

'Free Bird' (Allen Collins, Ronnie Van Zant) 7:29
Recorded in 1970, this version has Larry Junstrom on bass and includes a version of the outro solo, unlike the later Quinvy demo version, which fades out without the solo section.

'Need All My Friends' (originally released on Shade Tree Records, 1968) (Collins, Van Zant) 3:18
Despite being one of the first two Skynyrd compositions recorded, their style is recognisable, although Ronnie's vocal phrasing is a little less assured than it was in later years. The overdubbed strings are a surprise, and the drumming from Burns is certainly more basic than it became. The song captures a sentimental feeling, and the lyrics, not for the last time, tell of the hardships of a working musician's life, leaving loved ones behind, chasing opportunities, battling exhaustion and desperately wanting both success and a sense of home. These are themes the band would frequently return to. Although the song would be re-recorded for the Quinvy sessions, it was never returned to once the band were successful. There is a familiar line, however, 'It's been so long since I've been gone', which would become the opening line of 'Comin' Home'.

'Michelle' (originally released on Shade Tree Records, 1969) (Collins, Van Zant) 2:57
The playing and the recording are a little ragged in places, but the fact that this is another of their first songs written and recorded must be taken into consideration. The tempo isn't particularly solid. The outro solo pays homage to the British invasion with a feel not unlike some of the work of The Yardbirds. The lyrics are deeply personal and refer to Ronnie's daughter Tammy Michelle Van Zant, his daughter with his first wife, Nadine. She was born on 30 July 1967 and passed away on 11 July 2022. Ronnie Van Zant and Nadine Inscoe divorced in 1969 after being married in 1967.

'If I'm Wrong' (Collins, Gary Rossington, Van Zant) 5:29
In 2016, Vincent Lopez, writing for *Society Of Rock*, made the following assessment:

With haunting lyrics sung by the one and only Ronnie Van Zant, Lynyrd Skynyrd's 'If I'm Wrong' (Shade Tree Demo) is what we could consider the lost singer's personal anthem, with a line like 'I don't need no fame, I don't play no games'. Choosing to deliberately belt the sorrowing blues despite the consequences the character sensed, he shows no fear of death or loss in the song as he accepts his fate willingly and knowingly in the lyrics of the song. Recorded in 1970 at the Norm Vincent Studios in Jacksonville, FL, this demo is known as one of the first recordings in the band's history that displays pristine riffs that will carry you away by both Collins and Rossington, as well as incredible drumming by Burns, with Ronnie leading the mic effortlessly. Released in 2000 on the *Collectybles* album, featuring some of the band's earliest recordings, the world truly went too long without this sensationally sombre song. Fans who understood and accepted Ronnie as he was were aware that he sensed he wasn't going to live very long, for whatever reason, and this demo is just one of those incredibly and unfortunately accurate predictions of that fact. So, honour the rockstar as he was in all of his well-sung glory with what has to be one of the greatest demos recorded in history.

The song begins with an acoustic guitar and a plaintive, short solo. Ronnie sings well, and the first main solo has slightly better phrasing than the intro. To this listener, the praise Lopez gave the song is not really warranted. Decent as the song is, there really aren't any pristine riffs, there is no awesome drumming and the guitar work falls short of what Rossington and Collins became capable of. However, that is not to decry its merit. It is certainly interesting to hear the song, which is enjoyable, but it is also important to remember that this was a young, developing band and there were shortcomings.

'No One Can Take Your Place' (Collins, Rossington, Van Zant) 5:25
'No One Can Take Your Place' is about grief and longing after losing someone deeply loved. Ronnie's love of country music has been noted several times, and this song offers further affirmation. In Mark Ribowsky's *Whiskey Bottles And Brand-New Cars*, he talks about Allen Collins' 'weeping slide guitar', but there is no evidence that this is Allen. There is only one other claimed incidence of Allen playing slide, which is on 'I've Been Your Fool', and that is something that in itself seems just as unlikely. The slide lines are doubled and panned left and right, though, so, however unlikely, it is possible one of these lines is Allen rather than a Rossington overdub.

Of all the songs in the Skynyrd repertoire, this is the purest country song, with the possible exception of 'When You Got Good Friends', but that featured several guest musicians from .38 Special and not all of the Skynyrd band.

Quinvy Recordings (1970)
'Hide Your Face' (Rossington, Van Zant) 2:59
This is another song that has an early Blackfoot feel, but, of course, the vocals are instantly recognisable as Ronnie. The mix is a little crude with the guitars hard panned left and right, including the fills and solo, but it does have a live feel and captures an energetic performance of a rocking song with a slightly funky groove. The fills and solos sound like Allen, and the dominant rhythm guitar is Gary. This was an early example of what became a common template. It is often the case in Lynyrd Skynyrd's catalogue that the song author didn't get the solo.

'Bad Boy Blues' (Rossington, Van Zant) 7:48
It is probably fair to say that you could get away with some lyrics in the past that you couldn't do today. It is difficult to imagine the latter-day incarnation of Lynyrd Skynyrd getting away with 'Lord wanna bring your long legs here/ Oh yeah/So you can ride on my pony honey/Lord for your bridle you can use my ears/Oh yeah'. This gives the line about the 'big sister' in 'Gotta Go' (from *Best Of The Rest*) a run for its money. Double entendres and risqué lyrics have always been common in blues music, which in turn influenced rock 'n' roll and rock music. Hokum blues, characterised by humorous and risqué lyrics, emerged in the 1920s and was popularised in the early 1930s. This style of blues often dealt with sex, alcohol and drugs, although the music was typically upbeat and danceable. If we can forgive Tampa Red for 'Let Me Play With Your Poodle' and Lucille Brogan for the outrageous 'Shave 'Em Dry', we can certainly forgive Ronnie.

What we have here is a 12-bar blues with Ronnie turning his hand to singing the blues in an impassioned growl and Rossington and Collins delivering some familiar chord progressions and turnarounds. The subtler and more authentic chord work seems to come from Gary, perhaps unsurprising as he co-authored the song with Van Zant. At 2.02, Allen takes his first solo and conjures his inner Clapton through to 2:53. He takes a second solo before Gary takes a turn at 3:51. There are some familiar blues motifs, but both players are clearly having fun. There is no new ground broken here, but it's a good listen, rather than just a curiosity.

'Need All My Friends' (Complete Version) (Collins, Van Zant) 5:11
A more assured vocal delivery from Ronnie is augmented by a band who are a little tighter than they were on the Shade Tree recordings. The song is better without the strings and includes some creditable lead guitar. The bends in the first solo aren't perfect, but the faster soloing is spirited and gives a hint of what was to come.

'Michelle' (Complete Version) (Collins, Van Zant) 5:43
This is again more solid than the Shade Tree version, with notable improvements in the band's playing and timing. The drums and the bass are

tighter, but Allen's trill between 2:56 and 3:13 is too long. The outro solo does still recall the British Invasion but has a more mature delivery. Had 'Need All My Friends' and 'Michelle' been revisited just a year or two later, they could have sat alongside the rest of the music Skynyrd recorded quite comfortably. Both are still well worth listening to, though, in both the Shade Tree and Quinvy incarnations.

Second Helping Outtake (1974)
'Memphis' (Ed King, Rossington, Van Zant) 3:21
This is an instrumental demo recording of a song that was never completed, and that was recorded during the sessions for *Second Helping*. The title is inspired by the trip to Memphis for the WMC-FM broadcast. The band loved Memphis and took the opportunity to visit Graceland. There is perhaps limited value in the inclusion of this demo; it is just a bare-bones backing track with no vocals, solos, or fills. Musically, it is slow and bluesy in style, perhaps reminiscent of Free to a degree. Ultimately, it is little more than a curiosity.

Live On WMC – FM (1973)
Regional Radio promo man John Scott was present at Skynyrd's legendary Sounds Of The South party that saw the premiere of 'Workin' For MCA'. He was blown away by the performance, so, with Dick Williams, MCA Director of Special Projects, he arranged for the band to make a live promotional broadcast on WMC-FM in Memphis, Tennessee. The show, on 30 October 1973, could be picked up all over the Southern states and a recording survived. Notably, the recording includes several tracks from their first album and several songs that would be included on *Second Helping*. Of particular interest, though, is the only known version of 'Woman Of Mine', which was never recorded in the studio. The recording has historical significance and would have been representative of what The Who fans got to experience from the Lynyrd Skynyrd support slots.

'Woman Of Mine' (Van Zant, Leon Wilkeson) 6:33
This live recording was a great find. Although a studio version was never recorded, and the band were probably playing the composition to gauge fan reaction, the song sounds quite well-developed and gig-ready. Billy takes an extended solo on the electric piano, probably largely an ad-lib performance and reflecting the fact that guitar solos hadn't been worked up and arranged fully. There are a couple of lead breaks and a longer slide solo from Ed King, but a signature of Lynyrd Skynyrd was that solos were worked out and played note-for-note each time. The bassline is quite hypnotic, and the song has a very different feel to most Skynyrd music, which is probably why it was not taken into the studio. It does maybe sound a little dated now in terms of style, but its serendipitous survival and discovery enabled its worthy addition to this collection.

Street Survivors Outtake (1977)
'Jacksonville Kid' (Haggard, Van Zant) 4:09
According to the sleeve notes for the 2008 expanded version of the *Street Survivors* album, this was the last lyric that Ronnie ever wrote and performed. Having been inspired by the presence of engineer Barry Rudolph (sent by Tom Dowd, who was finishing a session with Rod Stewart), who had previously worked with Waylon Jennings, they decided to cut a version of Merle Haggard's 'Honky Tonk Night Time Man'. As an afterthought, Ronnie went back and wrote an alternate autobiographical lyric to the tune, which he called 'Jacksonville Kid'. What became his final musical statement sums up all of his unresolved feelings about his childhood on Jacksonville's west side and his perception of his rejection by his hometown. He felt isolated, despite his success. He also addressed the changing of the music scene and changing trends. It's as close as Ronnie got to working with Haggard, who Ronnie considered to be his favourite songwriter and performer in the world.

Thyrty (2003)
Tracklisting: 'Sweet Home Alabama', 'Need All My Friends', 'Blues Medley' ('Sweet Little Angel', 'How Blue Can You Get', 'I Got A Mind To Give Up Living') (Previously Unreleased), 'Down South Jukin'', 'Was I Right Or Wrong?', 'I Ain't The One', 'Tuesday's Gone', 'Gimme Three Steps', 'Workin' For MCA', 'The Ballad Of Curtis Loew', 'Call Me The Breeze', 'Saturday Night Special', 'All I Can Do Is Write About It' (Acoustic), 'Free Bird', 'Whiskey Rock-A-Roller' (Live), 'Simple Man' (Live), 'What's Your Name', 'That Smell', 'I Know A Little', 'You Got That Right', 'Comin' Home' (Live), 'Swamp Music' (Live), 'Gimme Back My Bullets' (Live), 'Smokestack Lightnin'', 'The Last Rebel', 'Things Goin' On' (Acoustic), 'Talked Myself Right Into It', 'We Ain't Much Different' (Live), 'Workin'', 'Mad Hatter'

'Blues Medley' (Previously Unreleased) (10:16)
'Sweet Little Angel' (B.B. King, Jules Taub)
'How Blue Can You Get' (Jane Feather, Leonard Feather)
'I Got A Mind To Give Up Living' (B.B. King and Cliff Adams)
This was the last of the Quinvy recordings to be released, more than 30 years after it was recorded in 1970 in Sheffield, Alabama. Even at this early stage of their career, it is apparent how expressive Ronnie could be with his vocal delivery. The album credits have Jane Feather as the author of 'How Blue Can You Get', but the song was co-written with her husband and jazz critic Leonard Feather. 'I Got A Mind To Give Up Living' is credited as 'traditional' but is the name given to the Butterfield Blues Band's 1966 version of the song 'All Over Again', which was originally released by B.B. King in 1965 and written by Donald Eugene Adams and B.B. King.

Rossington's bends in the song intro lack his trademark precision, but he seems quite at home, like on 'Bad Boy Blues', with the rhythm guitar and blues chord voicings. Allen seems happy to primarily add fills and solos, and his trademark vibrato is evident. Allen's blues phrasing and facility with pentatonic scales are apparent. There is a strange vocal stutter at 4:07 that must be deliberate, although it sounds like a needle stuck on a vinyl record because the music is uninterrupted. At 5:04, there is a shift and a swing from the bass and drums, which is welcome. At 5.24, Allen shows his ability with the wah pedal, a skill that would be recognised many years later when his wah solo in 'Needle And The Spoon' was ranked number 19 in 2015 by *Guitar World* magazine in their list of best wah solos of all time.

At 7:02, the song's ending begins, with Ronnie stopping mid-line with the word 'on' and the band pausing before Allen launches into a solo guitar performance where he pours out his Clapton and Hendrix influences for the next three minutes until 10:03, where the band resume the ending. Ronnie never did finish his sentence, though; he had probably forgotten by the time Allen finished. There is an organ buried in the mix, but there is no artist credit for this.

FYFTY (2023)

CD1: 'Comin' Home' (Original Version), 'I Ain't The One, Gimme Three Steps', 'Tuesday's Gone', 'Simple Man', 'Sweet Home Alabama', 'The Ballad Of Curtis Loew', 'Workin' For MCA', 'On The Hunt', 'Made In The Shade', 'Whiskey Rock-A-Roller' (Live), 'All I Can Do Is Write About It' (Acoustic Version), 'Gimme Back My Bullets', 'Double Trouble'

CD2: 'Saturday Night Special' (Live), 'T For Texas' (Blue Yodel No. 1) (Live), 'Travelin' Man' (Live), 'Free Bird' (Live – Unreleased), 'What's Your Name', 'You Got That Right', 'I Know A Little', 'Down South Jukin'', 'White Dove', 'Was I Right Or Wrong?', 'Georgia Peaches', 'Mr. Banker'

CD3: 'Call Me The Breeze' (Live), 'That Smell' (Live), 'Smokestack Lightning', 'Southern Women', 'The Last Rebel', 'Born To Run', 'Devil In The Bottle', 'Talked Myself Right Into It', 'Berneice, Voodoo Lake', 'Tomorrow's Goodbye'

CD4: 'Mad Hatter', 'Pick 'Em Up', 'Red, White & Blue', 'Skynyrd Nation', 'Simple Life', 'Still Unbroken', 'God & Guns', 'Gifted Hands', 'Start Livin' Life Again', 'Mississippi Blood', 'Last Of A Dyin' Breed', 'Last Of The Street Survivors', 'Gimme Three Steps' (Live – Unreleased)

This is the most comprehensive Skynyrd overview since 1991's 3CD *Lynyrd Skynyrd – The Definitive Lynyrd Skynyrd Collection*. It was housed in 12x12 vinyl-style packaging, and the gatefold jacket houses a 40-page booklet with photos, opening notes by filmmaker-journalist Cameron Crowe and track-by-track liner notes from music historian Gary Graff. The songs were drawn from studio albums plus rarities and live recordings, as well as two previously unreleased tracks: a 7 July 1976 performance of 'Free Bird' at Atlanta's Fabulous Fox Theatre – in place of the studio original – and a 13 November 2022 live take of 'Gimme Three Steps' from Nashville's storied Ryman Auditorium from what proved to be Gary Rossington's final performance with the band. Subsequently, this concert was released on CD and DVD. Also included is the 2020 digital single, 'Last Of The Street Survivors'.

'Last Of The Street Survivors' (J. Van Zant, Medlocke, Rossington, Hambridge) 4:15
The group released the song digitally on 24 April 2020, in the wake of the postponement of a series of *Street Survivor* concert dates because of the coronavirus pandemic. *The Last Of The Street Survivors Farewell Tour* began in May 2018. The first physical release of the track was for this compilation album, *FYFTY*, released in 2023. The song is an autobiographical reminiscence about their long, successful and storied career.

Arpeggiated guitars and slow, atmospheric slide guitar set a familiar tone. The sound is full, with great production, and the song is heavy with sentiment, evoking the spirit of the lost but not forgotten members. All three lead guitarists fittingly contribute to the final solo before the song closes at 4:15. When Skynyrd were preparing for what was planned to be a farewell tour, prior to the pandemic, they were looking for new material and found a demo of this song that they decided to work up. For Johnny, the song was all about Gary: 'We always thought of Gary as being the last survivor of the originals who started this band. For that to be the last (studio) song that we recorded is pretty wild, isn't it?'

Associated Track
'Free Bird' (Collins, Van Zant) 10:45
In 2023, Dolly Parton released her 49th studio album, *Rockstar*, which included a near 11-minute version of 'Free Bird' to close the album. The song was notable for the inclusion of Ronnie Van Zant's vocals, permission for which was granted by his widow, Judy, and for the contributions of Gary Rossington and Artimus Pyle. Sadly, this version served as an epitaph for Rossington, who had died earlier in March 2023.

Live Albums

One More From The Road (1976)

Released: 13 September 1976

Label: MCA

Formats: 2LP

The recording took place over three nights at the Fox Theatre in Atlanta. Tom Dowd oversaw the production. He recalled the recording being 'a comedic set of circumstances', firstly with Artimus disappearing for three days parasailing and missing rehearsals, causing postponement of the recording, and secondly, when he did the same again but broke his leg. Dowd's recollections were that, with songs selected from three nights, overdubs were minimal. He recalled redoing some backing vocals with the girls, touching up a couple of Ronnie's vocals and Allen wanting to redo the 'Free Bird' solo completely unnecessarily. This contradicts Garry Rossington's recollections, when he told Mike Estes that there was quite a lot of work done. In 1976, Ronnie stated his intent for the album, 'An intact recording of the band in concert. No overdubbing, no 'Lynyrd Skynyrd Comes Alive' for us. All we had to do was find a new guitarist.' Here, Ronnie is suggesting that Peter Frampton's seminal live album *Frampton Comes Alive* had been partially overdubbed in the studio. This is quite a harsh comment, as the overdubs on that album were not extensive and were only used to make up for technical faults. The new guitarist turned out to be Steve Gaines, and at the time of recording, he had only been with the band a few weeks, so he didn't even play on all the songs, at times miming, according to Rossington. However, the resulting live album is a masterpiece. A more complete 25th Anniversary Deluxe Edition was released in 2001. Two singles were released from the album in 1976. 'Gimme Three Steps' was released with 'Travelin' Man' as a B-side and did not chart. 'Free Bird' was backed by 'Searchin'' and reached 38 in the US charts.

Southern By The Grace Of God (1988)

Released: 21 March 1988

Label: MCA

Formats: CD

Recorded during the *Lynyrd Skynyrd Tribute Tour* in 1987, these live concerts were a tenth anniversary tribute by Lynyrd Skynyrd to the members of the band who had died in the 1977 plane crash. The band consisted of all the surviving members except for Allen Collins, who was present but no longer able to play after being paralysed in a car accident. He chose his replacement, Randall Hall. Ed King returned on guitar, and Johnny sang in tribute to his brother. There are several guests on the album, which is also notable for the extended version of 'Free Bird' that the crowd sang, Johnny feeling unable to do so at that time. Instead, a spotlight was put on a mic stand on which hung Ronnie's hat.

Southern Knights (1996)

Released: 1 July 1996
Label: SPV
Formats: CD
This album was a European release, but significant insofar as it represented Ed's last recordings with the band. Mike Estes was soon to exit, too, but he shared these recollections of the album in September 2025:

Southern Knights was a live album that was really mostly live. I think Johnny re-did some vocals, mostly because he just wanted to, not because the live vocals were bad. They could have been used, in my opinion. As far as the band, there were very few fixes. I was there for a lot of the mixing, and I mixed 'Devil In The Bottle', 'Free Bird' and 'What's Your Name' myself. Ed Hopson was our front-of-house guy, and he recorded it over a few shows on ADAT format, which I was very familiar with. So, Ed had me come down to Atlanta to help him mix and fix a few things. I think we had a mic go out on the drums, and Owen came down to put a few overdubbed hits in, only for technical reasons. I was kind of proud that it was mostly live, because Gary had told me there was a lot of fixing and overdubbing done on One More From The Road.

Lyve From Steel Town (1998)

Released: 2 June 1998
Label: SPV
Formats: CD, DVD

Lynyrd Skynyrd Lyve: The Vicious Cycle Tour (2004)

Released: 22 June 2004
Label: Sanctuary Records
Formats: CD, DVD

Live From Austin Texas (2006)

Released: 2006
Label: New West Records
Formats: DVD

Lynyrd Skynyrd Live, Cardiff Capitol Theatre – Cardiff, Wales 4 November 1975 (Authorised Bootleg) (2009)

Released: 2009
Label: Geffen Records
Formats: CD

Live At Winterland, San Francisco 7 March 1976 (Authorised Bootleg) (2009)

Released: 2009

Label: Geffen Records
Formats: CD

Live From Freedom Hall (2010)

Released: 22 June 2010
Label: Roadrunner Records
Formats: CD, DVD

One More For The Fans (2015)

Released: 2015
Label: Loud & Proud Records
Formats: CD, DVD

Pronounced Leh-Nerd Skin-Nerd & Second Helping, Live From Jacksonville At The Florida Theatre (2015)

Released: 2015
Label: Eagle Records
Formats: CD, DVD

Live In Atlantic City (2018)

Released: 2018
Label: Ear Music
Formats: CD, DVD

The Last Of The Street Survivors Farewell Tour (2019)

Released: 2019
Label: Curtis Loew Records
Formats: CD, DVD

Live At Knebworth '76 (2021)

Released: 2021
Label: Eagle Records
Formats: 2LP/CD/DVD

A welcome release of the famed Knebworth show, supporting The Rolling Stones. The release is somewhat let down by the fake crowd overdubs, but otherwise, it is a great document of a moment in time. Skynyrd met and hung out with several A-list celebrities and played a superb show, but for many, the defining moment is when Ronnie sends his 'mules' (the guitarists) out onto the tongue at the front of the stage, against the express wishes of Mick Jagger.

Celebrating 50 Years: Live At The Ryman (2025)

Released: 2025
Label: Frontiers Music SRL
Formats: 2CD, 2LP, 2CD+DVD, Blu-Ray Video

This is a significant release as it sadly features the final performance of Gary Rossington. Skynyrd had a new label for the release. The last word belongs to Johnny:

Fifty years for Lynyrd Skynyrd. Wow! We are so grateful to the devoted fans for their support throughout the years of transitions and losses. Last year, we lost the great Mr. Gary Rossington. We unknowingly were able to have captured his final performance with us. It's bittersweet, but what a special place to have had his final performance, the mother ship of music, The Ryman Auditorium!

Facing page: 1975 tour personnel (*Authors Collection*)

Sir Productions

March 17th - May 5th, 1975

****

<u>Lynyrd Skynyrd Traveling</u>

Allen Collins
Ed King
Billy Powell
Artemus Pyle
Gary Rossington
Ronnie Van Zant
Leon Wilkeson
Gary Bouchard - Road Manager
Joe Barnes -   Stage manager
John Butler -   Personal manager / guitars
Kevin Elson -   Crew Chief
Chuck Flowers -   Keyboard Tech.
Dean Kilpatrick -   Valet
Joe Osborne   Sound Engineer
Kenny Roberts -   Moniters
Craig Reed -   Drums

Andy Tannis   Sound Company
Gerry Smith   Sound Company

Scott Parsons   Lighting
Bob O'Neill   Lighting
****

Note:

1.   Road money will be $20.00 daily

2.   Rock N' Roll Audio   901 274 0056

3.   Continental Design Lighting   901 526 4101

130 West 57 Street, Suite 5D, New York, N.Y. 10019 / (212) 765-7620

On Track series

AC/DC – Chris Sutton 978-1-78952-307-2

Aerosmith – Andrew Rooney 978-1-78952-364-5

Allman Brothers Band – Andrew Wild 978-1-78952-252-5

Tori Amos – Lisa Torem 978-1-78952-142-9

Aphex Twin – Beau Waddell 978-1-78952-267-9

Asia – Peter Braidis 978-1-78952-099-6

Badfinger – Robert Day-Webb 978-1-878952-176-4

Barclay James Harvest – Keith and Monica Domone 978-1-78952-067-5

Beck – Arthur Lizie 978-1-78952-258-7

The Beat, General Public, Fine Young Cannibals – Steve Parry 978-1-78952-274-7

The Beatles 1962-1996 – Alberto Bravin and Andrew Wild 978-1-78952-355-3

The Beatles Solo 1969-1980 – Andrew Wild 978-1-78952-030-9

Black Sabbath The Dio Years – Chris Sutton 978-1-78952-409-3

Blue Oyster Cult – Jacob Holm-Lupo 978-1-78952-007-1

Blur – Matt Bishop 978-178952-164-1

Marc Bolan and T.Rex – Peter Gallagher 978-1-78952-124-5

David Bowie 1964 to 1982 – Carl Ewens 978-1-78952-324-9

David Bowie 1983 to 2016 – Don Klees 978-1-78952-351-5

Bucks Fizz – David Waterfield 978-1-78952-448-2

Kate Bush – Bill Thomas 978-1-78952-097-2

The Byrds – Andy McArthur 978-1-78952-280-8

Camel – Hamish Kuzminski 978-1-78952-040-8

Captain Beefheart – Opher Goodwin 978-1-78952-235-8

Caravan – Andy Boot 978-1-78952-127-6

Cardiacs – Eric Benac 978-1-78952-131-3

Wendy Carlos – Mark Marrington 978-1-78952-331-7

The Carpenters – Paul Tornbohm 978-1-78952-301-0

Nick Cave and The Bad Seeds – Dominic Sanderson 978-1-78952-240-2

The Chic Organisation – Chris Sutton 97801-78952—366-9

Eric Clapton Solo – Andrew Wild 978-1-78952-141-2

The Clash (revised edition) – Nick Assirati 978-1-78952-325-6

Leonard Cohen – Opher Goodwin 978-1-78952-359-1

Elvis Costello and The Attractions – Georg Purvis 978-1-78952-129-0

Crosby, Stills and Nash – Andrew Wild 978-1-78952-039-2

Creedence Clearwater Revival – Tony Thompson 978-1-78952-237-2

Crowded House – Jon Magidsohn 978-1-78952-292-1

The Cure – Matthew R. Davis 978-1-78952-347-8

The Damned – Morgan Brown 978-1-78952-136-8

Deep Purple and Rainbow 1968-79 (new ed)– Steve Pilkington 978-1-78952-411-6

Deep Purple from 1984 – Phil Kafcaloudes 978-1-78952-354-6

Def Leppard – Scott Robinson 978-1-78952-447-5

Depeche Mode – Brian J. Robb 978-1-78952-277-8

Dire Straits – Andrew Wild 978-1-78952-044-6

The Divine Comedy – Alan Draper 978-1-78952-308-9

The Doobie Brothers – Andrew Wild 978-1-78952-462-8
The Doors – Tony Thompson 978-1-78952-137-5
Dream Theater – Jordan Blum 978-1-78952-050-7
Duran Duran – Karen Windle 978-1-78952-368-3
Ian Dury – Opher Goodwin 978-1-78952-374-4
Bob Dylan 1962-1970 – Opher Goodwin 978-1-78952-275-2
Eagles – John Van der Kiste 978-1-78952-260-0
Earth, Wind and Fire – Bud Wilkins 978-1-78952-272-3
Electric Light Orchestra – Barry Delve 978-1-78952-152-8
Emerson Lake and Palmer – Mike Goode 978-1-78952-000-2
Fairport Convention – Kevan Furbank 978-1-78952-051-4
Focus 1969 to 1985 – Stephen Lambe 978-1-78952-463-5
Peter Gabriel – Graeme Scarfe 978-1-78952-138-2
Genesis – Stuart MacFarlane 978-1-78952-005-7
Gentle Giant – Gary Steel 978-1-78952-058-3
Gong (new edition)– Kevan Furbank 978-1-78952-340-9
Green Day – William E. Spevack 978-1-78952-261-7
Dave Grohl and Foo Fighters – Ben L. Connor 978-1-78952-363-8
Steve Hackett – Geoffrey Feakes 978-1-78952-098-9
Hall and Oates – Ian Abrahams 978-1-78952-167-2
Peter Hammill – Richard Rees Jones 978-1-78952-163-4
Roy Harper – Opher Goodwin 978-1-78952-130-6
Hawkwind (new edition) – Duncan Harris 978-1-78952-290-7
Jimi Hendrix – Emma Stott 978-1-78952-175-7
The Hollies – Andrew Darlington 978-1-78952-159-7
Horslips – Richard James 978-1-78952-263-1
The Human League and The Sheffield Scene – Andrew Darlington 978-1-78952-186-3
Humble Pie –Robert Day-Webb 978-1-78952-2761
Ian Hunter – G. Mick Smith 978-1-78952-304-1
Iggy and the Stooges – Robert Day-Webb 978-1-78952-360-7
Iggy Pop 1977 to 1999 – Hans Meertens 978-1-78952-446-8
The Incredible String Band – Tim Moon 978-1-78952-107-8
INXS – Manny Grillo 978-1-78952-302-7
Iron Maiden (new ed) – Steve Pilkington 978-1-78952-380-5
Joe Jackson – Richard James 978-1-78952-189-4
The Jam – Stan Jeffries 978-1-78952-299-0
Jefferson Airplane – Richard Butterworth 978-1-78952-143-6
Jethro Tull – Jordan Blum 978-1-78952-016-3
J. Geils Band – James Romag 978-1-78952-332-4
Elton John in the 1970s – Peter Kearns 978-1-78952-034-7
Billy Joel – Lisa Torem 978-1-78952-183-2
Journey – Doug Thornton 978-1-78952-337-9
Judas Priest – John Tucker 978-1-78952-018-7
Killing Joke – Nic Ransome 978-1-78952-273-0
The Kinks – Martin Hutchinson 978-1-78952-172-6

Korn – Matt Karpe 978-1-78952-153-5
Led Zeppelin – Steve Pilkington 978-1-78952-151-1
Level 42 – Matt Philips 978-1-78952-102-3
Little Feat – Georg Purvis 978-1-78952-168-9
Lynyrd Skynyrd – Chris Salisbury 978-1-78952-472-7
Love – Emma Stott 978-1-78952-4642
Magnum – Matthew Taylor 978-1-78952-286-0
Aimee Mann – Jez Rowden 978-1-78952-036-1
MC5 – Richard Butterworth 978-1-78952-377-5
Ralph McTell – Paul O. Jenkins 978-1-78952-294-5
Metallica – Barry Wood 978-1-78952-269-3
Joni Mitchell – Peter Kearns 978-1-78952-081-1
The Moody Blues – Geoffrey Feakes 978-1-78952-042-2
Motorhead – Duncan Harris 978-1-78952-173-3
Nektar – Scott Meze 978-1-78952-257-0
New Order – Dennis Remmer 978-1-78952-249-5
Nightwish – Simon McMurdo 978-1-78952-270-9
Nirvana – William E. Spevack 978-1-78952-318-8
Laura Nyro – Philip Ward 978-1-78952-182-5
Oasis – Andrew Rooney 978-1-78952-300-3
Phil Ochs – Opher Goodwin 978-1-78952-326-3
Mike Oldfield – Ryan Yard 978-1-78952-060-6
Opeth – Jordan Blum 978-1-78-952-166-5
Pearl Jam – Ben L. Connor 978-1-78952-188-7
Tom Petty – Richard James 978-1-78952-128-3
Anthony Phillips – Alan Draper 978-1-78952-356-0
Pink Floyd – Richard Butterworth 978-1-78952-242-6
The Police – Pete Braidis 978-1-78952-158-0
The Pretenders 1978 to 1990 Richard Butterworth 978-1-78952-358-4
Porcupine Tree (Revised Edition) – Nick Holmes 978-1-78952-346-1
Procol Harum – Scott Meze 978-1-78952-315-7
Queen – Andrew Wild 978-1-78952-003-3
Radiohead – William Allen 978-1-78952-149-8
Gerry Rafferty – John Van der Kiste 978-1-78952-349-2
Rancid – Paul Matts 978-1-78952-187-0
Lou Reed 1972-1986 – Ethan Roy 978-1-78952-283-9
Renaissance – David Detmer 978-1-78952-062-0
REO Speedwagon – Jim Romag 978-1-78952-262-4
The Rolling Stones 1963-80 – Steve Pilkington 978-1-78952-017-0
Linda Ronstadt 1969-1989 – Daryl O. Lawrence 987-1-78952-293-8
Roxy Music – Michael Kulikowski 978-1-78952-335-5
Rush 1973 to 1982 – Richard James 978-1-78952-338-6
Rush 1984 to 2015 - Richard James 978-1-78952-372-0
Sensational Alex Harvey Band – Peter Gallagher 978-1-7952-289-1
The Small Faces and The Faces – Andrew Darlington 978-1-78952-316-4

The Smashing Pumpkins – Matt Karpe 978-1-7952-291-4

The Smiths and Morrissey – Tommy Gunnarsson 978-1-78952-140-5

Soft Machine – Scott Meze 978-1078952-271-6

Sparks 1969-1979 – Chris Sutton 978-1-78952-279-2

Spirit – Rev. Keith A. Gordon 978-1-78952- 248-8

Bruce Springsteen - David Starkey 978-1-78952-471-0

Stackridge – Alan Draper 978-1-78952-232-7

Status Quo the Frantic Four Years – Richard James 978-1-78952-160-3

Steeleye Span 1970-1989 – Darren Johnson 989-1-78952-369-0

Steely Dan – Jez Rowden 978-1-78952-043-9

The Stranglers – Martin Hutchinson 978-1-78952-323-2

Talk Talk – Gary Steel 978-1-78952-284-6

Talking Heads – David Starkey 978-178952-353-9

Tears For Fears – Paul Clark 978-178952-238-9

The Temptations 1960 to 1978 – George Haffenden 978-178952-373-7

The The –Brian J. Robb 978-178952-370-6

Thin Lizzy – Graeme Stroud 978-1-78952-064-4

Tool – Matt Karpe 978-1-78952-234-1

Toto – Jacob Holm-Lupo 978-1-78952-019-4

U2 – Eoghan Lyng 978-1-78952-078-1

UFO – Richard James 978-1-78952-073-6

Ultravox – Brian J. Robb 978-1-78952-330-0

Van Der Graaf Generator – Dan Coffey 978-1-78952-031-6

Van Halen – Morgan Brown 9781-78952-256-3

Suzanne Vega – Lisa Torem 978-1-78952-281-5

Jack White And The White Stripes – Ben L. Connor 978-1-78952-303-4

The Who – Geoffrey Feakes 978-1-78952-076-7

Steven Wilson – Insurgentes-To The Bone – Nick Holmes 978-1-78952-317-1

Wishbone Ash 1970 to 1982 978-1-78952-413-0

Roy Wood and the Move – James R Turner 978 1 78952 008 8

The Yardbirds – Andrew Darlington 978-1-78952-362-1

Yes (new edition) – Stephen Lambe 978-1-78952-282-2

Neil Young 1963 to 1970 – Oper Goodwin 978-1-78952-298-3

Frank Zappa 1966 to 1979 – Eric Benac 978-1-78952-033-0

Warren Zevon – Peter Gallagher 978-1-78952-170-2

The Zombies – Emma Stott 978-1-78952-297-6

10CC – Peter Kearns 978-1-78952-054-5

Decades Series

The Bee Gees in the 1960s – Andrew Mon Hughes et al 978-1-78952-148-1

The Bee Gees in the 1970s – Andrew Mon Hughes et al 978-1-78952-179-5

The Bee Gees in the 1980s – Andrew Mon Hughes et al 978-1-78952-497-0

Black Sabbath in the 1970s – Chris Sutton 978-1-78952-171-9

Britpop – Peter Richard Adams and Matt Pooler 978-1-78952-169-6

Phil Collins in the 1980s – Andrew Wild 978-1-78952-185-6

Would you like to write for Sonicbond Publishing?

We are mainly a music publisher, but we also occasionally publish in other genres including film and television. At Sonicbond Publishing we are always on the look-out for authors, particularly for our two main series, On Track and Decades.

Mixing fact with in depth analysis, the On Track series examines the entire recorded work of a particular musical artist or group. All genres are considered from easy listening and jazz to 60s soul to 90s pop, via rock and metal.

The Decades series singles out a particular decade in an artist or group's history and focuses on that decade in more detail than may be allowed in the On Track series.

While professional writing experience would, of course, be an advantage, the most important qualification is to have real enthusiasm and knowledge of your subject. First-time authors are welcomed, but the ability to write well in English is essential.

Sonicbond Publishing has distribution throughout Europe and North America, and all our books are also published in E-book form. Authors will be paid a royalty based on sales of their book. Further details about our books are available from www.sonicbondpublishing.com. To contact us, complete the contact form there or email info@sonicbondpublishing.co.uk

Doctor Who: The David Tennant Years – Jamie Hailstone 978-1-78952-066-8
James Bond – Andrew Wild 978-1-78952-010-1
Monty Python – Steve Pilkington 978-1-78952-047-7
Seinfeld Seasons 1 to 5 – Stephen Lambe 978-1-78952-012-5

Other Books
1967: A Year In Psychedelic Rock – Kevan Furbank 978-1-78952-155-9
1970: A Year In Rock – John Van der Kiste 978-1-78952-147-4
1972: The Year Progressive Rock Ruled The World – Kevan Furbank 978-1-78952-288-4
1973: The Golden Year of Progressive Rock – Geoffrey Feakes 978-1-78952-165-8
1974: The Year Progressive Rock Came Of Age – Kevan Furbank 978-1-78952-473-4
1977: How Progressive Rock Defied Punk – Kevan Furbank 978-1-78952-367-6
Apple Of My Eye: The Story Of Apple Records – Andrew Wild 978-1-78952-379-9
Eric Clapton Sessions – Andrew Wild 978-1-78952-177-1
Constellation Heroes – Hans Meertens 978-1-78952-498-7
Dark Horse Records – Aaron Badgley 978-1-78952-287-7
Derek Taylor: For Your Radioactive Children – Andrew Darlington 978-1-78952-038-5
Ghosts – Journeys To Post-Pop – Matthew Restall 978-1-78952-334-8
The Golden Age of Easy Listening – Derek Taylor 978-1-78952-285-3
The Golden Road: The Recording History of The Grateful Dead –
John Kilbride 978-1-78952-156-6
Hoggin' The Page – Groudhogs The Classic Years – Martyn Hanson 978-1-78952-343-0
Iggy and The Stooges On Stage 1967-1974 – Per Nilsen 978-1-78952-101-6
Jon Anderson and the Warriors – the Road to Yes – David Watkinson 978-1-78952-059-0
Magic: The David Paton Story – David Paton 978-1-78952-266-2
Misty: The Music of Johnny Mathis – Jakob Baekgaard 978-1-78952-247-1
Music in the 1980s – Peter Woolliscoft 978-1-78952-347-8
Nu Metal: A Definitive Guide – Matt Karpe 978-1-78952-063-7
Phish- Baker's Dozen – Brent Waltz 978-1-78952-361-4
Philip Lynott – Renegade – Alan Byrne 978-1-78952-339-3
Remembering Live Aid – Andrew Wild 978-1-78952-328-7
Thank You For The Days - Fans Of The Kinks Share 60 Years of Stories –
Ed. Chris Kocher 978-1-78952-342-3
The Making Of Abba – Joe Matera -978-178952-378-2
The Sonicbond On Track Sampler 978-1-78952-190-0
The Sonicbond Progressive Rock Sampler (Ebook only) 978-1-78952-056-9
Tommy Bolin: In and Out of Deep Purple – Laura Shenton 978-1-78952-070-5
Maximum Darkness – Deke Leonard 978-1-78952-048-4
The Twang Dynasty – Deke Leonard 978-1-78952-049-1
Van der Graaf Generator – Pawn Hearts – Paolo Carnelli 978-1-78952-357-7

... and many more to come!